The Anti-Racism Linguist

Full details of all our other publications can be found on http://www.multilingual-matters.com, or by writing to Multilingual Matters, St Nicholas House, 31-34 High Street, Bristol, BS1 2AW, UK.

The Anti-Racism Linguist

A Book of Readings

Edited by
Patricia Friedrich

MULTILINGUAL MATTERS
Bristol • Jackson

DOI https://doi.org/10.21832/FRIEDR2859
Library of Congress Cataloging in Publication Data
A catalog record for this book is available from the Library of Congress.
Names: Friedrich, Patricia, editor.
Title: The Anti-Racism Linguist: A Book of Readings/Edited by Patricia Friedrich.
Description: Bristol; Jackson: Multilingual Matters, [2023] | Includes bibliographical references and index. | Summary: 'This book explores language at the intersection of race and ethnicity and the institutional practices that still make for uneven access to education, resources and a sense of belonging. The book is a thoughtful reflection on how teachers and scholars can incorporate anti-racism pedagogy and thought into their practice' – Provided by publisher.
Identifiers: LCCN 2022046818 (print) | LCCN 2022046819 (ebook) | ISBN 9781800412842 (paperback) | ISBN 9781800412859 (hardback) | ISBN 9781800412873 (epub) | ISBN 9781800412866 (pdf)
Subjects: LCSH: Racism in language. | Racism in education. | LCGFT: Essays.
Classification: LCC P120.R32 A58 2023 (print) | LCC P120.R32 (ebook) | DDC 408.9 – dc23/eng/20221214
LC record available at https://lccn.loc.gov/2022046818
LC ebook record available at https://lccn.loc.gov/2022046819

British Library Cataloguing in Publication Data
A catalogue entry for this book is available from the British Library.

ISBN-13: 978-1-80041-285-9 (hbk)
ISBN-13: 978-1-80041-284-2 (pbk)

Multilingual Matters
UK: St Nicholas House, 31-34 High Street, Bristol, BS1 2AW, UK.
USA: Ingram, Jackson, TN, USA.

Website: www.multilingual-matters.com
Twitter: Multi_Ling_Mat
Facebook: https://www.facebook.com/multilingualmatters
Blog: www.channelviewpublications.wordpress.com

Copyright © 2023 Patricia Friedrich and the authors of individual chapters.

All rights reserved. No part of this work may be reproduced in any form or by any means without permission in writing from the publisher.

The policy of Multilingual Matters/Channel View Publications is to use papers that are natural, renewable and recyclable products, made from wood grown in sustainable forests. In the manufacturing process of our books, and to further support our policy, preference is given to printers that have FSC and PEFC Chain of Custody certification. The FSC and/or PEFC logos will appear on those books where full certification has been granted to the printer concerned.

Typeset by Riverside Publishing Solutions.

For Tomas Mesquita

Contents

	Contributors	ix
1	Anti-Racist Linguistics *Patricia Friedrich*	1
2	TEIL as a Tool for Anti-Racist Pedagogy: Exploring its Potential *Aya Matsuda*	26
3	On (Dis)Inventing Language as a Zone of Non-Being: Black Teachers in ELT and Linguistic Racism in Brazil *Gabriel Nascimento*	44
4	Confessions of a Sociolinguist: A Linguistic Autoethnography *Chatwara Suwannamai Duran*	65
5	Narratives of Invisibility: Racism and Anti-Racism in Academic Spaces in Brazil *Clarissa Menezes Jordão, Juliana Zeggio Martinez and Eduardo Henrique Diniz de Figueiredo*	85
6	Positionality, Creativity and Linguistic Prejudice: The Challenges of Honoring Multiple Identities and Being an Anti-Racist *Patricia Friedrich*	106
7	'No One Can Say it Anyway': Personal Names in the Classroom *Tracey McHenry*	119
8	Anti-Racist Linguistic Practices in the History Curriculum *Luciana C. de Oliveira and Joy Beatty*	135
9	On Human and Linguistic Dignity *Patricia Friedrich*	146
	Appendix: Q&A with Contributors	152
	Index	158

Contributors

Joy Beatty is a doctoral student in the PhD in Education, Concentration in Curriculum, Culture and Change, in the School of Education at Virginia Commonwealth University. She is a Southern Regional Education Board (SREB) Doctoral Scholars University Award recipient. She was a curriculum writer at CodeVA and has taught history and English for over 10 years. She has taught in Virginia and Maryland. Additionally, Joy taught English in South Korea as she was sponsored by the Rotary Club. Her passion is developing curricula for teachers so they can challenge dominant narratives as a way to support diverse learners.

Eduardo H. Diniz de Figueiredo is a tenured Professor of English at Universidade Federal do Paraná in Curitiba, Brazil. He holds a PhD in Applied Linguistics from Arizona State University and an MA in English from Universidade Federal de Santa Catarina. His work has appeared in such publications as *World Englishes, Brazilian English Language Teaching Journal* and *Applied Linguistics*. He co-authored *The Sociolinguistics of Digital Englishes* with Patricia Friedrich. His research interests lie in the areas of English as an international language, critical applied linguistics and language teaching.

Chatwara Suwannamai Duran is Associate Professor of Applied Linguistics at the University of Houston where she teaches and researches in the field of sociolinguistics and English Language Teaching. Her work has appeared in *Journal of Language, Identity, and Education, Linguistics and Education, TESOL Quarterly* and several edited volumes. Her recent book *Language and Literacy in Refugee Families* (2017) presents her multi-year ethnographic study with Karenni families originally from Myanmar but resettled in the United States.

Patricia Friedrich is Professor of Sociolinguistics and Provost Fellow at Arizona State University. She holds a PhD from Purdue University and has held temporary appointments in universities in Latin America. She is the author/editor of 12 books (fiction and academic), including *Applied Linguistics in the Real World* (Routledge), *The Sociolinguistics* *of Digital Englishes* (Routledge, with Eduardo Henrique Diniz de Figueiredo) and *English for Diplomatic Purposes* (Multilingual Matters), *The Art of Always* (TWRP), and over 40 articles in journals/chapters in edited volumes. Her research interests include social justice, disability studies, world Englishes, language and power, critical applied linguistics and attitudes toward language and language users. A founding member/chair of the anti-racism council (NewARC) in her academic unit, she is a lifetime member of the International Association for World Englishes.

Aya Matsuda is Associate Professor of Applied Linguistics in the Department of English at Arizona State University, USA. Her research interests include the use of English as an international language and the pedagogical implications of the global spread of English. Her work focusing on these issues have appeared in various books and journals including *English Today*, *JALT Journal*, *TESOL Quarterly* and *World Englishes*, and her edited volumes, *Principles and Practices of Teaching English as an International Language* (2012) and *Preparing Teachers to Teach English as an International Language* (2017) were published by Multilingual Matters. Matsuda has served on the Board of Directors for TESOL International Association (2014–2017) and as a secretary/treasurer of the International Association for World Englishes (2016–2019).

Juliana Zeggio Martinez is a full-time tenured Professor of English at Universidade Federal do Paraná, in Curitiba, Brazil. She holds a PhD in Applied Linguistics from Universidade de São Paulo with a doctoral internship taken at the University of British Columbia, in Vancouver, Canada. She is also the coordinator of a Centre for Continuing Language Teacher Education (NAP-UFPR), which was created to enhance collaboration among teacher educators, pre-service and in-service teachers. Her research interests lie in critical applied linguistics, language teacher education, internationalization of Higher Education, the coloniality/modernity Latin American research group and decoloniality.

Tracey McHenry is Professor of English at Eastern Washington University in Washington State, USA, where she teaches introduction to linguistics, English grammar, research methods and teaching English to ESL students. Her MA and PhD are from Purdue University in 1995 and 1999. Her research interests include English for tourism, world Englishes, Native language interests in the United States and English sociolinguistics and grammar.

Clarissa Menezes Jordão holds a PhD in literary education and a Master's degree in English language literatures, both from Brazil. She currently teaches at postgraduate level at the Federal University of Paraná, supervising doctorate and master students. Her main research interests are English as a Lingua Franca, decoloniality, southern epistemologies and critical applied linguistics.

Gabriel Nascimento is an Assistant Professor at the Institute of Humanities, Arts and Science of the Universidade Federal do Sul da Bahia. He has also been a Visiting Scholar at the Graduate School of Education of the University of Pennsylvania. He holds a Master's degree in Applied Linguistics from the University of Brasília and a PhD in Language Studies from the University of São Paulo. He authored several books, such as *Linguistic Racism* (Letramento Publishing House). His research interests revolve around the interplay of language and racism in language studies.

Luciana C. de Oliveira is Associate Dean for Academic Affairs and Graduate Studies in the School of Education and a Professor in the Department of Teaching and Learning at Virginia Commonwealth University, Richmond, VA, USA. Her research focuses on issues related to teaching multilingual learners at the elementary and secondary levels. She served in the presidential line of TESOL International Association (2017–2020) and was a member of the Board of Directors (2013–2016). She was the first Latina to ever serve as President (2018–2019) of TESOL.

1 Anti-Racist Linguistics

Patricia Friedrich

> In this introduction, I will discuss the relationship between anti-racism work and linguistics, especially those areas within linguistics (e.g. sociolinguistics, applied linguistics, world Englishes) that are already engaged (or at least have great potential to be involved) with social issues and social justice. I will introduce the other chapters and describe the common thread that runs through the book as well as the challenges of editing a book on the topic, one that can represent the diversity of voices, perspectives and lived experiences in this space.

Introduction

I hope I do not sound hyperbolic when I say we are at a crossroads moment in the history of the world. As I write this introduction, we are dealing with variants of the virus that changed the world, as we slowly come out of the social distancing of almost two years due to the COVID-19 pandemic. Within a few months, COVID completely changed our modes of interaction, work, study and living. At the same time, we have been faced with growing racial, ethnic and gender tensions, perhaps at a scale (at least in the US, from where I write) not seen since the Civil Rights movement of the 1960s. And maybe these two occurrences are not unrelated at all. The pandemic has caused us to confront the reality that people of color and historically underserved minorities deal with greater challenges, worse outcomes and disproportionate injustices in a time of crisis,[1] and for many of us, this has been the most serious and salient crisis of our lifetimes. Educational outcomes have reflected this reality, with members of minoritized groups facing more challenges to complete work and study remotely. Women have been disproportionately affected by the employment crisis and more often hit with the double duty of children learning from home and work that is not confined to an office anymore. We have come to realize that environmental injustice affects members of historically minoritized groups more intensely than they affect white, cis, middle-class/wealthy, neurotypical and able-bodied men.

Writing about the intersection of language, race, ethnicity, gender and disability in this context is an urgency. Taking action that starts to address some of the most serious forms of inequity in our time is even more urgent. We are both observers and subjects of this reality, given that we, for the most part, put this book together during and immediately after the most critical part of the COVID-19 pandemic outbreak.

For those of us who study, track, critically address and hope to positively impact language use, the possible areas of action have only multiplied. From questioning and revising our vocabulary when it comes to how we speak of gender, disability, race and ethnicity to finding new ways to teach language and linguistic awareness in a world both united and separated by digital spaces, we have a lot to do. While the challenges have been enormous, there has also been more institutional openness to change and to reimagining language, communication and interaction (and, in some domains, equally strong pushback). What is more, I hope we have reassessed the value of applied disciplines and understood that one can be theoretically rigorous and at the same time work so that such knowledge results in material outcomes and meaningful action.

From visual arts, to movies, to books of fiction and non-fiction, our forms of 'entertainment' gained new meaning. Once we could not go to the movies, the theater, concerts and shows, we contemplated what it would be like to be in the world without these seemingly 'superfluous' media, and the truth is that we did not like what we saw. At the same time, we found renewed respite and those activities that we could engage in, such as reading, writing, painting, planting, learning. The importance of art, knowledge, science, poetry, language in all their forms for our well-being as social creatures has being made very clear in this time of adversity and should inform how we choose to move forward. I am well aware too of the privilege that allowed people like me to engage with art and learning even in isolation at a time when so many were struggling for work and basic necessities.

For a long time, institutions have framed their efforts in creating more just environments under the label of 'diversity and inclusion'. The words have been uttered in human-resources contexts, written about in academic work and taught in classrooms and business seminars. Yet the fragility of some of our institutions and practices have caused us to consider that not only do we have to reaffirm our commitment to these constructs, but we also need to expand them. As time went by, the need to emphasize equity, justice and belonging as part of our efforts became more obvious. As a consequence, the notion of equality was increasingly replaced with the more contextual concept of equity, and we have introduced the concept of belonging to express that it is not sufficient that someone be present but especially crucial that they feel they are valued, seen and their contributions are recognized, understood and welcome. Belonging reflects a sense of justice and inclusion in context. Someone that belongs feels a sense of peace in being in a particular environment.

They can lower their defenses and feel comfortable. Belonging means feeling you are home. We bring equity by providing to each according to their needs, aspirations and their positionality; we create belonging by valuing people as they are and letting them know we do.

Of course, the backlash to these ideas has been swift. Threatened by the notion of competition on a more equitable (however far from equal) footing, some groups have started to frame their efforts in regaining an upper hand in terms of a misguided longing for a past when white cis men were (almost exclusively) in charge (or at least perceived to be). Such efforts often rely on nonsensical, pseudo-academic notions of a natural order of things and a hierarchy where men are in command because they are inherently predisposed to leading. For example, it is hard to think of something more perplexing than reading in 2022 that, 'The people who hold that our culture is an oppressive patriarchy, they don't want to admit that the current hierarchy might be predicated on competence'.[2] And yet, this is one of the 'milder' quotes by psychologist Jordan Peterson, beyond which I am too uncomfortable to even cite.

Lest we think this is a small, fringe point of view, we only need to remember that Peterson has a huge following, one eager to hear that DEIB (diversity, equity, inclusion and belonging) efforts are just a way of upsetting the natural order of the world, often represented by a look back to the 1950s as emblematic of a model to be followed. According to that view, rather than starting (barely) to create some measure of equity for woman, people of other genders, BIPOC (black, indigenous and people of color) and other minoritized populations, DEIB efforts only create a situation in which 'merit' is not rewarded. This is certainly a tempting proposition for individuals who, despite certain levels of privilege, fail to meet either societal or self-prescribed goals and objectives. There is a long, unfortunate tradition of blaming women and members of minorities for one's own shortcomings, and in a world that has seen a proliferation of efforts to discredit objective reality (e.g. 'that the earth is round is just your opinion'), this type of discourse comes as one additional hurdle for those seeking a measure of equity and inclusion.

Language and its Challenges

As social beings, we are also aware of the challenges inherent to language use. We linguists, for example, learn early on that communication (e.g. the Shannon-Weaver model) involves such elements as the interlocutors, the channel of communication, the message, etc. Any disconnect in any element of this dynamic process of interaction, and clashes can occur. It might be that the channel has a problem (e.g. the phone connection is bad due to proximity to the mountains); it could also be that the interlocutors do not share a language (e.g. one is a monolingual user of English and the other a monolingual user of French). It could also be that one of the interlocutors has a cultural orientation so different from that of the other party that they have trouble establishing some common ground. The potential for breaks in communication are enormous. Yet, a willingness to come together in conversation should help build a communicative bridge in ways that would otherwise be impossible to achieve.

I would like to establish some common ground by spending a bit of time on a few of the terms that are sure to be reflected in the various chapters of this book. It is a challenging undertaking. As linguists, we know that as I register these words on the page, they are already changing (time being another important element in the outcome communication, as noted by anyone who tries to read in Old English for the first time). When I read this book in five years, some of the terms used here might have fallen completely out of use, some might have switched in meaning or implication, and certainly new terms will have been adopted. Two year ago, I could not speak of 'long howlers' in the context of COVID-19, those patients who months after infection continue to experience symptoms or consequences of the virus. As I write, the term has currency in the US, and it would be recognized by many. Yet, should this book be read in 20 years, will the readers readily recognize that term as current, or would the same people be referred to by different terms?

While I cannot provide a definitive answer as to exactly which words will morph in what ways, my experience as an applied linguist informs me that my words here will age, transform and acquire new meanings. Some will become charged and will have been co-opted by groups in an attempt to ridicule or disempower 'the Other'. Some of those attempts will have worked, thus leading to the creation or the employment of new words. Others will be further strengthened by positive uses. As individuals, we have little control over which words will make it (unless one of us is really famous, in which case a tweet can go a long way in causing language change). However, the work of a linguist is (also) to document what happens in a particular point in time for future reference and consideration, and at this point in time, the terms used here refer to important concepts. So rather than ask the reader to agree with the definitions below or even to agree that those concepts are the central ones in this discussion, I am asking that the readers consider that those terms with those meanings were on my mind and the minds of the contributors as we put this book together. Below, I explain and exemplify how they are used in this book and in this moment in time.

Abyssal Lines

In quite an organic way, the idea of abyssal lines started to permeate some of the most important discussions in this book. The term, as used by de Sousa Santos (2007), establishes that:

> Modern Western thought is an abyssal form of thought. It is a system of visible and invisible demarcations, being that the invisible ones work as the bases for the visible ones. The invisible demarcations are established through radical lines that divide social reality into two different universes: the universe 'this side of the line' and the universe 'that side of the line.' The division is such that 'that side of the line' disappears as a form of reality, becoming non-existent, and is indeed taken to be inexistent. Inexistence means not existing in any form that is relevant or understandable.[3] [my translation]

As I think of abyssal lines, one of the first examples that come to me (and I believe it is pertinent here, given so many of us who contribute to this book are originally from South America) is the line that separates the so called 'western world' from the rest of what is, for lack of a better word, the west. The world map – as most of us experience it in Europe and the Americas – is drawn so that Europe lies in the center (not by chance), to the east of which is Asia, Oceania, etc. and to the west of which are the Americas. Oftentimes, the scale of the north and south differs, so that Europe is made to look disproportionately big in comparison to Africa, in the same maneuver that makes most north Americans extremely surprised to learn that Brazil is larger than the continental US. Yet, the Western world only includes western Europe and parts of North America. Since in this classification, given the demarcations of this particular map, South America, for instance, cannot reasonably be classified as being in the east, it virtually ceases to exist. It becomes a zone of non-being.

More recently, South America became part of the construction of what is known as the 'Global South' (another abyssal line). Yet, in the binary east–west, it simply does not exist. The consequences of the demarcation that puts South America on 'that side of the line' are many: what happens to the scientific knowledge produced in an area that does not exist? How about its literature? The dialogic exchange that knowledge entails becomes severely compromised. Note that while I am using the example of South America, the world is full of other zones of non-being, and geopolitical lines are but one example of the many abyssal lines created.

Linguistically speaking, abyssal lines have unique consequences as well, some of which are thoroughly discussed in Chapter 3. We can argue that abyssal lines separate, for example, users of more standard forms of language from those associated with dialectal variations as well as those who use languages of wider communication and those who use more local languages. It is not uncommon for the latter to inhabit such zones of non-being that eventually the languages actually cease to exist, as seen by so many languages that have disappeared or are in the process of extinction. One of the necessary reflections, as we read the pages that follow becomes: In what ways am I in my practice, or in the institutions

I serve, further stressing these abyssal lines and/or helping create new ones?

Anti-Racism

In this book, anti-racism is any thought, theory or action which aims to positively affect individuals and institutions so that more equity of access and opportunity as well as a necessary change of attitude toward and treatment of ethnic and racial minorities can be effected. The ultimate goal is that all members of a given society enjoy respect, dignity and equitable opportunity and access to housing, education, employment, health, nourishment and all other benefits that living in society should afford. Anti-racism action and scholarship in the specific context of linguistics means removing the linguistic barriers, the preconceptions, the linguistic prejudice and negative attitude toward language varieties that might adversely affect our attempt to achieve the afore-mentioned equity, and in turn building institutions and practices that facilitate access, opportunity and achievement for all.

Belonging

Belonging or belongingness is a psychological construct with a long history of use and investigation, but more recently it appears in humanistic and other social sciences contexts with renewed strength, and together with diversity, inclusion, equity and sometimes justice as important goals for anti-racism and LGBTQ+ activism and education. Baumeister and Leary (1995: 497) comment on how, in his highly influential *Toward a Psychology of Being*, Maslow (1968)

> ranked 'love and belongingness needs' in the middle of his motivational hierarchy; that is, belongingness needs do not emerge until food, hunger, safety, and other basic needs are satisfied, but they take precedence over esteem and self-actualization.

This seems to indicate that a sense of belonging is quite important for human beings in our attempts to lead fulfilling and heathy lives. Evolutionary psychology (refer to Malone *et al.*, 2012, for example), would postulate that our fear of being excluded from the social milieu has its roots in an inherent sense that, left to our own devices, without the acceptance and protection of our community, we would face great adversity, the inclement nature of weather, the search for nourishment and shelter all potentially affected by whether we belong or not. While rationally we might argue that we live in conditions that are different from those of earlier human civilizations, the brain with which we perceive potential dangers and obstacles is still the same, and the need for community just as strong.

BIPOC

The social movements of 2020 saw an increase in the use of the term BIPOC as a shortcut to represent several populations advocated for through anti-racism action. Leonard (2021: 219), for example, explains that in his work he uses the term BIPOC 'in recognition of the several shared experiences (despite key differences) and benefits of coalition-building among racialized groups'. The term, which stands for 'Black, Indigenous, People of Color', aims to highlight the urgency of addressing issues of racism, diversity, equity and belonging within these communities and to underscore that, at least within the US, black and indigenous populations are the ones most at risk of having their human rights (and, as a consequence, their linguistic rights) infringed upon. Like with the use of language elsewhere and the capacity/incapacity of terms to reflect reality perfectly and/or stay the same over time, the term BIPOC is not universally endorsed. It is, nevertheless, a step in the direction of highlighting that particular groups have been more often and to greater extents minoritized in certain contexts.

Decoloniality

After almost 20 years in my current institution, I finally realized that I have been carrying around certain practices, however nominal they might feel, that have been with me from my early upbringing in Brazil, and which have come to represent to me small disruptions of the fabric of colonial institutionalization. I am, nonetheless aware that, as a member of a privileged group in my birth country, and in many respects in my adopted country as well, I too have perpetuated practices that speak to coloniality there; and yet, some of the cultural elements that I have continued to incorporate in my professional life, feel, in my current environment, decolonial.

For example, I instinctively never set a detailed, formal agenda for the meetings that I lead. It is intuitive to me to arrive at the meetings and 'feel the room' before deciding how much time to dedicate to what topic and even if a topic should be breached at all. The idea that we will have five minutes for an 'ice breaker', followed by 10 minutes dedicated to the first topic and so on, does not match the elasticity of time with which I was raised and acculturated into the world. However minimal these differences might seem, they offer us a peek into the fact that oftentimes practices that have been instituted as default and sometimes the 'obvious choice' are not obvious or default at all; rather, they have been passed down to us as a given, and we perhaps did not have the latitude or the bird's eye view to question them. Societies that are more mindful of their environment, that live with the seasons rather than fight them, tend to observe more how that environment will facilitate our action in the world. Small acts, such as letting the participants of a meeting feel the direction of the conversation, seem to me in tandem with those considerations.

Therefore, decoloniality to me encompasses all manner of thought and practice that questions colonial institutionalization as default and implements other actions instead. A decolonized curriculum does not default to a Western knowledge base, but rather includes knowledge created by scholars from a diversity of geographies and backgrounds at the same time that it values the knowledge brought by the students and their lived experience. A decolonized classroom relies on oral histories, storytelling, music and other forms of knowing that a more positivist environment might neglect. The decolonized language classroom honors and reaffirms the languages and varieties the students bring from home as valuable, complete, functional and altogether an asset, whereas a colonialized classroom might see students linguistic performance from a deficit perspective (with a colonial language and status varieties as the only acceptable goals for learning).

Speaking of feminist geographies in Latin America, and, more specifically, in Brazil, Silva *et al.* (2020: 272) explain that:

> Scientific practice capable of making visible the subjects produced as invisible in geography is only possible when we understand that invisibility is not by chance, but rather is produced by the power of tradition of the theoretical and methodological elements that delimit a certain world view and what questions can be formulated about a given spatial reality.

Power of traditional is key here, as it is often confounded with 'better' as if better were not a context-specific judgement of value, imbued with all forms of privilege and bias. I am aware that this brief section on decoloniality is not able to even scratch the surface of its complexity, but I wanted to give the reader a sense that the topic is constantly on our minds, and that as scholars who have transposed a variety of cultures and geographies, we too many times live in the in-between created by the dynamics of colonialism, sometimes as the Other, sometimes as those who perpetuate the very structures we would like to modify. It is a positionality that both informs and gives great awareness, but that also frustrates us, especially when we engage, aware or unaware of them, the very practices that we wish to make better.

I want to close this short section, with the powerful words of the seminal work by Anibal Quijano (2000: 574) on coloniality, power and Latin American, a quote made further apropos in this book because so many of the contributors are originally from and/or work and teach in the region: '… it is time to learn to free ourselves from the Eurocentric mirror where our image is always, necessarily, distorted. It is time, finally, to cease being what we are not'. Arguably, that is the biggest goal of a decolonial practice.

Disability

The concept of disability as a feature of the environment as opposed to of a person is the basis of most Disability Studies (DS), an (inter)disciplinary area I am proud to be associated with and to have combined with my linguistics scholarship. Placing disability in the environment differentiates the Disability in DS from the medical concept of impairment (a deficit, ailment or disorder that medical practice needs to act upon). Furthermore, placing disability in the environment restores a sense of power to those who experience forms of disability, be it visible, invisible, temporary or permanent, because we can affect the environment in ways that augment the possibilities of self-fulfillment and expression for all people, including those in this community. A person is disabled by the environment if, for example, they are a wheelchair user and there is no ramp to the area they are trying to reach. Another might be disabled by the environment if they experience a form of learning disability that requires extended periods for the completion of a task and they are not granted such extension. Yet another might be disabled by a working environment that requires that they use technology not designed for their particular needs or talents. In sum, we can, through individual action, institutional change, better design of physical spaces and availability of adaptive technology, affect disability if it is located in the environment.

I mention disability in the context of a book on anti-racism because (1) I believe work on anti-racism offers an important platform for the consideration of all forms of injustice and lack of inclusion and equitable treatment, of which disability is certainly a part; and (2) I am aware of the many intersectionalities between race, ethnicity, gender, age, socioeconomic status and disability, and the need to address them as they occur in the world: hardly ever in isolation and made more complex by the possible layers of disenfranchisement that many who embody several of these identities are subjected to. In that sense, therefore, when we deal with anti-racism in the context of linguistics, it is important to consider how those at the intersection of different forms of identity experience the world and what we as scholars and teachers can do honor and amplify those experiences as best as we can. For more on disability studies, please refer to Linton (2005), and disability and linguistics, Friedrich (2015).

Diversity

I would like to enter this topic with a quote from a recent study on the availability of technologies and their flexibility toward different languages (Joshi *et al.*, 2021: 6282):

> Language technologies contribute to promoting multilingualism and linguistic diversity around the world. However, only a very small number

of the over 7000 languages of the world are represented in the rapidly evolving language technologies and applications.

That seems to be the crux of the matter when it comes to diversity, here represented by language, but ultimately applicable for other constructs as well – diversity only implies a variety of elements in the same category: languages, people, plants in an ecosystem. It does not guarantee that access to resources, attention to specific needs and belonging are automatically available. In the case of languages, as described by Joshi *et al.*, when one considers how new technologies are designed to fit the needs of language users for the about 7000 languages of the world, some are clearly 'winners' (the fifth and top category in their 5-tier taxonomy) while others are 'the left-behinds' (the first and bottom-tier category), with others still somewhere in between. Of course the availability or not of tech resources for different languages ultimately affects the users of those languages, widening the gap between the winners and the left-behinds even more over time. We can say the same about education, housing, food, and so many aspects of human life when we consider diversity as a starting point.

So to acknowledge diversity as existing and important for the maintenance of healthy communities is, in itself, not sufficient to guarantee the evening out of conditions for those populations that need it the most. This is part of the reason why diversity hardly ever appears by itself in conversations about access. Most likely, it is in the very least paired with inclusion, and in more thought-out environments further grouped with equity, belonging and sometimes justice.

Epistemological Racism

This section speaks directly of the work of Kubota (2020) in which racism is contextualized not only in what applied linguistics is concerned but also in the role researchers can have in perpetuating the very structures they aim to denounce. According to Kubota (2020: 715):

> In most cases, [however], the critical gaze is cast on language users, learners, and professionals rather than on us as researchers who are implicated in epistemological racism in our knowledge production and consumption. It is necessary to critically examine how our own scholarly activities produce and maintain racial hierarchies and inequalities of different academic knowledges, further impacting the institutional status of racialized scholars.

Kubota goes on to exemplify through several anecdotes what this looks like in academic environments, from scholars in the Global South being advised their paper was not 'global enough' (2020: 719) to concerns about how authors, whose names are considered non-Western, might be also questioned in their ability to sell a book (2020: 720). The latter is a concern I have heard often from colleagues whose last names are not Anglo-American.

It would be possible to fill a book with anecdotes from scholars on this very topic (and maybe we should), and I narrate some of my own tales in my chapter later in this volume, but here I would like to offer a slightly different one, which nonetheless speaks to the difficulties that those of us whose careers involve language and whose work is located partially or totally within geographies other than the North America–Western Europe axis have to face.

While my primary job is that of an academic, researcher and university professor, as part of my practice, I also write novels. A couple of years ago, while querying publishers with one of my manuscripts – a split narrative in which half of the book takes place in early 20th-century Brazil whereas the rest takes place in the US – I received some overall generous feedback from the editor in a very reputable publishing house that indicated that although I was an excellent writer, who had written a very well-told story, they would have to pass on my book. The reason, they continued, was that books like the one I wrote sold (to readers) on the basis of escapism, and it was the publisher's belief that the part about Brazil did not have as much local color as they would have liked (there were no comments about local color regarding the US part of the story).

Being originally from Brazil, I was unable and unwilling to tell a story in which my country of birth was represented in its stereotypical version, and unfortunately this translated to some as lacking in Brazilian-ness (or at least their perception of it). Luckily, when this volume goes to press, my novel will have already been out for several months as it was purchased by another publisher, but the impression I was left with was that to tell a story about the Global South (and I wonder if others have had this experience about other geographies as well) one must conform to pre-conceived notions (by outsiders) of what that place is like, especially if they want to be commercially viable. This is exactly the kind of situation that our epistemic lenses need to confront and help change.

Going back to the realm of scholarship, Kubota suggests that:

> First, we need to validate alternative worldviews and marginalized voices that challenge white Euro-American knowledge in our scholarship. A question to explore is what alternative conceptualizations and descriptions are possible regarding language use, acquisition, learning, teaching, and other topics within our field. (2020: 726)

I see a strong parallel between what happened to me in fiction and what happens to scholars who propose scholarship that puts into question stereotypical perceptions, for example, of language use and its users in different parts of the world. Furthermore, while there is an unspoken assumption that information about Anglo-American linguistic and cultural contexts will be generalizable and of interest beyond the US and Europe, the opposite movement (i.e. the generalizability of and interest in what happens elsewhere in the world within the US and Europe) is not assumed to be true.

Works written by scholars whose identities speak to a variety of linguistic experiences within and outside of the West have the potential to challenge these long-held beliefs and it is very much in that spirit that this book was put together.

One of the big-picture challenges is that when you try to move away from the very practices that have been institutionalized as the 'right' ones, you run the risk of being perceived as non-rigorous, a-technical, non-scholarly, even when the meaning behind those words is very much connected to the dynamics you are trying to dismantle. Singh (2018: 21) writes about this conundrum when discussing the idea of 'mastery' and its connection to oppressive colonial systems:

> Failure is absolutely crucial to my attempts, and to the ways that the texts I engage across this book invite practices of reading that confront and question our subjectivities. ... In failing to master, in confronting our own desires for mastery where we least expect or recognize these desires, we become vulnerable to other possibilities for living, for being together in common, for feeling injustice and refusing it without the need to engage it through forms of conquest.

This seems like a much more hopeful and helpful proposition than just alternating who is in the position of oppressed and oppressor. On a related note, this book attempts to thread a precarious balance between theorizing that relies heavily on existing literature/theoretical knowledge, and experiential knowledge that disengages from its milieu because, while overreliance on the former would send us right back to the very dynamics we are trying to avoid, exclusive attention to the latter might give the impression that there are not institutional and institutionalized practices that generate an experience of oppression and exclusion for many people.

Equity

In this book, as in many other contexts, equity means 'to each according to their own needs'. For a long time, we struggled to make the idea of equality fit, but embedded in it is a natural challenge: 'to each the same' means a disregard for people's unique circumstances, talents, difficulties, needs, profiles, identities, etc. If five individuals, each a monolingual user of one of five languages – English, Portuguese, Farsi, Japanese and Swahili – are given an instructional manual on how to operate a machine and that manual is written exclusively in Japanese, they were given equal treatment but hardly an equitable one, and their ability to operate the machine will suffer as a consequence. Our job, linguistically and otherwise, is to try and create contexts that are as equitable as possible, even if we know that in many circumstances we will fall short. Had all of those same individuals been second language users of English and had we provided the manual in that language, conditions might not have been perfectly equitable still, given that their level of proficiency might have varied, and yet we would have certainly taken a step in the right direction.

Gender

The social construction (and, as a consequence, the significance of gender as a spectrum) has been evolving rapidly in the last decade, in many respects facilitated by online discourses and by the advocacy by members of underserved populations, who now, because of digital technologies, have a more far-reaching platform. As a result, there is a considerable gap between the understanding of gender by those more engaged populations and some other linguistic networks. Autoethnographies, personal narratives, autobiographies and memoirs help bridge that gap in understanding, and so does scholarship.

Linguistically significant elements from these developments include the self-assignation of pronouns, often times communicated during introductions (e.g. 'Hi, my name is Taylor and my pronouns are they/them') and the practice of self-naming with proper nouns that more closely match a person's gender identity than those names assigned at birth. Likewise, there is significant change going on in other languages: in Brazilian Portuguese, for example, where nouns, grammatically speaking, take a masculine (*o*) or feminine (*a*) article even when they refer to inanimate objects or ideas (*a cadeira*, the chair, as feminine; *o sofa*, the sofa, as masculine), significant movement exists to utilize *e* as a neutral alternative. Therefore, *o menino* (the boy), or *a menina*, (the girl), become *e menine* in their neutral form. In 2015, as part of several linguistic changes and additions, the official dictionary of the Swedish language (Sweden has a Swedish Academy that oversees such matters) introduced a gender-neutral pronoun.[4] *Hen* came to exist alongside *han* (he) and *hon* (she) as viable alternative to refer to non-binary individuals, for those situations when the gender of the person is unknown, or for when the interlocutor deems it unnecessary to acknowledge a person's gender.

Whether these changes across all languages that are seeing some movement will remain might be a little early to tell. Some will likely be definitive, others might change as our understandings continue to change, others still might be the subject of even more profound reformulations. Nevertheless, they speak to central considerations about gender that are taking place currently, and they evidence the fact that languages change as societies change, but they also help shape societal changes.

In a recent dinner with friends, I was asked what causes some linguistic changes to stick and others to fade away. Trying to come up with an easy analogy, I said that it was not very different from what happens to a viral post: we cannot always tell what will go 'viral' on the internet, but usually a combination of collective agreement, timeliness, large-platform reach and some opinion-makers' endorsements tend to help.

Because of important intersections with issues of race and ethnicity, gender is featured in this book in those terms: as part of a continuum of self-identities that interact dynamically with other identities a person may have. While not a central subject in this book, the linguistic rights and existing challenges facing members of the LGBTQ+ community present an important intersection with the issues of racism, diversity, inclusion, equity and belonging presented here, and I acknowledge the need for linguistic research and advocacy to continuously operate in that space and in particular to do field work that addresses the linguistic status and the linguistic needs of people who identify beyond the cis, straight male and cis, straight female binary.

Inclusion

Inclusion has been used in many contexts as a catch-all term for the practice of incorporating individuals from certain groups to particular linguistic networks, communities of practice, classrooms and work environments. At a certain point, awareness arose that diversity in itself did not guarantee that individuals with different talents, needs, backgrounds, cultures, etc. felt and indeed were made full participants of given systems. Then as scholars, practitioners and people interested in more just societies, we went a step further and realized that for diversity and inclusion to work, they needed to be aligned with equitable practices.

That is, it was not sufficient to invite individuals from diverse backgrounds and orientations into the networks and to make them full members of those groups; we also had to provide to each according to their needs and talents. Finally, the ideas of belonging and justice came along as an almost natural consequence (I say almost because we have to work for those as well) of establishing diverse, inclusive, and equitable environments. In language that means, accepting persons with different linguistic expressions into networks (e.g. publishing books by authors of color or individuals with a number of different language varieties), valuing the richness they bring to the group (e.g. creating a book club to discuss the contributions of that book or recommending that book to others), providing to each according to their linguistic needs (e.g. helping a student add to their linguistic repertoire in the classroom when that enhances their linguistic possibilities) and finally achieving a sense of belonging and justice (e.g. having that student become proud of their home language and their ability to code switch).

Institutions

This book carries what I hope is a productive tension between the individual and the institutions within which they work and live. The reason this tension exists is that prejudice, racism and other forces described here operate at these two, often-intertwined levels. The term 'institutions' in this book refers to all of the normative bodies, both physical and intangible, that drive, regulate, rule, constrain, inform and guide human behavior. The legal system is an institution, as are schools and universities. Some societies have institutions that operate within the realms of language and literature, whereas in others, people gravitate more toward schools, grammarians and dictionaries as the institutions that regulate language (our incapacity to fully regulate language notwithstanding).

Language itself is an institution, and, as such, it is susceptible to social forces such as prejudice, racism, power, policy, access, inclusion, etc. Recently, I had an interaction with someone who, as is common among non-specialists, described someone else's variety of language as 'accent free'. Of course no variety – individual or otherwise – is accent free. This is an utter impossibility. What this layperson's shortcut might mean is that the variety the individual in question uses is close enough to the idea of a 'standard' language to be perceived as not accented. What they are actually describing is how far from 'the norm' a variety is perceived to be, and the norm is nothing but the abstract notion of the language of the most powerful. In Brazil, the 'accent free' version of Brazilian Portuguese is that of formally educated people in the city of São Paulo. Not coincidently, this is the area of the country with the highest concentration of banks, international companies, institutions of higher education and just capital. And as a human institution, language and the perception that people have about it, is not invulnerable to attitudes that have little to do with practical matters such as linguistic functionality (i.e. the purposes that a variety serves in the real world).

Another important point about institutions in this book is that they are not viewed here as intrinsically good or bad, but rather that the way institutions operate within democratic systems is complex, full of challenges and up for continuous modification and amelioration.

In worst-case scenarios, institutions can limit action and exacerbate issues of prejudice, lack of access and inequality across populations. In more hopeful cases, institutions can help project the aspirations of those populations onto new levels of achievement.

Intersectionality

When I started to write research based upon scientific surveys, I quickly learned that multi-dimensional constructs would make my work much more meaningful. If I could investigate attitudes, perceptions and beliefs about language from a variety of angles, my work would come to life. The image that stuck with me was going to the movies and wearing those blue and red disposable glasses that made the otherwise two-dimensional screen at the movie theater pop. Multi-dimensions made my research nuanced and richer.

To me, intersectionality does something similar. It allows the experience of human beings to be understood multi-dimensionally because we are never just one identity. We are the place we were born, our socioeconomic realities, our racial and ethnic identity, our gender, our disability status, our citizenship. We are also our own personalities and characters. Without that sense of multi-sectional experience, we would be a generalization, one unable to capture the richness but also the challenges of our human condition.

The term intersectionality was coined by Kimberlé Crenshaw (1989). She explains its importance in the context of the life experiences of black women in the following terms:

> Because the intersectional experience is greater than the sum of racism and sexism, any analysis that does not take intersectionality into account cannot sufficiently address the particular manner in which Black women are subordinated. (1989: 140)

When it comes to racism, prejudice, discrimination, it becomes necessary to understand and act upon the reality that the more underserved and underrepresented identities a person carries, the greater chances that they will face more challenges when it comes to access, inclusion, justice and belonging. That is of course unfair and unjust, but the path to changing that situation requires that we acknowledge the situation exists in the first place. Kubota (2020: 717) reminds us that 'Intersectionality invites us to understand how racism is experienced differently by people from diverse backgrounds'. In terms of language, that might mean that a person whose first language is used by a small number of individuals, who is a member of a BIPOC community and who lives with a disability will face more barriers to advancement, access and inclusion (and experience racism differently) than an individual who carries none of those identities. Our effort as scholars, teachers, advocates and, in fact, fellow human beings, should be to identify those barriers and then bring them down.

Linguistic Justice

The idea of linguistic justice is often associated with the work of Van Parijs (for example, 2002, 2011). It can refer to the imbalance brought forth by asymmetrical bilingualism (i.e. many of us learned English to communicate with a wider audience, but members of the English-as-a-first-language community do not often reciprocate by learning other languages), but I believe it becomes more interesting when taken in its broadest meaning. Van Parijs himself (2002: 60) argues that 'it makes sense to think of linguistic justice as a form of intercommunity cooperative justice, and not only as an aspect of interindividual distributive justice'. His model relies heavily in the idea of cost-benefit dynamics (according to which individuals who have to learn a dominant language bear the costs alone, whereas those who already speak the dominant, as a first language, bear no costs).

To me, the matter of linguistic justice gets complicated by the fact that 'having to learn' a language actually carries great benefits. I believe I am a better person intellectually, socially, spiritually, and culturally for having chosen to learn three languages in addition to my mother tongue. As a consequence, to me (and I do acknowledge that my view is skewed given the privileges that I have enjoyed), the most important operational word is 'choice'. While the career I chose did require the acquisition of in the very least English, the other forms of privilege I enjoyed (being raised in the middle class, having access to great schooling, arts, etc., having attended university, having as a mother tongue another dominant language) would have allowed me to pursue many interests even if I had remained monolingual. Becoming bilingual and later multilingual certainly enhanced my options, but I was never faced with an all-or-nothing situation because of monolingualism.

The same is not true of everyone else, especially for first-language users of minority languages, endangered languages, primarily oral languages and languages with very few native speakers. It is those populations that we have to consider the most when we speak of linguistic justice, which in turn cannot be separated from the matter of access (please refer to the matter of 'access paradox', which Matsuda discusses in Chapter 2).

Another important group that should not be forgotten in relation to this topic is that of users of varieties that enjoy relatively less prestige, even within dominant languages. Attitudes towards and perceptions of their varieties can influence everything, from access to jobs to educational opportunities.

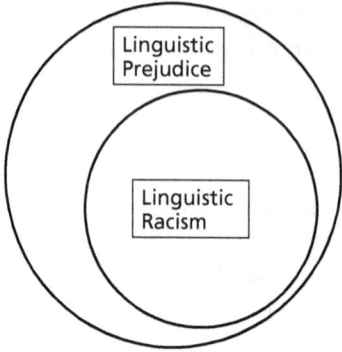

Figure 1.1 Linguistic racism in relation to linguistic prejudice

Linguistic Prejudice

The term linguistic prejudice is used here in a broader sense than linguistic racism, as shown in Figure 1.1. In my view, in a Venn diagram, linguistic racism would be completely within a bigger, linguistic-prejudice circle. That is because other factors besides race and ethnicity can be a part of linguistic prejudice. For example, a person who uses English as an additional language might suffer linguistic prejudice in the US because of their variety even if the prejudice is in this case not related to their race.

Linguistic prejudice can manifest itself in many ways: it can be in the lower acceptance rates of papers by second-language users in certain journals (even when the papers are not about language), or the false belief in the relationship between certain varieties and academic achievement or yet in non-hiring of people whose names 'sound' as possibly from another country. Our unconscious biases can also lead us to forms of linguistic prejudice. Think of the times we subconsciously adapted our speech to slower or louder when we detected a non-native accent even if there was no evidence of the person's difficulty in understanding or any sign of hearing impairment. But those biases themselves are not the problem. Our thinking that we are not impacted by them is.

Minoritized Individuals

The term 'minoritized' used as an adjective can be attributed to Yasmin Gunaratnam (2003: 17), who explains its adoption in the following terms:

> ... I do not use the term 'ethnic minority' in any unproblematic, descriptive sense. I prefer to use the term either in quotation marks, or more often I use the term 'minoritized' to give some sense of the active

processes of racialization that are at work in designating certain attributes of groups in particular contexts as being in a 'minority'.

This is a very important consideration. The term gives away the fact that someone – an individual, an institution, a social practice – is *actively* disadvantaging certain people and certain groups, and that the process is often related (at the receiving end) to one's racial, ethnic, gender, sexual orientation, disability status, socioeconomic standing and other identity markers or the intersection of any of them.

While the term is not universally endorsed – an opinion piece[5] in *The Baltimore Sun* called it 'violent' – it is important to remember why it makes us uncomfortable and to also realize that our discomfort should not be the criterion by which we decide if a linguistic element is useful or not. The fact that members of society are routinely given fewer opportunities, access, sense of belonging and social justice than others should always make us uncomfortable enough to work toward change. The word 'minoritized' is not violent; instead, it is violent to minoritize individuals. To call attention to that is a necessary part of anti-racism practice and anti-racism linguistics. Therefore, several of us choose to use this useful and telling term in our chapters.

The Work in this Book

Several of the chapters in this book offer a personal take on the matters discussed in this introduction, both overtly and in an implied manner. Some have autoethnography elements to them. This was part of our commitment and intention. As linguists, we know that subjectivity, interpretation, biases and agency are necessary elements of our accounts. They will be present whether we openly acknowledge them or not. Some disciplines 'ban' first-person pronouns in an attempt to make the text more 'neutral' and the evidence 'speak for itself'. We know it is not the case: evidence, statistics, graphs do not speak for themselves. In fact, they do not speak at all. They require our interpretation, our storytelling, our making sense of them: in this book, as in many others in the social sciences and the humanities, we are simply more overt about recognizing that such is the case. As Clarissa Menezes Jordão, Juliana Z. Martinez and Eduardo Henrique Diniz de Figueiredo explain in Chapter 5, this erasure of the first-person account can in itself be seen as a colonial practice, and if we are to be anti-racist, we have to remember that more 'subjective' storytelling is at the heart of knowledge and learning in many cultures that are otherwise excluded from academic discourse.

But changing ourselves, telling our stories and those of minoritized groups and making space for the stories of others to be told as well is only one part of the journey, albeit an important one. For long-lasting change to take effect, it is important to systematize this shift, as posited by (Welton *et al.*, 2018: 2), who indicate that

> ... to achieve racial equity in education not only do individuals' mindsets need to be shifted to a more anti-racist ideology, but the institutions in which they work need to make profound anti-racist changes as well.

Throughout this book, the reader will at times notice that some of the contributors place emphasis on the body as the locus of research, as it is, I would suggest a more developed practice in the Global South than in the so-called Western world. This makes sense in a volume that brings together language, race, ethnicity, etc. It is clear that the use of language by certain bodies is much more monitored than by others as is also the case of the use of the body by certain peoples in certain domains, especially if their biotype (as well as their language varieties) is not deemed to be the standard. For example, dancers who do not conform to prototypical ideas of what the body of one who dances 'should' look like are more monitored than those whose body does conform. Women's bodies tend to be more scrutinized than men's bodies and one can speculate that trans women are subject to even more scrutiny than cis women and so on.

A great challenge is to not reproduce the same practices that have been passed down as default to so many of us. When we engage in discourse that comments on the physical type of a dancer rather than their artistic merit, are we not perpetuating those ideas about the body? And when we fail to acknowledge that every living linguistic variety is functional, are we not doing the same? This becomes a dilemma for an editor of a book such as this one. Academic discourse can and indeed often does opine on what counts as 'appropriate' language for the medium, and the line between editing for cohesion and coherence, on the one hand, and disrespecting the variety of the contributor, on the other, is a very tenuous one. For every change I made to the pages that followed I, therefore, asked myself whether I was making the change for the sake of general intelligibility and access or to homogenize the discourses contained herein. If I detected the later, I refrained from the edit, and I hope the reader, even in their minds, will do the same. In the end, each chapter received my editorial suggestions, while every effort was made to maintain the language variety of the authors represented as intended by them.

This is also true of ways of knowing in these pages. Even though many of us come from cultures that privilege storytelling and personal experience as sources of wisdom and knowledge, academic discourse as established by Western thought tends to disregard personal narratives, first-person accounts and storytelling, especially when combined with 'scientific thought'. Yet these are not opposed ways of knowing; they are in fact embedded in one another, so in this book we subvert that idea to bring both storytelling and more 'objective' knowledge into the nuanced crafting of each chapter.

My preoccupation is in doing this work with integrity, knowing that I have to fight the forces of racism in language that would cause the very things that we are trying to contest here to show up in my own editorial practice while I know fully well that racism is so institutionalized that given my own positionality, I am continually falling for it without even realizing. How do I make suggestions to the contributors of this work without erasing their voice, so as to make their voice shine in coherent ways but that do not diminish their authority or inflict pain or intrude on their right to their own language and right to English? How do I for example, make editorial suggestions that point to prescriptive notions of English when we are saying some of those very practices are racist and privilege one language or variety over another?

When this awareness of my own limitations brings me anxiety, I ultimately rely on my original reason for proposing this book: to amplify the voices of these wonderful researchers and teachers. I then make my editorial decisions by asking myself: does this move help me amplify or does it cause me to diminish the impact of their voices?

When it comes to codified world Englishes, the decisions tend to be easier: multiplicity is key and everyone's original WE variety should be displayed. When it comes to standardization of outer-circle varieties, things become fuzzier: what is the line between mistake and variation? Who gets to decide, and how will readers perceive it? These are for sure difficult questions with elusive answers, and I certainly cannot claim to have gotten it right at all times, but my rationale was clear: amplify as many voices as possible and value people's varieties as they arrived to me.

In **Chapter 1**, I tried to set some of the parameters of the work and give the reader the rationale behind my writing and my editorial choices in this volume. This is of course a short glimpse, which I hope will be expended several fold by the discussions that follows. As the name of the volume indicates, this is a book of readings; there is no finality in what we say here – just hope that what we bring to the conversation can serve as a springboard to other important considerations.

Chapter 2 offers Aya Matsuda's personal and professional take on Teaching English as an International Language as a tool for anti-racist pedagogy. She argues that this can be achieved

> by moving away from some ELT practices based on colonial assumptions (e.g. native speaker bias in assessment and teacher qualification), and *explicitly* by creating space (and necessities) for learners and teachers to reflect on and fight coloniality and racism in their English learning and teaching experience.

Many of us started our careers at a time, or after a time, when concerns about linguistic imperialism (Phillipson, 1992) were at the forefront of our considerations, but many of us too found that the frameworks of that decade did not fully reflect our perspective on imperialism and coloniality (see, for example, Berns et al., 1998). This anti-racism platform has given us a renewed opportunity to frame our concern and work in ways that resonate not only with the ideas of our previous selves, but also with the times we now live.

In **Chapter 3**, Gabriel Nascimento presents an impressive account of language as a zone of non-being for black scholars but also reflects on our capacity to disinvent language as such. He argues that 'language cannot be interpreted as if it were an autonomous entity regardless of the world and social reality it convenes' and that 'it is through naming that racism imposes its mastery upon the way the Other is racialized'.

Chapter 4 arrives with the premise that 'a language ideology that privileges Standard American English and its "correct forms" subordinates other forms of Englishes' as Chatwara Suwannamai Duran presents, through an autoethnography, her own experience of personal and professional change facilitated by linguistic awareness.

Chapter 5 continues in the same vein of combining research and personal narrative by presenting 'Narratives of Invisibility: Racism and Anti-Racism in Academic Spaces in Brazil' as a discussion space for the many ways in which multiple voices in academia can be made unheard. Clarissa Menezes Jordão, Juliana Z. Martinez and Eduardo Henrique Diniz de Figueiredo posit that, given the ways in which race and ethnicity are constructed in different parts of the world,

> we experience race (and racism) in convoluted, often confusing ways, since our bodies, ways of speaking and gesturing, and the manners in which we relate to people as a whole index very different identities and ways of knowing and being (both to those with whom we relate and to ourselves).

In **Chapter 6**, I discuss positionality, creativity and linguistic prejudice with a view of distinguishing between linguistic prejudice and linguistic racism given that I believe – as expressed above – that the former encompasses the later, and then applying that to linguistic examples. This chapter also represents my own reflection on the challenges I have faced coming to terms with my positionality given that, depending on my locus of residence and work, I have had my race and ethnicity assigned to me by others (sometimes in quite disparate ways), according to their perception of my linguistic ability, variety and performance. I hope those reflections resonate with readers who face similar circumstances. Some of the issues that come to light are congruent with what contributors have expressed in Chapter 5, so I believe those chapters work well in sequence.

In **Chapter 7**, Tracey McHenry discusses the reluctance of many to used names deemed as 'difficult to pronounce' in the context of American classrooms and how that relates to linguistic prejudice and linguistic racism. She offers simple ways to bring awareness and healthier practices to the classroom.

In **Chapter 8**, Luciana C. de Oliveira and Joy Beatty explain, through the example of a History curriculum, how to apply an anti-racism linguistic framework to the disciplines.

Finally, in **Chapter 9**, I offer my concluding remarks and my thoughts on my strong-held beliefs about the role of honoring human dignity in our pursuit of anti-racism practice.

There are two instances of unresolved tension in this book (probably more), and while I do not necessarily believe they need to be resolved, I agree that they should be addressed. The first has to do with the dichotomy of institutional racism and individual racist beliefs/actions. In our context, institutional racism refers to policies, practices, beliefs and systems at the societal or institutional level which tend to affect particular racial or ethnic groups disproportionately. For example, practices that have facilitated schooling, voting, housing, employment obtention by members of certain groups in detriment of others operate within the realm of institutional racism. They can be affected by awareness raising that leads to changes in policy, the law, etc. On the other hand, there are individual acts towards and beliefs about race and ethnicity at the individual level that can affect others at that specific level as well. Many times those actions are juxtaposed against environments that not only make them possible but condone them. For example, if there is no law in a particular environment making it illegal to deny someone housing on the basis of their race, ethnicity, or national origin, the individual racism of a particular property owner can exist unchallenged. In this book, we oscillate between considerations at the social level and at the individual level exactly because of that juxtaposition, and not always do we call the reader's attention to what form of racism is at center of a discussion because of this fluidity.

The second point of tension has to do our academic focus on historically minoritized populations (a more scholarly focus) as the subject of concern in our writing and a more legalistic approach to discrimination that applies and defends the rights of any person of any race and gender not to be discriminated against. That is to say that if a white, cis male alleges discrimination at a place of work based on his race, his case is legally no different from that of any other person seeking legal action. On the other hand, academics, when writing about discrimination, more often than not focus on populations that have been historically disenfranchised and minoritized. Accordingly, in this book our general focus is on BIPOC populations and their intersections with other identities (e.g. gender, sexuality, disability status) that might lead to positions of greater vulnerability in our societies.

I hope this book inspires its readers to adopt an anti-racist stance in their research and practice, one that recognizes all of our shared humanity and intrinsic value. Work on anti-racism is never finished, is never passive, and is always worthwhile.

Notes

(1) Centers for Disease Control (2021) Health Equity Considerations and Racial and Ethnic Minority Groups. See https://www.cdc.gov/coronavirus/2019-ncov/community/health-equity/race-ethnicity.html.
(2) Bowles, N. (2018) Jordan Peterson, custodian of the patriarchy. *The New York Times*, 18 May. See https://www.nytimes.com/2018/05/18/style/jordan-peterson-12-rules-for-life.html.
(3) O pensamento moderno ocidental é um pensamento abissal. Consiste num sistema de distinções visíveis e invisíveis, sendo que as invisíveis fundamentam as visíveis. As distinções invisíveis são estabelecidas através de linhas radicais que dividem a realidade social em dois universos distintos: o universo 'deste lado da linha' e o universo 'do outro lado da linha'. A divisão é tal que 'o outro lado da linha' desaparece enquanto realidade, torna-se inexistente, e é mesmo produzido como inexistente. Inexistência significa não existir sob qualquer forma de ser relevante ou compreensível.
(4) See https://www.theguardian.com/world/2015/mar/24/sweden-adds-gender-neutral-pronoun-to-dictionary for more information on the Swedish pronoun addition.
(5) Cummings, K.W. (2019) 'Minoritized:' A violent word. *The Baltimore Sun*. https://www.baltimoresun.com/opinion/op-ed/bs-ed-op-0328-minoritized-word-20190320-story.html.

References

Baumeister, R.F. and Leary, M.R. (1995) The need to belong: Desire for interpersonal attachments as a fundamental human motivation. *Psychological Bulletin* 117 (3), 497–529.
Berns, M., Barrett, J., Chan, C. and Chikuma, W. (1998) (Re)experiencing hegemony: The linguistic imperialism of Robert Phillipson. *International Journal of Applied Linguistics* 8 (2), 271–282.
Crenshaw, K. (1989) Demarginalizing the intersection of race and sex: A black feminist critique of antidiscrimination doctrine, feminist theory and antiracist politics. *University of Chicago Legal Forum*: 1989 (1), Article 8.
de Sousa Santos, B. (2007) Para além do Pensamento Abissal: Das linhas globais a uma ecologia de saberes. *Revista Crítica de Ciências Sociais*. http://journals.openedition.org/rccs/753.
Friedrich, P. (2015) *The Literary and Linguistic Construction of Obsessive-Compulsive Disorder: No Ordinary Doubt*. New York: Palgrave.
Gunaratnam, Y. (2003) *Researching Race and Ethnicity: Methods, Knowledge and Power*. London: Sage.
Joshi, P., Santy S., Budhiraj, K., Bali A. and Choudhury, M. (2021) The state and fate of linguistic diversity and inclusion in the NLP world. *Proceedings of the 58th Annual Meeting of the Association for Computational Linguistics* (pp. 6282–6293), July 5–10, 2020.

Kubota, R. (2020) Confronting epistemological racism, decolonizing scholarly knowledge: Race and gender in applied linguistics. *Applied Linguistics* 41 (5), 712–732.

Leonard, W.Y. (2021) Toward an anti-racist linguistic anthropology: An indigenous response to white supremacy. *Journal of Linguistic Anthropology* 31 (2), 218–237.

Linton, S. (2005) What is disability studies? *PMLA/Publications of the Modern Language Association of America* 120 (2), 518–522.

Malone, G.P., Pillow D.R. and Osman, A. (2012) The general belongingness scale (GBS): Assessing achieved belongingness. *Personality and Individual Differences* 52 (3), 311–316.

Maslow, A.H. (1968) *Toward a Psychology of Being*. New York: Van Nostrand.

Phillipson, R. (1992) *Linguistic Imperialism*. Oxford: Oxford University Press.

Quijano, A. (2000) Coloniality of power, Eurocentrism, and Latin America (trans. M. Ennis). *Nepantla* 1 (3), 533–580.

Silva, J.M., Ornat, M.J. and Mason-Deese, L. (2020) Feminist geographies in Latin America: Epistemological challenges and the decoloniality of knowledge. *Journal of Latin American Geography* 19 (1), 269–277.

Singh, J. (2018) *Unthinking Mastery: Dehumanism and Decolonial Entanglements*. Durham, NC: Duke University Press.

Van Parijs, P. (2002) Linguistic justice. *Politics, Philosophy & Economics* 1 (1), 59–74.

Van Parijs, P. (2011) *Linguistic Justice for Europe and for the World*. Oxford: Oxford University Press.

Welton, A.D., Owens, D.R. and Zamani-Gallaher, E.M. (2018) Anti-racist change: A conceptual framework for educational institutions to take systemic action. *Teachers College Record* 120 (14), 1–22.

2 TEIL as a Tool for Anti-Racist Pedagogy: Exploring its Potential

Aya Matsuda

Teaching English as an International Language (TEIL) is a relatively new approach to English Language Teaching (ELT) informed by world Englishes and English as a Lingua Franca studies, and it embraces the plurality of English and diversity of its users and uses (e.g. Alsagoff *et al.*, 2012; Matsuda, 2012). Although it has been promoted mostly as a way to meet the pragmatic needs of English language learners in the heterogeneous and complex sociolinguistic reality of English, rather than a political movement or activism, I argue that TEIL can function as decolonizing and anti-racist practices in two ways: *implicitly* by moving away from some ELT practices based on colonial assumptions (e.g. native speaker bias in assessment and teacher qualification), and *explicitly* by creating space (and necessities) for learners and teachers to reflect on and fight coloniality and racism in their English learning and teaching experience. In this chapter, I substantiate this argument by taking examples of ELT practices that have been repeatedly criticized for their coloniality and racism – the conceptualization of legitimate forms of English, cultures of English and users of English – and demonstrating how TEIL challenges, deconstructs and redefines their meaning and places in ELT. TEIL by any means is not neutral or immune from the coloniality of ELT. As with anything else that is related to ELT, it is inherently colonial, at least in the ways ELT is envisioned and practiced today. TEIL does not solve or eliminate the problem of coloniality or racism in the field either. However, it has the potential to diffuse them by deconstructing the problematic dichotomies that often underlie the taken-for-granted colonial and racially unequal relationships found in different dimensions of the field and can serve as an accessible entryway for ELT professionals who are new to this effort.

Introduction

I have been working with the idea of Teaching English as an International Language (TEIL) for almost 20 years but never explicitly talked about it in relation to the issue of race and Teaching English to Speakers of Other Languages (TESOL)[1] (Curtis & Romney, 2006; Kubota & Lin, 2006) or in terms of its role in anti-racist pedagogy (e.g. Motha, 2014). In fact, I have explicitly said that TEIL was not created to promote any particular ideology and resisted bringing the discussion of race into the discussion of TEIL.

I did so for several reasons.

First, TEIL, in my view, is a framework primarily to meet the pragmatic needs of leaners and something one should consider adopting regardless of their language or political ideology. TEIL certainly is not ideology free, and it is in fact based on some specific assumptions (such as that outer-circle varieties are legitimate) that may not be shared by all TESOL professionals. But my stance has been that one should adopt the framework even if one does not personally share those assumptions because it benefits our students. As a result, my efforts have been to promote TEIL as something not tied to a particular ideological goal and to appeal to more practitioners to adopt it in a way that makes sense in their local contexts. Bringing a race-informed perspective seemed to contradict such efforts.

Second, I hesitated to engage in the conversation around race and TESOL in general. Discussions of race and TESOL involve (and in a sense, rely on) various categories and dichotomies that have been critiqued for their essentializing tendencies, among other things (e.g. white vs non-white, native English speakers (NESs) vs non-NESs (NNESs)[2]). A degree of essentialization is inevitable when talking about categories, but talking about them while acknowledging the diversity and complexity within each category is quite challenging and it can lead to the marginalization of individuals who do not quite fit the criteria (Kubota & Lin, 2006). In other words, by engaging in talks that attempt to challenge and deconstruct the problematic categorizations and resulting practices, I could end up further promoting them. I could not figure out how to get around that.

More specifically, I could not figure out how to discuss race and racialization in the context of English Language Teaching (ELT) without getting caught in the paradox of centering whiteness in the process of critiquing whiteness. I understand that whiteness does not refer to simply one's pigmentation or phenotype but one's social and political standing. It is not a natural, biological category but a social category (Kubota & Lin, 2006, 2009; Luke & Lin, 2006). As my colleague, Lee Bebout, a leading scholar in critical whiteness theory, reminded me, Irish immigrants and their descendants were often not considered white in the US until the late 19th and early 20th century although they are now.

And to complicate the matter further, in the early 1900s, Irish-Americans were considered white in some places like Arizona but not in some other places like New York City. Such an example shows the pliability of whiteness and demonstrates that race is 'all about social and historical context' (personal communication, 1 April, 2021).

But as someone who is new to this idea, I find it impossible to separate the term 'whiteness' from one's skin color, and consequently, Europeanness, Anglo-Americanness and the worldview that centers around them. For example, colonization is often equated as white oppressing non-white, which applies to most cases of military and political colonization that are associated with the spread of English and ELT (i.e. the expansion of the British empire). But they are *European* colonizations. There are cases such as the Japanese colonization of Taiwan and Korea that do not quite fit the picture of white oppressing non-white, in terms of their skin color. Then, in a sense, the practice of equating the powerful/oppressor with white and the powerless/oppressed with non-white is based on and enforces Eurocentric perspectives; it can erase or marginalize the history of colonization and stories of colonized peoples that do not fit the criteria although they are equally real to those who experienced it. I understand that that is not the intention of those who critique race dynamics in ELT, and that my struggle may simply be a result of not quite grasping the concept of whiteness. But for whatever reason, the incongruence I saw discouraged me from pursuing this line of inquiry.

Furthermore, talking about race is hard. It is complicated and requires a thorough understanding of the concept and nuanced use of language to engage in a productive discussion. I was too intimidated at first, and then, as the time passed and the conversation moved forward, it seemed impossible to catch up. Besides, some smart and invested scholars were tackling these issues anyway, so why not leave the challenge to them?

But I always felt that I was not doing all I could. I knew I was in a unique position to make a difference if I wanted to. 'A woman of color' is a label I do not quite identify with because I find it homogenizing; there are other labels such as 'Japanese', 'teacher', 'scholar', '(single) mother' and 'runner' that speak more loudly about me. But I realize that I am a woman of color, after all, and more specifically, a woman of color who has been successfully working in the field of TESOL at a US institution (i.e. contexts in which whiteness prevails). Because of this, I have a unique perspective that I can bring into the conversation, and I'm in the privileged position that allows me to act on this. But how do I enter the conversation?

Then two things happened. One was a conversation with Suhanthie Motha, one of the most prominent and influential scholars of race and ELT, in February 2020. I admire her both as a person and a scholar and always find her work eye-opening and inspiring. She was a plenary speaker at the Linguistics and Applied Linguistics/TESOL Symposium put together by graduate students at Arizona State University, and in her talk, she reminded us that not doing anything about racism in TESOL means that we are complacent and supporting it (Motha, 2020); she also urged each of us to think what we can do about it. I felt like she was speaking to me, and I promised myself that I would do something about it.

In the same year, in the US, where I live and work, there was a series of incidents involving police force and minoritized citizens that lead to the 2020 Black Lives Matter[3] protests. Although such incidents were occurring prior to that year, there was a sudden increase in awareness about structural racism among the general public. At my university, this prompted conversations about anti-racist pedagogy in general – how we could address the issue of structural racism in our curricula and what changes we could bring to the world through our teaching – and I was inspired by the ideas shared by colleagues outside of my own field.

These two forces pushed me to reflect on my role in promoting or resisting racism, specifically in the field of TESOL, which is my scholarly home. And my thinking brought me back to TEIL, an approach to ELT I have helped develop and advocate for. In this era, when we are searching for ways to fight racial injustice through teaching, it only makes sense for me to examine the potential of this familiar framework as a tool for anti-racist pedagogy.

This chapter begins with a brief review of how the issue of race has been investigated, problematized and critiqued in the field of ELT. I then introduce the framework of TEIL and unpack how this pedagogical approach allows us to move away from the mindset and practices that reflect and reinforce structural and institutional racism in the field. The chapter ends with a reflection on the opportunities TEIL provides us, TESOL professionals, to combat racism in a way that makes sense to each practitioner and their local contexts.

Race and/in TESOL

When Ryuko Kubota and Angel Lin edited a special topic issue on race and TESOL for *TESOL Quarterly* in 2006, they observed that 'inquiry into ideas of race [had] not yet earned significant visibility in TESOL scholarship' (2006: 472). Multiple factors, including the discourse of colorblind racism (Bonilla-Silva, 2013) and liberal multiculturalism (Kubota, 2004) that presents TESOL as a race-neutral space, discouraged open discussion about issues of race and inequality (Motha, 2014).

Fifteen years later, however, I think it is fair to say that there is increased awareness, interest and dialogue among ELT practitioners concerning race, racism and racialization. For example, a Google Scholar article search using the key terms 'racism' and 'TESOL' yielded

242 entries with the publication year of 2005 and 930 entries with the publication year of 2020. There are also books (e.g. Kubota & Lin, 2009; Motha, 2014; Rosa, 2019) that critique structural and institutional racism in ELT today and call for anti-racist pedagogy in TESOL.

Moreover, as I mentioned earlier, a series of tragic events involving police violence on minoritized citizens in 2020 led to an increased awareness among the general public about structural racism, and educators began (if they hadn't had already) pondering how to fight it through their teaching. In response, the TESOL International Association, whose headquarters are in the US, issued a statement against racial injustice and inequality (TESOL, 2020b) and issued a joint *TESOL Quarterly-TESOL Journal* publication (TESOL, 2020a) that curated articles on race, identity and ELT that were published in the journals in the past five years. While the triggering events were local (US) events, their effects are not only local in the discourse in TESOL where people, ideas and practices are heavily transnational.

Racism in TESOL

The word racism may be used synonymously with or be closely associated with bigotry in lay conversation, but that is not the primary focus of the discussion of racism in TESOL. Rather, the focus is on structural racism, or practices and thinking patterns that are supported by and perpetuate 'a specific power dynamic that excludes certain racialized groups as the inferior Other while maintaining the status quo of the Self' (Kubota & Lin, 2006: 478)

Typically, the group(s) with power and privileges are (racialized as) white and the oppressed group(s) are (racialized as) non-white, which reflects the Anglo-European history in which white Europeans colonized and/or dominated non-white populations and enjoyed a number of privileges not available to others. These categories may have been based on the notion of biological race historically, but they are now *racialized* – that is, as I stated earlier, their whiteness is a social construct associated with the power and privilege rather than an individual's skin color. What that means is that I, as an East Asian person, may not identify as or be perceived as 'white' or Caucasian, based on appearance, but I could be part of a privileged group or category associated with whiteness.

I have already mentioned earlier that I am still struggling with this way of thinking because I cannot seem to separate the 'skin color' aspect of race from the social construction of the category, and consequently, cannot let go of the fear that the discussion of whiteness can perpetuate the white-centric view of the world that it attempts to critique. Having said that, however, I agree completely there is a race-based structural inequity in ELT. I also acknowledge that, because it has been part of the profession throughout its history and manifestations and is reinforced in all facets of ELT practices, such inequity is often implicit and invisible, making it difficult to address.

Coloniality of ELT

ELT, both past and present, is inherently colonizing and cannot escape from its coloniality (Pennycook, 1994, 1998, 2007). Political and military colonization by the UK and the US in the 1500s through the 1900s was the major force behind the global spread of English, and 'ELT was a vehicle by which to privilege British and American colonizers, and create colonial subjects modeled after their own image (Kumaravadivelu, 2003, Pennycook, 2010)' (Yazan & Rudolph, 2018: 2). The current use and status of English as an international and global language is also supported by – and reinforces – today's idea of globalization, in which Eurocentric values and epistemologies continue to dominate and are privileged. And, by extension, TESOL can be defined as a profession that is supported by, perpetuates and even promotes coloniality.

From the critical race perspective, then, this implies that ELT comes with racism and racialization. Motha (2006: 496), for example, has argued that '[b]ecause the spread of the English language across the globe was historically connected to the international political power of white people, English and whiteness are thornily intertwined (Kumaravadivelu, 2003; Pennycook, 2001)'. Likewise, identities shaped within the construct of ELT are inherently racialized (Motha, 2006), where the privileged groups – e.g. teachers over students, speakers of a 'standard' variety over others – are associated with whiteness (e.g. Ruecker & Ives, 2015). In fact, ELT is embedded within a context of inequitable racial relationship and thus 'the mere act of teaching ESOL reproduces racism' (Motha, 2014: 77). In other words, if you take a position that ELT is inherently racist, it is also the case that ELT is built upon, reinforces and further promotes structural racism, and we cannot get away from the coloniality and consequently, racism, as long as we are engaged in ELT (Motha, 2020).

In addition, coloniality (and racism) is a layer that coats the entire ELT industry, and its presence can be observed in all aspects of ELT (e.g. Brittain, 2020; Kiczkowiak *et al.*, 2016; Mohamed, 2015). It may not be visible because it has been normalized (Lowe, 2020), and it may not always be the most prevalent or influential factor; but it is always there.

What is TEIL?

In this chapter, I am using TEIL as an umbrella term to refer to an emerging paradigm in ELT, following the common usage among many researchers (e.g. Alsagoff *et al.*, 2012; Marlina & Giri, 2014; Matsuda, 2012; Matsuda & Friedrich, 2011; McKay, 2002; Sharifian, 2009). TEIL, and other approaches included in this paradigm, such as *English as a Lingua Franca* (ELF)*-aware pedagogy* (Bayyurt & Sifakis, 2015; Sifakis, 2014) and *Global English Language Teaching* (GELT) (Galloway, 2013; Galloway & Rose, 2015), all draw from the study of world Englishes (WE), English as an international language (EIL) and English as a lingua franca (ELF) studies and embrace the plurality of English and diversity of its users and uses.

TEIL does not assume or promote one variety of English dedicated to or preferred in international communication. Rather, it assumes that there will be multiple varieties of English accompanied by different cultural frames of reference brought to the table by participants, and that participants employ various strategies to negotiate differences to make themselves mutually intelligible. And thus, the goal of TEIL is not to make English language learners similar to NESs but rather to prepare them for the heterogeneous, dynamic and contextually defined use of English as a global lingua franca.

In practice, TEIL typically encourages, among other things:

- exposure to, awareness of and respect for different varieties of English and their users;
- use of and critical engagement with the cultural materials from diverse sources; and
- understanding of the politics of EIL among teachers and students.

The uniqueness of TEIL, however, is not merely a new set of practices that are more inclusive of and in sync with the diversity and heterogeneity in the English-speaking world today. Rather, it is the way TEIL challenges the traditional notion of language legitimacy, ownership and norm, which has driven and shaped the field of ELT throughout history. In other words, it calls for a shift in the mindset and a new conceptualization of the target model(s), correctness, teacher qualifications and so forth that have implications for overall ELT practices.

How Can TEIL Be Used to Fight Racism?

From the perspective of anti-racist pedagogy, the virtue of TEIL is that it challenges the traditional notion of language legitimacy and ownership and the troubling colonial relationships and whiteness embedded in them. In one of TEIL's parenting disciplines – WE studies – the colonial past is understood as one of the driving forces behind the global spread of English and influential factors in determining the place of the language in different countries around the world. More specifically, it recognizes how local users of English have dissociated the language from its Anglo-European background (Hino, 2009; Kachru, 1992b) and nativized the language to meet their own communicative and identity needs (Kachru, 1992a). By legitimizing the local forms and users of English, WE studies – and, consequently, TEIL – deconstruct the exclusive power and privileges from the UK and the US in the context of ELT and creates a more pluricentric view of the language.

Because of this, TEIL has the potential to tackle racism in ELT. Implicitly, because TEIL promotes practices that are based on the view of language and language users in which the power, legitimacy and agency are more diffused, adopting it as the guiding framework, by definition, redirects us from engaging in the racist and racialized practices of the past. It can rewrite or reprogram our ELT practices by embracing the reality of English-speaking world and recognizing the critical role played by various minoritized groups. Explicitly, TEIL creates opportunities to directly confront racism and racialization as they relate to the use, learning and teaching of English today and affords space for students to engage in critical thinking and activism.

Racialization of NESs/NNESs

One way in which racism manifests in ELT is the racialization of NESs and NNESs. The categories of NES and NNES, their dichotomous positioning and the uncritical privileging of NESs that accompany them have been heavily criticized in the field of TESOL, with or without reference to race (see the resource page of the TESOL NNEST interest section, 2019, for a collection of publications on this topic). And the NES bias has ripple effects on all aspects of ELT, from the way standard English is defined to the reality created in the teaching materials to teacher qualification to assessment to the construction of an English learner identity. From the race perspective, the racialization of NESs and NNESs is not only one manifestation of racism in TESOL but also the fuel behind the practices that perpetuate it. That is, various practices that have been criticized as racist seem to come back to the racialization of NESs and NNESs.

In the context of ELT, the most influential privilege that is associated with the category of NES is that they are perceived and presented as the only *legitimate* speakers of English (Lowe, 2020). They are the ideal speakers who have rich linguistic and cultural knowledge related to English and they are the people English learners expect to interact with. Additionally, there is often – although not always – a desire or perceived need on the part of the learners to become like them in order to be part of the English-speaking community that English learners imagine. Motha (2014), for example, points out that the only type of English-as-a-second-language (ESL) student in US schools that is represented in the social imagination of US Americans is the assimilated one, sending a message that the only way they can become part of this society is through learning English and becoming a whitewashed American. This positioning of NESs and NNESs perpetuates the inequality between the two because, if NESs are the only legitimate users of English, English learners, by definition, are promised only to be illegitimate users of English.

To clarify, again, that NESs and NNESs are 'racialized' does not mean that all NESs are of one race and all NNESs are that of another/ others. Rather, it refers to the tendency to equate the NESs with white and NNESs with non-white, including all privileges, power, oppression, etc. that are associated with each racial/racialized group in a society. In other words, a non-white NES enjoys the privilege of their white counterparts, although possibly not to the fullest extent (e.g. Charles, 2019), not because of their self-identified or perceived 'race' but because the category they belong to due to their language background (NESs) can (at times) lead to forms of white privilege.

The NES/NNES dichotomy and the NES bias are explicitly deconstructed and problematized in TEIL. Insights from WE studies, for example, challenge the dichotomy by shedding light on a group of language users that do not quite fit into these binary, specifically proficient (and even L1) users of nativized varieties of English from the outer circle. WE studies also show the 'cline of proficiency' (Kachru, 1992a: 57) or the range of proficiency among English users in one context, questioning the essentialized view of NESs and NNESs that enables this dichotomous thinking. Similarly, EIL and ELF research, both of which inform TEIL, explicitly challenge the assumption that NESs are the most competent users of English in the global use of English.

Based on these scholarly insights, TEIL advocates for adopting successful EIL users as the target, regardless of their 'nativeness' as an English user. TEIL emphasizes the importance of the exposure to a variety of English users – both so-called NESs and NNESs – not only as a way to prepare learners for future interlocutors who would come from diverse contexts but also to help learners see themselves as future legitimate users of English. Proficient NNESs, when included and represented in English classrooms, can potentially serve as a role model for English language learners. Even more, they can create an opportunity to have students reflect on their own beliefs about (N)NESs and how they change over engagement with NNESs. In assessment, too, the norm can be defined not in terms of how closely the use approximate NESs but rather how effective the language use will be in EIL/ELF communication. For example, in traditional assessment, mixing non-English words and phrases is typically perceived as a demonstration of a gap in one's English lexical knowledge because that is not something NESs – who are often assumed to be monolingual in the context of ELT – are expected to do. However, it is something that is often observed in EIL/ELF communication, with a different degree of success; that is, in some contexts, the audience may understand the non-English expression without any explanation, but in other contexts, it may require different levels of linguistic and cultural translation, and EIL/ELF users may not be always successful in assessing the required level of contextualization. If so, then the use of non-English expressions should not automatically be regarded as an error but instead can be assessed in terms of how effectively it is done – focusing on the appropriateness in the context provided in the assessment or whether the response demonstrates the speaker or writer's ability to contextualize non-English expressions appropriately and use them to achieve their communicative goals successfully.

In other words, the reality envisioned in TEIL does not rely on the racialized, problematic categorization and dichotomy of NESs and NNESs, at least to the extent that the traditional approaches to ELT do. As a result, the consequent practices can contribute to taking down the instructional racism in TESOL that gets repeated and reinforced every day.

Racialization of 'standard' English

If the category of NESs is racialized, what about the language they speak? The notions of legitimate speakers and legitimate varieties of English are in a tautological relationship: English spoken by *legitimate* speakers is *legitimate*, and those who speak *legitimate* English are *legitimate* users of English. More specifically, in ELT worldwide, it is the mainstream varieties of American and British English that are considered standard. They are presented as the target model, they are the varieties most textbooks are written in and they are the varieties students are tested on. They are privileged in the classroom and carry currencies outside of the classroom, which leads to more privileging in the classroom. And this privileged status is closely tied to the status of speakers of those varieties: it is widely accepted in sociolinguistics that the power and status of a language does not rest in the language itself but in the power and status of its speakers.

From a critical race perspective, it can be said that both NESs of the standard English and their English are racialized, and their racializations extend to each other because of the aforementioned tautological relationship. 'Standard English' is associated with the variety spoken by mainstream white people with certain power and privileges in so-called English-speaking countries (e.g. the inner circle in Kachru's concentric circle model), but the variety itself also has been racialized and enjoys power and privileges. Nero (2005), for instance, has argued that 'while the ESL class might celebrate cultural diversity in theory, it requires linguistic uniformity in practice' (2005: 198). *White English* is the legitimate variety of English that is privileged in real society and as well as in ELT curricula.

These two scales of whiteness – NESs and 'Standard English' – also intersect with each other. Thus, a NES of standard English – someone who is entitled to double whiteness – may enjoy more privileges than someone who has only one – a NES of 'non-standard' English or a NNES who speaks 'standard English'. And they all are likely to enjoy more privilege than NNESs whose English is not recognized as standard.

And within each category, realities such as the difference between self-perceived whiteness and perceived whiteness and the situated nature of whiteness complicate the matter even further. In fact, Motha (2006: 507) has argued that 'race is implicated in the construct of native English, standard English, WEs, and AAVE' and that 'the idea that nativeness in English is more desirable than fluent, comprehensible NNES speech and an unquestioned belief in the necessity of passing in order to be truly successful are rooted in both racism and colonialism' (Motha, 2014: 94).

TEIL directly challenges this line of thinking by arguing that 'non-white' varieties – such as new Englishes in former colonies of the US and UK – are also legitimate, and the correctness of each variety is determined not by how closely it resembles a white variety of English but rather by the local usage. It urges teachers and program designers to stop selecting varieties associated with whiteness as the target variety merely to maintain the status quo and instead to re-examine their selection based on the appropriateness for the specific group of learners and contexts where teaching is taking place. Furthermore, TEIL emphasizes the importance of exposure to and awareness of different varieties of English, the receptive proficiency in those varieties (i.e. one does not have to be fluent in multiple varieties but must be able to understand them) and the respect toward varieties of English that differ from the variety they are learning. After all, the chosen target variety may be considered the 'best' variety in that particular context, but it may not be a preferred choice in other contexts.

In actual practice, the assumption that all varieties are equal plays out in a complicated way. In an ideal world, all varieties of English would be respected and accepted equally. But the reality is that there is always a hierarchy in each context where the instruction takes place. And not giving students access to the privileged variety of English – standard, white or western centric – is not necessarily in the best interests of students because, for students of the oppressed groups, NNESs being one of them, proficiency in a privileged variety is often the most powerful weapon to overcome the oppression and to have their voice heard in the fight against such oppression. So TEIL practitioners must take into consideration such local factors as the needs of learners and the status of different varieties of English, and as a result, they often end up selecting a variety/varieties associated with privilege as the target variety.

The dilemma described here is what Lodge (1997) called the *access paradox*:

> If you provide more people with access to the dominant variety of the dominant language, you contribute to perpetuating and increasing its dominance. If, on the other hand, you deny students access, you perpetuate their marginalization in a society that continues to recogni[s]e this language as a mark of distinction. You also deny them access to the extensive resources available in that language; resources which have developed as a consequence of the language's dominance. (Janks, 2004: 33)

In other words, in the context of EIL, selecting the 'standard' or 'privileged' variety as the target variety feeds into the privileging of white English, the variety with *linguistic capital* (Bourdieu, 1991), adding to the spiral process of adding more privilege to the variety and, thus, contributing to further inequity. But, denying access to such a variety is unfair to learners because the lack of proficiency in the privileged variety will conveniently keep them in their current position/situation, also perpetuating the inequity.

To work around this, teachers 'need to find ways of rejecting a unitary view of English and a normative view of communicative competence' (Janks, 2004: 36). Encouraging students to *add* a privileged variety to their linguistic repertoire, rather than to *replace* what they know with the new variety of English, is one way to mitigate this problem. Another is to foster a critical awareness of how the linguistic hierarchy plays out in different contexts. While helping students develop fluency in the privileged variety, we can also help them think critically about in what contexts and with which audience such a variety is preferred and why. Janks (2004) argues that teachers must reduce the power of education to maintain a language's symbolic power, especially when it is detrimental to the languages students speak. TEIL does not protect us from engaging in colonializing practices but can influence how Englishes are understood and presented in TEIL, which in turn provides some possibilities to be more empowering than oppressing.

Racialization of (N)NESTs

One area within TESOL where the implication of the racialization of (N)NESs is most studied and critiqued is probably in the discussion of teacher qualification and hiring. Research in NNEST studies over the past two decades, as well as numerous anecdotes, has shown, among other things, that 'native speakers of English have a privileged status in employment, a privilege that is increased by having white skin' (Kubota & Lin, 2006: 479; see also Ruecker & Ives, 2015; Sawyer & Ligget, 2012). Lin shares her own experience (Kubota & Lin, 2006) where she was passed over for an opportunity which was then given to her less-qualified NES colleague; not only that, her supervisor justified it by saying it was a better PR move. Stories such as that present examples of practices that show and perpetuate the NES bias which extends to teachers.

There are several assumptions that enable NEST bias, including a belief that NESs have 'perfect' linguistic knowledge of English and rich knowledge of 'English-speaking' culture, which automatically make them better teachers than their non-native counterparts. Some may even argue that it is good for English learners to become accustomed to the NESs who represent their future interlocutors. However, NNEST research as well as our experiences debunk such myths. Just reflecting on our own experience with our 'native' language, we quickly realize that we do not have 'perfect' or complete knowledge of the language and culture(s) associated with it. Just having acquired a language as a native language alone does not adequately equip us to be effective teachers, either. In fact, if we acknowledge the fact that much of English use today takes place exclusively among NNESs, even the idea that NESs represent the future interlocutors no longer holds true.

Moving away from the NES/NNES dichotomy in relation to teachers does not mean to compromise and settle for less-than-NES teachers. Rather, it is to redefine teacher qualification and effectiveness by closely examining what is required and preferred for a teacher in a particular context. For instance, in most contexts in which TEIL is adopted, proficiency in intercultural communication is critical for teachers because the use of English for which learners are being prepared often involves intercultural communication. Whether one is a NES or NNES is not the best way to measure or predict proficiency in this area; depending on their prior living circumstances, some have more experience than others, and some are more apt in this skill than others. Some hiring committees may decide that experience of teaching abroad is a good way to assess one's proficiency in this area; others may decide that experience working with a multicultural group within a local community is a better indicator. Whatever the criteria they decide to use, they can use them in the job description and candidate screening, instead of using the term NEST with a hope that the NES candidates happen to bring such experiences.

Unpacking the idea of competent EIL users and teachers and looking specifically for those identified qualities in hiring and teacher evaluation are goals clearly compatible with TEIL. Their implementation increases the TEIL's efficacy as an anti-racist pedagogy tool by weaning ELT practitioners from the NES(T)/NNES(T) dichotomy.

Concluding Remarks

In this chapter, I explored TEIL's potential as a tool for anti-racist pedagogy in ELT. Because of its fundamental assumptions and resulting practices, TEIL, by definition, moves away from some ELT practices that are considered racist. It also creates space – and sometimes necessity – to engage students in critical thinking about the coloniality and racialization in their own English learning experiences, construction of their identity as an English learner and user and in their lives in general.

I do, however, want to clarify a few things. First, adopting TEIL alone may make our practice less racist or help us diffuse it to some extent, but it does not necessarily make it *anti*-racist. TEIL is not immune to racism in TESOL because it is, after all, a form of ELT, which is considered inherently colonial and racist. If we think of it as a pair of scales, something that is explicitly decolonizing and anti-racist must be added to counterbalance the inherit racism of ELT. Specific ways to facilitate this would vary, depending on specific ways in which race and racism affect students. But regardless of the contexts, abilities to think critically to engage in difficult, contentious, risky conversations need to be fostered in the classroom, and teachers need a good understanding of anti-racist pedagogy as well.

I also believe that TEIL – or any framework for that matter – cannot be expected to be used as THE only way to fight racism through teaching in a society. Structural racism is not exclusive to ELT; while some examples of racism in ELT are uniquely tied to the history and practices of ELT, it is also a part of a larger system that has its own structural racism, which influences and feeds into teaching and learning. Furthermore, although structural racism is everywhere, the way it plays out and is perceived and processed by teachers and learners varies from one context to another – i.e. it is not as simple as 'whites oppressing non-whites' because each community has its own way of constructing and privileging different races. Each teacher and learner also has their unique way of understanding their own race and its meaning in their community. If so, then, it is expected that the impact of a particular pedagogical framework would vary across the contexts and that it needs to be implemented in tandem with other pedagogical efforts to fight racism effectively.

In terms of the message to my colleagues, this is what I hope I have accomplished in this chapter. For my colleagues who are enthusiastically looking for new ways to fight racism through teaching – the category most readers of this volume probably belong to, given the focus of the book – I hope I have shown that TEIL is compatible with your vision and has the potential to assist you in achieving your goal if you are in the field of TESOL. I hope that you would consider giving it a try.

For readers who want to make their practices less racist but are not quite ready or equipped to engage in an active anti-racist pedagogy, I want to suggest TEIL as a starting point. As I explained earlier, there are aspects of TEIL that reduce the extent of racism by their design. Once such practices become the norm in your instructional context, you may start to see more opportunities within the framework and may feel more comfortable branching out.

And for those who do not believe that TESOL is racist or that is something that teachers need to fix, I still urge you to adopt TEIL. As I argued before (Matsuda, 2018), TEIL is a framework that all TESOL professionals should consider adopting regardless of their ideology, including their perspective on race and racism, for its pragmatic benefits. Even if you do not see racism in TESOL, you may decide to adopt it because it is better aligned with the sociolinguistic reality of English today. The less-racist approach you end up taking can help strengthen the current force to move the entire field to fight racism, even if the intention is not there.

Enthusiastic proponents of anti-racist pedagogy may argue that the last two of the three groups above are part of the problem because they are not taking a more active role in combating racism. And I, who encourage them to take such weak approaches, may be a coward enabler who allows racism in the field to continue and thrive. Should all teachers engage in anti-racist pedagogy? Ideally, yes. Racism exists, and teachers as the agent of societal changes should do everything they can to address the unfairness, inequity and discrimination that exist in their community. But the reality is that not all teachers feel the same need, readiness or power to enact such changes.

One approach to this varying degree of commitment and readiness is to try to convince all teachers to see themselves as an active gamechanger and accept that not doing so is feeding into racism. What is likely to happen is that people will respond with different degrees of enthusiasm, and the work of fighting racism in TESOL ends up on the shoulder of a selected group of passionate and committed TESOL professionals, as it has been. Another approach, which I have taken in this chapter, is to work toward a big change in the field by engaging everyone in the less-racist (and eventually anti-racist) practices that they can actually practice in their own context so that the wind would shift slowly but steadily toward the direction of less-racist and anti-racist practices. Although the changes brought by this approach may be less drastic, there is a power of mass and a sense of shared ownership among more individuals. Besides, smaller changes are better than no change at all.

Neither TEIL nor anti-racist pedagogy is something that can be implemented overnight. They both involve not just changes in procedure but also changes in the mindset and assumptions that inform our pedagogical decisions. This involves objectifying, critiquing, denying, challenging, moving away from and replacing the familiar system that has created who we are as English users and teachers today, and it is not easy to acknowledge that our efforts to be better and to help others may have contributed to racism. What that suggests to me is that we must allow ourselves to implement changes on a small scale, in a way that is perhaps a bit uncomfortable but still manageable, without being judged for not doing it all the way right away. That, in my view, is a good place to start.

Acknowledgments

I am grateful to Patricia Friedrich, Lee Bebout, Suhanthie Motha, Matthew Prior and two anonymous reviewers for their constructive feedback, insightful comments and helpful suggestions.

Notes

(1) In this chapter, I use the term TESOL (Teaching English to speakers of other languages) and ELT (English language teaching) interchangeably to refer to the professional field, industry and practices.
(2) I am well aware that the concept of 'native speaker' has been extensively critiqued and contested in the field of applied linguistics. In this chapter, I use the terms NES and NNES in ways that reflect the common perceptions of different types of English users, but it is not my intention to promote or reinforce the NS/NNS dichotomy. See Matsuda (2014) for a critique of this concept in the context of ELT.
(3) The BLM movement itself started in 2013 (Black Lives Matter Website, see https://blacklivesmatter.com/).

References

Alsagoff, L., McKay, S.L., Hu, G. and Renandya, W.A. (eds) (2012) *Principles and Practices for Teaching English as an International Language*. New York: Routledge.
Bayyurt, Y. and Sifakis, N.C. (2015) Developing an ELF-aware pedagogy: Insights from a self-education programme. In P. Vettorel (ed.) *New Frontiers in Teaching and Learning English* (pp. 55–76). Newcastle upon Tyne: Cambridge Scholars Publishing.
Bonilla-Silva, E. (2013) *Racism Without Racists: Color-blind Racism and the Persistence of Racial Inequality in the United States* (4th edn). Lanham, MD: Rowman & Littlefield.
Bourdieu, P. (1991) *Language and Symbolic Power* (ed. J. Thompson). Cambridge: Polity Press.
Brittain, E. (2020) Reinforcement of White native-speakerism: An analysis of English language teaching training materials. *GATESOL in Action Journal* 30 (1), 16–31.
Charles, Q.D. (2019) Black teachers of English in South Korea: Constructing identities as a native English speaker and English language teaching professional. *TESOL Journal* 10 (4), 1–16.
Curtis, A. and Romney, M. (2006) *Color, Race, and English Language Teaching: Shades of Meaning*. New York: Routledge.
Galloway, N. (2013) Global Englishes and English language teaching (ELT) – Bridging the gap between theory and practice in a Japanese context. *System* 41 (3), 786–803.
Galloway, N. and Rose, H. (2015) *Introducing Global Englishes*. Abingdon: Routledge.
Hino, N. (2009) The teaching of English as an International Language in Japan: An answer to the dilemma of indigenous values and global needs in the Expanding Circle. *AILA Review* 22 (1), 103–119.

Janks, H. (2004) The access paradox. *English in Australia* 139 (1), 33–42.

Kachru, B.B. (1992a) Models for non-native Englishes. In B.B. Kachru (ed.) *The Other Tongue: English Across Cultures* (2nd edn, pp. 48–72). Urbana, IL: University of Illinois Press.

Kachru, B.B. (1992b) Teaching World Englishes. In B.B. Kachru (ed.) *The Other Tongue: English Across Cultures* (2nd edn, pp. 355–365). Urbana, IL: University of Illinois Press.

Kiczkowiak, M., Baines, D. and Krummenacher, K. (2016) Using awareness raising activities on initial teacher training courses to tackle 'native speakerism.' *English Language Teacher Education and Development Journal* 19, 1–9.

Kubota, R. (2004) Critical multiculturalism and second language education. In B. Norton and K. Toohey (eds) *Critical Pedagogies and Language Learning* (pp. 30–52). Cambridge: Cambridge University Press.

Kubota, R. and Lin, A. (2006) Race and TESOL: Introduction to concepts and theories. *TEOSL Quarterly* 26 (3), 471–493.

Kubota, R. and Lin, A. (eds) (2009) *Race, Culture, and Identities in Second Language Education: Exploring Critically Engaged Practice*. New York: Routledge.

Kumaravadivelu, B. (2003) A postmethod perspective on English language teaching. *World Englishes* 22 (4), 539–550.

Lodge, H. (1997) Providing access to academic literacy in the Arts Foundation Programme at the University of Witwatersrand in 1996 – The theory behind the practice. Unpublished MA research report, University of the Witwatersrand.

Lowe, R.J. (2020) *Uncovering Ideology in English Language Teaching: Identifying the 'Native Speaker' Frame*. Cham: Springer.

Luke, A. and Lin, A. (2006) Coloniality, postcoloniality, and TESOL ... Can a spider weave its way out of the web that it is being woven into just as it weaves? *Critical Inquiry in Language Studies* 3 (2–3), 65–73.

Marlina, R. and Giri, R.A. (eds) (2014) *The Pedagogy of English as an International Language: Perspectives from Scholars, Teachers, and Students*. New York: Springer.

Matsuda, A. (ed.) (2012) *Principles and Practices of Teaching English as an International Language*. Bristol: Multilingual Matters.

Matsuda, A. (2014) Beyond the native speaker: My life as an NJS, NNES, and bilingual user of Japanese and English. *NNEST Newsletter*. TESOL, September 2014. See http://newsmanager.commpartners.com/tesolnnest/textonly/2014-09-09/2.html (accessed 2 October 2014).

Matsuda, A. (2018) Is teaching English as an international language all about being politically correct? *RELC Journal* 49 (1), 24–35.

Matsuda, A. and Friedrich, P. (2011) English as an international language: A curriculum blueprint. *World Englishes* 30 (3), 332–344.

McKay, S.L. (2002) *Teaching English as an International Language: Rethinking Goals and Approaches*. Oxford: Oxford University Press.

Mohamed, M.A.S. (2015) The role of English language textbooks in the reproduction of racism. *International Journal of English Language & Translation Studies* 3 (1), 95–108.

Motha, S. (2006) Racializing ESOL teacher identities in U.S. K-12 public schools. *TESOL Quarterly* 40 (3), 495–518.

Motha, S. (2014) *Race, Empire, and English Language Teaching*. New York: Teachers College Press.

Motha, S. (2020) Is an antiracist and decolonizing applied linguistics possible? *Annual Review of Applied Linguistics* 40, 128–133.

Nero, S. (2005) Language, identities, and ESL pedagogies. *Language and Education* 19 (3), 194–211.

Pennycook, A. (1994) *The Cultural Politics of English as an International Language*. London: Longman.

Pennycook, A. (1998) *English and the Discourses of Colonialism*. London: Routledge.

Pennycook, A. (2001) *Critical Applied Linguistics*. Mahwah, NJ: Lawrence Earlbaum.
Pennycook A. (2007) ELT and colonialism. In J. Cummins and C. Davison (eds) *International Handbook of English Language Teaching* (pp. 13–24). Boston, MA: Springer.
Pennycook, A. (2010) *Language as a Local Practice*. New York: Routledge.
Rosa, J. (2019) *Looking Like a Language, Sounding Like a Race: Raciolinguistic Ideologies and the Learning of Latindad*. Oxford: Oxford University Press.
Ruecker, T. and Ives, L. (2015) White native English speakers needed: The rhetorical construction of privilege in online teacher recruitment spaces. *TESOL Quarterly* 49 (4), 733–756.
Sawyer, R.D. and Ligget, T. (2012) Postcolonial education: Using a duoethnographic lens to explore a personal curriculum of post/decolonization. In J. Norris, R.D. Sawyer and D. Lund (eds) *Duoethnography: Dialogic Methods for Social, Health, and Educational Research* (pp. 71–88). New York: Routledge.
Sharifian, F. (2009) *English as an International Language: Perspectives and Pedagogical Issues*. Bristol: Multilingual Matters.
Sifakis, N.C. (2014) ELF awareness as an opportunity for change: A transformative perspective for ESOL teacher education. *Journal of English as a Lingua Franca* 3 (2), 317–335.
TESOL International Association (2020a) Race, identity, and English language teaching – A joint *TESOL Quarterly* and *TESOL Journal* publication. See https://onlinelibrary.wiley.com/doi/toc/10.1002/(ISSN)1234-5678.race-identity-and-english-language-teaching.
TESOL International Association (2020b) TESOL statement on racial injustice and inequality. See https://www.tesol.org/news-landing-page/2020/06/01/tesol-statement-on-racial-injustice-and-inequality.
The NNEST Interest Section (2019) The NNEST interest section resources page. See https://nnest.moussu.net/resources.html.
Yazan, B. and Rudolph, N. (2018) Introduction: Apprehending identity, experience, and (in)equity through and beyond binaries. In B. Yazan and N. Rudolph (eds) *Criticality, Teacher Identity, and (In)Equity in English Language Teaching* (pp. 1–19). Cham: Springer.

3 On (Dis)Inventing Language as a Zone of Non-Being: Black Teachers in ELT and Linguistic Racism in Brazil

Gabriel Nascimento

> This chapter seeks to analyze Black scholar Frantz Fanon's contributions on language and racism as a way to embrace and understand the role of language as a zone of non-being, thus making a deal to call on applied linguistics to be further committed to an anti-racist agenda that can engage dis-invention of language as that zone of non-being. Fanon (2008) writes from postcolonial Martinique and rejects white-based humanism. He then chooses language able to address rising problems concerning the language of the colonized black. Moreover, he claims language is a way for black men to be whitened and removed from their local culture. In order to deepen the remarks on languaging and racism, I will position race as a sign in a realm that accommodates black individuals within a zone of non-being. My arguments are informed by Gates Jr (1988) and by previous work I authored (Nascimento, 2019). Finally, I will embrace Fanon's primary analysis on the zone of non-being to push for dis-inventing language as an element of that space while analyzing the status of language as a zone of non-being imposed on the career of black teachers of English language in Brazil.

Introduction

Much scholarship is being devoted to analyzing the complex naturalization of language that supports the existence of oppression as a natural phenomenon. Fields such as language ideologies (Blommaert, 2010;

Irvine & Gal, 2000; Silva & Lopes, 2019; Silverstein, 1979), language as invention (Makoni & Pennycook, 2007; Nascimento, 2019); linguistic human rights (May, 2014), investment in second language teaching (Darvin & Norton, 2017), translanguaging approaches (Canagarajah, 2011; García & Li, 2014), linguistic citizenship (Williams & Stroud, 2015) among others offer robust examples of how language cannot be interpreted as if it were an autonomous entity regardless of the world and social reality it convenes. With these core elements as evidence, I claim that it is through naming that racism imposes its mastery upon the way the Other is racialized (Nascimento, 2019). Within these dynamics, language is used to mandate colonial forces (Veronelli, 2016) for the colonized to obey. It is precisely language as a means of dehumanization of black people that constitutes the first empirical object of Frantz Fanon in his *Black Skin White Masks* (Fanon, 2008), a book originally authored decades ago and reclaimed here in this article.

Frantz Fanon was born in 1925 in Martinique, in the Caribbean. According to Faustino (2015), Fanon joined the French army during the German invasion of France. It was during the war that he first realized he was surrounded by only white soldiers who discriminated against him.

After his PhD dissertation was rejected, he wrote *Black Skin White Masks* (Fanon, 2008), which came to be used widely in the peak of postcolonial studies in the UK.

My close relationship with this particular paper results from my personal position as a black scholar speaking from the Global South, with my inquiries revolving around race, racism and racialization in language. My country is a place with the most concentrated population of formerly enslaved people in the world, making up 52% of total population. As I mentioned earlier (Nascimento, 2019) black people are the majority of the victims of both police brutality and criminal-group violence in the context of colonial violence in Brazil[1]; black individuals are also the majority of the out-of-school and university and inside-the-jail population; finally, they are also the largest population of unemployed persons. My entire life was pervaded by those data to the point that I myself have relatives within those racially vulnerable groups that I have just mentioned. I have nephews and cousins who got involved in violent situations and still are in a space of vulnerability in Brazil. They are black and are aware of their position as black men and black women in the country.

Since early childhood, I recognized that language and racism were an extension of the major violence my family and I suffered at school and from our white neighbors in my community. *Wrong speaking, no proper Portuguese* and accusations of black bodies as languageless people are among the frequent indictments I heard during my entire life. In this chapter, I draw on Frantz Fanon to explore the sense of linguistic racism through the lens of language as a zone of non-being. To carry out such a task, I embrace the definitions of language as invention to endorse the need for dis-invention as informed by Makoni and Pennycook (2007). Empirically, I will examine autobiographical narratives I collected from black teachers of English language, including my own narratives. These narratives will serve to support the idea of dis-invention of zones of non-being, which I claim to be the position delimited to black teachers of English in Brazil as well as to push for necessary redress in ELT.

Zone of Being and Zone of Non-Being

As said earlier, Fanon (2008) was concerned with how modernity, colonization, capitalism, etc. intrinsically entail the non-humanization of black peoples, a phenomenon which resulted from enslavement and the slave trade. This is a critique against the humanist interpretation that recognized the very existence of an European modernity in contrast with the rest of non-white and non-European world, which was considered as non-human. I thus argue that Enlightenment, capitalism, colonialism, liberalism, positivism are samples of colonial power because they originate from western humanism and are framed with a sense that the white world is humanized whereas the non-white world is racialized.

Frantz Fanon, later strengthened by Said (1990), claims that humanism is an European invention that served to dehumanize the rest of the world. Among various examples are *The Lusiads*, the epic poem by Portuguese poet Luís de Camões and the journal entries from the first colonizers to invade Brazil, which bring forth an Eurocentric view of themselves as white and human while regarding as non-human members of the local cultures they invaded and decimated. Relevant examples within these texts are the ways these colonizers look at local communities as stranger communities with no commonalities in terms of habits.

Dussel (1993), within the umbrella of a coloniality approach, argues that the colonial reason, the one that until now has been considered a modern reason, is a myth co-constructed in the naturalization of Europeanness as modern. In addition, he defines that myth as exactly the ruling vision from primitive to modern capital in Europe, wherein, in order to construct a modern nation state, European peoples had to invade, enslave and decimate. This perspective shaped the standpoint in defense of Europe as the center of the world, thus leading to what Castro-Gómez (2007) termed Europe *zero-point* hubris.

Fanon (2008), in turn, points out that (white) humanity is a zone of being, if compared with the so-called zone of non-being that others are relegated to the following:

> What does a man want? What does the black man want? At the risk of arousing the resentment of my colored brothers, I will say that the black is not a man. There is a zone of nonbeing, an extraordinarily sterile and

arid region, an utterly naked declivity where an authentic upheaval can be born. (Fanon, 2008: 2)

The opposite of zone of non-being, as a non-humanized region conceived by the European, consists of a zone of being, the locus of white people and their whiteness portrayed as human representation. Those signs of human representation are set under a veil of humanity and, according to Veronelli (2016) and Singh (2018), stem from diverse linguistic and colonial accounts that raise languaging as a capacity opposing the local practices as languageless. From there, it becomes an assumed idea that 'the black man [who] wants to be white. The white man enslaves to reach a human level' (Fanon, 2008: 3). Therefore, to be human, the black person must be white to be eventually acknowledged, after fulfilling a number of white-based alleged characteristics of a human. In fact, as Said (1990) later demonstrated, it is not the status of human, which is targeted and reached, but a reified position invented in western discourse that we consider to be that of a human, even under a hard context of violence.

Given this, the question becomes how to reconsider a number of progressive approaches coming from the criticism of modernity that still encompass humanism as if it were offered equitably. In doing so, progressive approaches such as those claiming a postmodern Europe (Bauman, 2001, 2005) do not appear to be protesting the consequences of modernity over former colonies. That helps us realize that, between white people and us, European peoples and us or even the postmodern and us, there exists a line (Grosfoguel, 2016), or more specifically an abyssal line (Santos, 2007) dividing us into humans and non-humans (Fanon, 2008), civilized and non-civilized, modern and pre-modern.

A way to recount the same history is by marking the unmarked in language (Menezes de Souza, 2018), which consists of bringing back our bodies (Menezes de Souza, 2019) into the locus of enunciation. Rosa and Flores (2017) push for a raciolinguistic perspective that in educational environments can mark the unmarked racializations that continue to occur. Therefore, since colonialism eliminated the bodies behind the creation of knowledge in the colonies, marking the unmarked is the meaning making towards recognizing white people not only as humans, but like white humans as it was designed by coloniality.

Language as a Zone of Non-Being

To me languaging in particular has to do with performances embedded in translingual practices (García & Li, 2014), and here I use it to address language practices in general, not only those likely to happen at transcultural contexts.

Fanon, who is not speaking about languaging or translanguaging particularly, chose language as the empirical object of inquiry he first analyzed in his *Black Skin White Masks*. He gathered the local French speakerism by black people in the Antilles (now Martinique) to illustrate how racism could use language as a way to racialize black Antilleans who, in order to exist, should master the colonial French language.

He demonstrates that the imitation of white patterns of French speakerism by black people, rather than dehumanizing them, was a means of neglecting their rights to be considered humans. The theorist implies that 'to speak is to exist absolutely for the other' (Fanon, 2008: 8), and that:

> To speak means to be in a position to use a certain syntax, to grasp the morphology of this or that language, but it means above all to assume a culture, to support the weight of a civilization. (Fanon, 2008: 8)

He goes on to confront linguistic structures by recommending taking language into account as a way to enact the weight of a civilization. All these ideas are gathered to reinforce the interplay of language as culture (Saylag, 2014), language and ideology (Irvine & Gal, 2000) and thus language and racism (Kubota & Lin, 2006), making sense of language as the co-naturalization of language and vice versa (Alim, 2016; Rosa & Flores, 2017). Actually, language as culture and language as ideology are analyzed here through the lens of how language studies are influenced by the power of racism. Taking language into account also means locating the way racism acts in language, through language, and due to language use, for example. Drawing on García (2009) and García and Li's (2014) uses of translanguaging, what they term as *trans* to mobilize languaging serves to also address languaging in colonial lenses.

Languaging in colonial terms means pervasive meanings to black bodies:

> The black man has two dimensions. One with his fellows, the other with the white man. A Negro behaves differently with a white man and with another Negro. That this self-division is a direct result of colonialist subjugation is beyond question. ... No one would dream of doubting that its major artery is fed from the heart of those various theories that have tried to prove that the Negro is a stage in the slow evolution of monkey into man. Here is objective evidence that expresses reality. (Fanon, 2008: 8)

As said earlier in this article, Fanon criticizes humanism as a white institution of the western world that mistreats black people by compelling them to behave differently among white people than they do with their own people. Intending to exist, or to perform a personhood, black people from Martinique used to speak like white people to exist absolutely, which endorses the racialism that identified black individuals as in a pathway to evolving toward becoming humans.

The racialism I refer to is about joint biased interpretations of race that supported white people racializing enslaved Africans by pervading their existence with horror, terror and fear. An example of racialist ideas is engaged through overt and covert forms of racism (Appiah, 1997). Likewise, racialism includes color-blind ideologies (Bonilla-Silva, 2010; Turra & Venturi, 1995) that represent black people as submissive to racism, without calling attention to their historical resistance, and demanding the interpretation of post-colonies as if they were racial democracies with no marked racism.

While rejecting humanism as the producer of racialism par excellence, Fanon points out that the 'The Negro of the Antilles will be proportionately whiter – that is, he will come closer to being a real human being – in direct ratio to his mastery of the French language' (Fanon, 2008: 8). This means that to speak like white people also denotes being human in language.

Importantly, this calls on black people to resist racism in language, but also to resist racism with the use of language, as follows:

> For the moment I want to show why the Negro of the Antilles, whoever he is, has always to face the problem of language. Furthermore, I will broaden the field of this description and through the Negro of the Antilles include every colonized man. Every colonized people—in other words, every people in whose soul an inferiority complex has been created by the death and burial of its local cultural originality—finds itself face to face with the language of the civilizing nation; that is, with the culture of the mother country. The colonized is elevated above his jungle status in proportion to his adoption of the mother country's cultural standards. (Fanon, 2008: 9)

Above all, what Frantz Fanon terms as zone of non-being, in accordance with whitening ruling of humanization, merits observation within what we call languaging. Languaging is thus the pathway of alleged evolution that makes black people remain under the tutelage of white people because it implies colonial dominance through language. Both Singh (2018) and Veronelli (2016) bring together language and coloniality to better illuminate colonial formations since old times. Singh (2018), more specifically, defines mastery as the category to separate colonizers from the colonized since early in the colonial invasion. Therefore, mastering a language is a significant feature of how to be proper in a language rather than speaking properly. What is at stake here are beliefs of who is articulate or speaks a language properly, in the context of a language that is itself based on monoglossic ideologies of language (García, 2009) shaped by colonial policies of language (Pennycook, 2002). These colonial policies, rather than restricted to colonialism, continue to impose their force with the use of a white listening subject that oversees all that we speak and hear.

Rosa and Flores (2017), drawing on Miyako Inoue (2003), describe the white-listening subject as the listening subject behind our linguistic attitudes that in turn point to produce dehumanization and co-naturalizations of language and race in the modern world; they reiterate a white pattern as the one to be followed. For example, Fanon (2008) presents the case of black officers from Senegalese regiments who served as interpreters of the masters' orders to their black fellows. Interestingly, as Fanon argues, speaking the pattern of language spoken and considered standard by white people made black people be interpreted by the lens of white people, allowing us to conceive of a white listening subject who is behind the linguistic practices in colonial contexts, but also nowadays, due to coloniality. I understand coloniality as the colonial power of colonialism existing after the so-called formal period of colonization.

Language and racism both go towards the direction of linking languaging and racialization, horror and pain. Languaging and racialization intersect, and both produce a listening subject that for Fanon (2008) was represented by the white colonizers. I seek here to distinguish between language and languaging, racism and racialization because that confusion often leads to color blindness (Bonilla-Silva, 2010; Turra & Venturi, 1995) that obscures the sense of racism on purpose by making it appear like an occasional discrimination whereas ignoring daily racialized practices as if racism were a simple fantasy in our black minds.

Fanon (2008) also warns of language as a zone of being performing when black people return from a stay in France. For him, it makes black individuals who returned be regarded as superior by their black fellows:

> Many of them, after stays of varying length in metropolitan France, go home to be deified. The most eloquent form of ambivalence is adopted toward them by the native, the one-who-never-crawled-out-of-his-hole, the *bitaco*. The black man who has lived in France for a length of time returns radically changed. To express it in genetic terms, his phenotype undergoes a definitive, an absolute mutation. (Fanon, 2008: 10)

That linguistic practice described by Fanon makes me return to my own linguistic experience in Brazil. When people (mostly black people) used to go from Bahia, the blackest state of Brazil, to São Paulo, a whiter one, their return to Bahia was permeated with mutations in their accent that made them be characterized by their black fellows as 'stuck up'.

On the other hand, a person who goes for the first time to the motherland of white colonizing people also faces the weight of language as a zone of non-being, as Fanon says:

> The Negro arriving in France will react against the myth of the R-eating man from Martinique. He will become aware of it, and he will really go to war against it. He will practice not only rolling his R but embroidering it. (Fanon, 2008: 11)

This also makes me turn to my personal stories. As I observed in Nascimento (2019), when we, black individuals who obtained a degree in English Language Teaching (ELT) in Brazil make the decision to pursue such a career and perform our identities in language at undergraduate and graduate programs, we are faced with the fact that the listening subject is white, either represented by mostly white English professors and teaching assistants in person or by linguistic patterns of the English language spoken by white US-Americans[2] (Smitherman, 1998) embraced within a market of accents (Blommaert, 2009).

In previous work (Nascimento, 2016), I put forward that ELT elitism, rather than related to racialization, originates from racialization as a process that has taken place throughout Brazilian history. Whereas English courses were being undermined during the dictatorship, for example, English language private centers expanded across the country. Albeit English was still present in language education in the country, it has been restricted to private schools, as Windle and Muniz (2018) present, where (mostly) only white people could afford the fees.

These are samples of how languaging can perform language as a zone of non-being for black individuals in colonized countries, such as Brazil and Martinique. In the following section, I will talk briefly about the term I bring so as to deepen the interplay of language and racism working as a zone of non-being for black people.

Linguistic Racism: On Inventing Languages as a Zone of Non-Being

Nascimento (2019) uses the term 'linguistic racism' to define each racialization that occurs with the use of a language, in language, and through language use. I attempt to cover the following: (i) the racialization that is spoken in language (when a white person uses a racial slur to offend a black person, for example), which I define primarily as linguistic racism with the use of a language; (ii) the racialization in language (when racist nouns are naturalized, and even the words *black* or *the N-word* are among those which were racialized and naturalized in language); and (iii) racialization through language (when a specific policy from language education comes in with racist consequences, as I mentioned earlier as being the case of ELT in Brazil) which then goes on to promote racial inequalities informed by language planning, language policies etc.

Much about the co-naturalization of language and race producing diverse kinds of racism has been said in a vast scholarship on language education and language teaching. Rosa and Flores (2017) advocate for a raciolinguistic perspective as a lens to read the inequalities of race and language rising from the modern/colonial world, that is based on a sense of Europeanness. Alim (2016) goes a step further by proposing raciolinguistics (language and race) as a way to deepen the ways language and race work in the modern word. In doing so, he connects racialization to transmodernity claims that rose from decolonial studies in Latin America (Dussel, 1993). The becoming black of the world (Mbembe, 2014) helps us understand the sense of transracialization in language studies if we interpret the neoliberal world as the force that racializes the world. Building on raciolinguistics (the area that works on the interplay of race and language), these scholars debunk the coloniality and color-blindness that make language education exist in the forms it has. Kubota and Lin (2006) come along with this idea by putting forward how their personal experiences were influenced by the imagery of racialization, as race in second language education was not always named but carried out in interpretations about their alleged incompetence.

Menezes de Souza (2018) insists on marking the unmarked while pointing to the loci of enunciation of each of the cited scholars, and making a point of stressing how the Global South, where he speaks from, produces local and 'glocal' shared notions of translation and perspectives constantly ignored within a global citizenship framework. The struggles against the racialization in the Global South, for him, point out the much-needed role of marking the unmarked (Menezes de Souza, 2018) and bringing our bodies back (Menezes de Souza, 2019) to the center of the discussion.

In other previous publications, Pennycook (2002), Phillipson (1992) and Windle (2019) have argued the entangled logics of language, coloniality, imperialism and conservatism in the contemporary world that resulted from a timelessness period of horror, invasion and globalization that led into totalitarian regimes of global capitalism (Santos, 2000). Although capitalism is often read as separate from colonialism, Mbembe (2014) brings both together. He forwards the idea that becoming black of the world means that capitalist regimes, in their neoliberal representations, shape every identity in the global world within a logic of exploitation historically of black bodies, a logic that has now become global.

Ladson-Billings and Tate (1995), Menezes de Souza (2004), Souza (2011), Ferreira (2014), Crump (2014) and Anya (2016) question the role of literacies embedded in monolingual practices of schools and communities and that perform an exclusionary agenda in language education. Informed by Critical Race Theory (CRT), Crump (2014), Ferreira (2014) and Anya (2016) draw our attention to the structures given in language that continue to feed a given framework of racism in language education, supporting the attempts to provide black people with monolingual practices of languaging.

Also remarkable for my career as a tenured English professor and a scholar from Brazil, in the Global South, has been the discussion that came to uncover the false arguments around the alleged superiority of native speakers. I have commented on that topic as racism because of the ways it impacts black teachers (Nascimento, 2019) who are always accused of being 'not good enough in English'. In this sense, Norton (1997), Byram (1997) and Pavlenko (2003) tackle all of these beliefs in their work. On the one hand, Norton (1997) and Pavlenko (2003), building on a post-structuralist means of analysis, protest the ownership of English as a property of native speakers by arguing for the right to speak by every person that wants to express themselves in the English language. These accounts are enacted in Byram's work (Byram, 1997) that explores and concludes that there are no findings that can prove a superiority in English language among speakers from countries where English is the major language. What is absent from those analyses is the power of racism to cause more violence to the daily lives of people who have been historically racialized.

Yet, what I frame as linguistic racism has to be considered alongside the concept of language. It first stirred me toward seeking to understand what I really thought of as a language. Makoni and Pennycook (2007) suggest that languages are invented and not social phenomena:

> When we argue that languages are constructed, we seek to go beyond the obvious point that linguistic criteria are not sufficient to establish the existence of a language (the old language/dialect boundary debates), in order to identify the important social and semiotic processes that lead to their construction. Social processes include, for example, the development of colonial and nationalist ideologies through literacy programs. (Makoni & Pennycook, 2007: 1)

Drawing on the invention of languages, this definition addresses languages as metadiscursive regimes that construct boundaries that we understand as speaking, writing and significance. To this extent, 'the concept of invention is relevant to both colonial and post-colonial metropolitan contexts' (Makoni & Pennycook, 2007) and addresses the various forms of seeing Africa beyond a given natural reality. Accordingly, they are those who embrace the idea of an invention of Africa, which means language and race were also invented (Mbembe, 2014).

According to Mbembe (2014), race has to do with a modern world. Its use is recent in the history of humanity and came to further appear during the long centuries of slave trade. I bring all these remarks to bear in what I set out to call linguistic racism because, albeit being performed continuously, it has been backed in history by the co-construction of modern names that, in the phonocentric tradition, came to characterize, not only words, but lived experiences (Fanon, 2008; Alcoff, 2006).

I assume linguistic racism is located in the structure of the modern world that, step by step, has managed to produce a set of inventions that become real, like race and racism. *Negro, black, mulatto* and *moreno* are more than words in their frames. They identify a range of classifications that never existed in the pre-colonial Africa within the logophonocentric approach (Derrida, 1973). The logophonocentric approach is the metadiscursive approach that overestimates sound-based languages which are represented into writing representations. That metadiscursive approach places writing-based languages as the symbol of civilization and modernity, whereas pre-modern languages, like those spoken by Africans, Asians or Native Americans (Americans ahead of the colonial invasion), are defined as dialects. Names and races are closely entangled within a structure of linguistic racism that defines all that exists. I mean that the names came to exist so as to classify, originate, and make believe a race in the Americas, in what is more than a simple naming act, but rather a scenario of real horror, pervasion and terror.

Dis-Inventing Languages as a Zone of Non-Being

The assumptions arising here are about how to tackle the issues surrounding the invention of language and of Africa by the European colonizers. Besides being informed by Fanon's contributions, I also draw on Makoni and Pennycook's (2007) work on invention and invention of languages. Accordingly, whereas Fanon's analysis dwells on the power of language as a zone of non-being that impairs the life story of black people, Makoni and Pennycook (2007: 6) posit the idea that 'Europeans sough to justify their presence and redefine the colonized societies in new terms'.

These *new terms* are the *raison d'être* of linguistic racism as I term it. In a broader sense, linguistic racism is loosely interconnected to a wide range of racial biases produced by uses of language that set racism in language, through language and with the use of language. However, as I am anchoring this term in a conception of language that is not tied to cognitive dimensions that bear out humanist approaches, I am also pointing to the struggles against appropriateness-based ideologies (Flores & Rosa, 2015) and monoglossic ideologies of language (García, 2009; García & Li, 2014) that, according to Canagarajah and Liyanage (2012), are not the landmark of pre-colonial communities in Africa – whose populations were multilingual before the colonial invasion – but instead to inventions of the modern world. As long as the world becomes whiter, monolingualism is more present than ever. In turn, appropriateness-based ideologies go on to reinforce racist ideologies while encompassing a way to speak properly based on white ways of speaking – what I term here as the white listening subject.

Additionally, as languages as a zone of non-being are invented, I call out the need for dis-invention as informed by Makoni and Pennycook (2007). Therefore, 'traditions have endured because (while creating the impression of timelessness) they survived owing to an ongoing dialogical tension between social and historical realities' (Makoni & Pennycook, 2007: 6).

It is to reinforce the argument of languages as invented that dis-inventions are given as hope and expectation in our collective imagination, but also as an epistemic basis for our work in areas such as applied linguistics and language education. If traditions are also inventions, they entail signs that can be reconfigured along with dialogical tensions.

Both Fanon (2008) and Mbembe (2014) state that the struggles against European-based humanism should focus on a future without the weight of race. The inquiries I have been raising in this direction are to position language more centrally, as opposed to what it has performed in the western world thus far, that is, to produce a counter-hegemony in language. This is about reinvention of language, but also reclaiming the identity of minoritized black teachers in ELT whose identities are premised to not occupy legitimately their position if they are not native speakers.

It implies that race, as produced by the European modernity, is configured and reconfigured into a double-sign (Gates Jr, 1988). Black peoples hijacked from Africa, beyond lamenting their forced condition, received *black* as a sign of oppression and reconfigured it into resistance. It has much to do with the way black peoples used language to express their body and embodiments, but also as the way they use languages, including a second language.

The meaning of *black* as a sign is situated within the idea of sign built on Bakhtin (1997), in which language itself does not exist but instantiates its representation through interaction.

Gates Jr (1988) explores such theorizations on proposing that *signifyin(g)* challenges the standard notion of sign Ferdinand Saussure gave rise to. As a consequence, it is on signifyin(g) that the black person produces a new double voice, resetting the sign previously given:

> signifyin(g) is black double-voicedness because it always entails formal revision and an intertextual relation, and because of Esu's double representation in art, I find it an ideal metaphor for black literary criticism, for the formal manner in which texts seem concerned to address their antecedents. (Gates Jr, 1988: 51)

This meaning then represents a disruption at the level of the signifier, which indicates that the signifier refers to a rhetoric figure for black people and that whether or not white people are using *the N-word* (or another racial slur) or even the word *black* to offend, a slur is reread as a double sign, representing both oppression while enacted by white supremacy and resistance for black people while recuperating the given frame of the sign and transforming it into resistance. Below is a scheme retrieved from Gates Jr (1988) that first showcases the white signifyin(g) of sign and second the black vernacular signifyin(g):

(i) *White sign sinifying* = <u>Signified</u> = <u>concept</u>
     Signifier = *sound-image*
(ii) *Black Vernacular Sign signifying* = <u>Signified</u> = <u>Rhetorical figure</u>
     Signifier = *sound-image*

Adapted from Gates Jr (1988)

Signifyin(g) is thus a black-voiced sign that understands the sign that creates *black* or *negro* (or, as I prefer, regarding the humanism that creates a human and a race as its counterpart, as I observed in Nascimento, 2019) as a rhetorical figure that, within a system of black signification, comes to mean some other ways of existing.

That scheme as informed by Bakhtin (1997) also resembles the most distinct means of resistance performed by black people in Brazilian history, one that backs the idea of signifyin(g) the black sign. Moura (2014) remarks that black people throughout Brazilian history shaped a concept of resistance by participating in various forms of resistance, such as quilombo-communities (rural areas with enslaved Africans who were released from their masters, like the revolutionary Palmares Republic,[3] a community that nearly reached 80 years of existence in a row with nearly 20 thousand Africans from different ethnicities), movements pro-independence in Brazil (that motivated thousands enslaved men and women to join such riots as a way to hope for their own freedom) and the guerrillas (armed squads who plotted around small towns to get the income of the masters of slave farms). I add to these forms of resistance the black sisterhoods in the catholic churches (groups of women that resisted colonization, such as the *Irmandade de Nossa Senhora da Boa Morte*), *The Capoeira* (an African-based dance originated in Brazil), *The Samba de roda* music (a musical and dance expression that originated in Bahia and was exported to the whole Brazil as one of the most important in the country). Many other forms of resistance not represented here include what González (1982) calls *black activisms*, in the plural, namely each act of resistance, institutionalized or not, that came to be developed by black people in Brazil to resist enslavement and colonialism.

My primary focus on black vernacular stems from black communities of resistance because they offer literacy lessons of (re)existence (Souza, 2011) that play a role in making us go further.

Therefore, Fanon's scholarship on language race signals the need for a reconfiguration of language studies. Whereas pioneering the idea of language and race, Fanon unveiled coloniality in language studies ahead of this time and also in a push for decolonizing language studies towards removing race as a center of decisions made in language education that continue to constraint black people to the same naturalized locations they (we) were imagined to occupy.

Black Teachers in ELT: Surviving Linguistic Racism and Language as a Zone of Non-Being

In order to engage reflections on the case of linguistic racism in Brazil, I will thus analyze the situation of black teachers in ELT who survive racism in the country and, more specifically, linguistic racism and language as a zone of non-being.

In fact, English language teaching is deemed as symbolic capital (Bourdieu, 1987) by which white people can get closer to the developed countries of the world. As Kubota (2016), Blommaert (2009), Windle (2018) and Nascimento and Windle (2020), among others, claim, language teaching has served a neoliberal market in the world. Especially in the Global South, ELT hegemony is bound to the existence of private schools where for the most part only white elites can afford course fees and material. Brazil, as a country with a non-white majority (over 50% of the population identify as black or of mixed race[4]), has seen private schools expand during the dictatorship while public schools did not have to teach English courses in secondary and post-secondary education anymore.

In previous work (Nascimento, 2019), I interpreted that phenomenon as being one of racialization in language studies in Brazil because it made ELT become exclusive to elitist areas where few to no black persons can live and afford their studies. Due to the reduction in the offer of ELT courses by public schools, private schools specialized in ELT were expanded across the country. As Beserra and Lavergne (2018) point out, public schools in Brazil are considered schools that serve those who cannot afford private education (which is widespread in many areas). Back to the slave trade context, the Decree n° 1.331 of 1854 issued by colonizers broadly prohibited slaves from attending public schools. Later, close to the end of slavery, black people were allowed to go to school at night, in a time when night courses were not widely available in the country.

Major consequences were expanded in language education. With no data provided by top officials of Brazilian government, we can only draw our conclusions from our visits to public and private schools, which help us conclude black people are enrolled in public schools with precarious ELT programs. Recent data[5] have shown that black teachers of English are only 23.7% of the total, and that is insufficient for engaging more students and stimulating more equitable classes.

Since the return of democratic governments in Brazil, ELT was reinserted in educational policies. However, what could be a rather attractive proposition was then blended into neoliberal policies of education. Media companies and entrepreneurial initiatives linked language studies to the market of accents (Blommaert, 2009) where solely north global countries could be alluded to as a model of English language to be taught. Accordingly, students could not be provided with varieties of Jamaican, Nigerian and other Englishes with more historical and racial connections to Brazil. While revolving around a context of privatization and access to capital of world companies in Brazil, language teaching became even whiter.

As a result, black teachers are not only in low proportion in development programs for language teachers, but also in schools. Investigating how a second language affects the matter of race and language in Brazil steams from my occupation as an English professor and, previously, a black teacher at public schools. It also unveils both linguistic racism and language as zone of being to mean the same in the biographies of these teachers, as I will show.

Methods and Participants

My main argument in the case of language as a zone of non-being, what I consider here to be a form of linguistic racism, is that black teachers remain underrepresented and non-being in ELT in Brazil. Thanks to low levels of representation, many teachers give up their careers and go on to find jobs as teachers of Portuguese language.

English language is set as a zone where black teachers do not exist in Brazilian education because they rarely are included in educational policies and demands from the government. Indeed, after centuries of omission, the Paulo Freire Program finally broadened the presence of black teachers in development programs for ELT. While not designed to help engage solely black teachers, the scheme resulted in motivating small-town in-service teachers without a diploma to go to universities to pursue a degree.[6]

As said earlier, black teachers, even though not targeted, ended up being those who made up the population of that program. I collected data from three teachers, including myself, which are described below.

Participants were chosen because they are black teachers who persisted in ELT in one of the states with the largest population of black individuals, but where ELT professionals nonetheless are white in their majority. Additionally, participants obtained a degree (bachelor's or master's) from the same institution, a public university in the Northeast region of Brazil.

Back then, students from ELT development programs were white in their majority and from middle-class private education. A great deal to be discussed here is that only people who studied at private schools were expected to demonstrate high performance in courses. When affirmative-action quotas became part of the policy in Brazilian universities, lots of politicians, principals of private schools and white students doubted black students would participate properly in classes. One of the aspects questioned was the language used by these students. As this ELT case can bring us into reflection, the two other students, Ana and Rosana (pseudonyms), and I were learners 'not supposed to be able to meet the standards' of English classes. As Ana pointed out:

> My colleagues doubted I could be competent in English classes. Sometimes I had to agree with my colleagues at the university. Professors used to teach as if everybody were fluent in English. As such, they did not want professors to teach students who presented with more difficulty.

That performance of racism in language education programs for pre-service teachers can be also found in my own narrative:

> We [black people] were in low proportion. I am one of the lighter-skinned ones. My black colleagues could not understand English well and professors did not want to help them with this. They simply spoke in English only. Most of my black colleagues dropped out of language education.

Difficulties at their work are another point they have in common. Both Rosana and I were taken for teachers of History because that field presents with more black people as in-service teachers, as follows with Rosana's case:

> In fact, language is a means for emancipation also. If you consider this, we have a way to fight racism. They usually think I am teacher of history, for example. People often ask me: 'did you graduate in History?' I have been the opposite.

As Rosana reports, being black in ELT is a way to fight racism because we are not being what racism demands that we be. Being an ELT professional, therefore, becomes a form of resistance. It helps elucidate the key aspect I am advocating for here. Not recognizing us/them as able to teach English has to do with how we are not supposed to exist in the teaching of English because we are constructed as incompetent.

In another short anecdote, I shed light to the fear black professors and teachers feel whenever they have to prove they can be English language teachers:

> His second job in education was at a private school. In there, he used to have his ability questioned. There was a class where he should prove he could master every little detail of English grammar so that students could be sure he was really competent. Because he was often taken for a teacher of history due to his hair and phenotype, he avoided speaking about history altogether.

This introduction to the participants' experience has the goal of ensuring we consider tackling racism while doing our job as professionals in ELT. In the next section, we will look more specifically at how linguistic racism leads black teachers in ELT to a zone of non-being.

Black Teachers on Surviving a Zone of Non-Being

Broadly endangered in the world of English language teaching, black teachers of English do not look like teachers or professors for most of the people, as we saw earlier, so they do not exist in language because they are restricted to the idea of a zone of non-being. More evidence of this is the report of criticism Ana suffered from her colleagues at the university, criticism that does not encourage a black teacher to pursue a career as an English teacher.

Ferreira (2014) gathered narratives from teachers who do not seem to be aware of how race affects language teaching. To further understand how teachers portray their identities in second language education, she suggests the use of autobiographical narratives to be built in class and to be used for reflection by teachers and colleagues.

The autobiographical narratives I collected in this article form a parallel that covers the following premises:

- English language teaching in Brazil is restricted to white people who could afford courses.
- Black people are only 23.7% of teachers of English language in Brazil, which makes black people minoritized in ELT.
- Black teachers' careers are not given the respect they deserve because black teachers are not considered good teachers by the community.

A point that could be reclaimed or one could wonder about is the social position that each teacher is set to hold in a society, thus reflecting sophisticated forms of racism. On the contrary, data collection showed that the tree participants reported disrespect.

Although Ana and Rosana did not say they had students disregarding their knowledge, Rosana was questioned about international travel. On the other hand, Gabriel was a victim during a class when a white student doubted him publicly during a lesson when the verb *to advertise* was being used. Importantly, *advertise* is a false cognate with the Brazilian Portuguese verb *advertir* that means *to warn* or to *admonish*. In fact, he used that rationale to say that Gabriel was wrong about the translation he was using with students. As Gabriel interprets it, being black in that context meant not be able to even teach false cognates because a white student, often taken for granted as wealthy because of his racial white profile, would be superior and more knowledgeable.

Major consequences of research were actions taken by teachers to dis-invent their positions in the zone of non-being that is the English language. Rosana utilizes their suggestions for political actions to create projects she develops at school as a way to call the attention of students to these issues. Gabriel is a professor at university, teaching students who are mostly from Southern Bahia. Many are black and indigenous. He engages language teaching with a focus on the regional context, where local languages were not disregarded. Quite the opposite – indigenous students valued local multilingualism and engaged their use.

Therefore, not only do black teachers appear to survive language as a zone of non-being or linguistic racism, but they also help their students negotiate their identities and then survive linguistic racism.

Conclusion

The aftermath I put forward in this chapter is that dis-invention may also result in reinvention of a language as a zone of being for black teachers and consequently their community, and in this way, they get to better positions of power from which they are able to demand new terms in the context of language teaching.

I see in language the very possibility of existence for black people if we change the terms of engagement in and through language. In existing contexts, however, black teachers are examples of what happens against black people in micro and macro contexts.

In this chapter, I explored threads that together can make us be aware and also act against race as a given sign imposed on black populations and also fight racism as a key aspect of modernity that permeates social relations in the educational contexts.

As also analyzed, black teachers can go from invention and dis-invention to also reinvention of language, rather than a zone of non-being. They can create a zone of their being and their existence in language teaching.

Notes

(1) A report lunched many years ago declared that a black youth is murdered every 23 minutes in Brazil. Available at https://face2faceafrica.com/article/a-black-youth-killed-every-23-minutes-the-dangers-of-being-black-in-brazil.
(2) I write US-American on purpose to sustain a claim before the indiscriminate use of Americans to refer solely to the people from the US.
(3) Although I am using 1597–1710 as a reference number for the records used here, more information from the web (https://www.britannica.com/place/Palmares) often informs a narrower time, what means it is still difficult to know what really was such a community that bravely resisted to enslavement. And albeit they are not calling it a republic, the Palmares was a range of quilombo-communities and not only one. This very correction is needed to the official records.
(4) See more at https://www.ibge.gov.br/.
(5) See additional information at https://www.correiobraziliense.com.br/euestudante/cultura/2020/12/4892614-observatorio-reune-dados-sobre-ensino-de-ingles-no-brasil.html.
(6) In fact the program received nearly no attention after Brazil's president Bolsonaro took office and was then interrupted.

References

Alcoff, L.M. (2006) *Visible Identities: Race, Gender, and the Self*. Oxford: Oxford University Press.
Alim, H.S. (2016) Introducing raciolinguistics: Racing language and languaging race in hyperracial times. In H.S. Alim, J.R. Rickford and A.F. Ball (eds) *Raciolinguistics: How Language Shapes Our Ideas about Race* (pp. 1–30). Oxford: Oxford University Press.
Anya, U. (2016) *Racialized Identities in Second Language Learning: Speaking Blackness in Brazil*. New York: Routledge.
Appiah, K.A. (1997) *Na casa de meu pai: a África na filosofia da cultura*. Rio de Janeiro: Contraponto.

Bakhtin, M.M. (1997) *Marxismo e filosofia da linguagem: Problemas fundamentais do método sociologico na ciencia da linguagem* (8th edn). São Paulo: Hucitec.
Bauman, Z. (2001) *Modernidade Líquida*. Rio de Janeiro: Zahar.
Bauman, Z. (2005) *Identidade: Entrevista a Benedetto Vecchi*. Rio de Janeiro: Zahar.
Beserra, B. de L.R. and Lavergne, R.F. (2018) *Racismo e educação no Brasil*. Recife: UFPE.
Blommaert, J. (2009) A market of accents. *Language Policy* 8 (3), 243–259.
Blommaert, J. (2010) *The Sociolinguistics of Globalization*. Cambridge: Cambridge University Press.
Bonilla-Silva, E. (2010) *Racism Without Racists*. New York: Rowman & Littlefield Publishers.
Bourdieu, P. (1987) *A Economia das Trocas Simbólicas* (2nd edn). São Paulo: Perspectiva.
Byram, M. (1997) *Teaching and Assessing Intercultural Communicative Competence* (1st edn). Clevedon: Multilingual Matters.
Canagarajah, S. (2011) Translanguaging in the classroom: Emerging issues for research and pedagogy. *Applied Linguistics Review* 2 (2011), 1–28.
Canagarajah, S. and Liyanage, I. (2012) Lessons from pre-colonial multilingualism. In A. Blackledge and A. Creese (eds) *The Routledge Handbook of Multilingualism* (pp. 49–65). London: Routledge.
Castro-Gómez, S. (2007) Descolonizar la universidad: La hybris del punto cero y el dialogo de saberes. In S. Castro-Gómez and R. Grosfoguel (eds) *El giro decolonial: Reflexiones para una diversidad epistémica más allá del capitalismo global* (pp. 79–91). Bogotá: Siglo del Hombre Editores.
Crump, A. (2014) Introducing LangCrit: Critical language and race theory. *Critical Inquiry in Language Studie*, 11(3), 207–224.
Darvin, R. and Norton, B. (2017) Language, identity, and investment in the 21st century. In T. McCarty and S. May (eds) *Language Policy and Political Issues in Education* (pp. 1–15). Cham: Springer.
Derrida, J. (1973) *Gramatologia*. São Paulo: Perspectiva.
Dussel, E.D. (1993) *1492: O Encobrimento do Outro: A Origem do Mito da Modernidade*. Petrópolis, RJ: Vozes.
Fanon, F. (2008) *Pele negra máscaras brancas [Black Skin White Masks]*. Salvador: Edulfba.
Faustino, M. (2015) Por que Fanon? Por que agora? Frantz Fanon e os fanonismos no Brasil. PhD Dissertation, Universidade de São Carlos.
Ferreira, A.J. (2014) Teoria racial crítica e letramento racial crítico: Narrativas e contranarrativas de identidade racial de professores de línguas. *Revista da Associação Brasileira de Pesquisadores(as) Negros(as) – ABPN* 6, 236–263.
Flores, F. and Rosa, J. (2015) Undoing appropriateness: Raciolinguistic ideologies and language diversity in education. *Harvard Educational Review* 85 (2), 149–171.
García, O. (2009) *Bilingual Education in the 21st Century: A Global Perspective*. Oxford: Wiley-Blackwell.
García, O., and Li, W. (2014) *Translanguaging: Language, Bilingualism and Education*. Basingstoke: Palgrave Macmillan.
Gates Jr, H.L. (1988) *The Signifying Monkey: A Theory of African-American Literary Criticism*. Oxford: Oxford University Press.
González, L. (1982) Movimento negro ou movimentos negros? In L. González and C. Hasenbalg (eds) *Lugar de Negro* (pp. 18–20). Rio de Janeiro: Marco Zero.
Grosfoguel, R. (2016) What is racism? *Journal of World-System Research* 22 (1), 9–15.
Inoue, M. (2003) The listening subject of Japanese modernity and his auditory double: Citing, sighting, and siting the modern Japanese woman. *Cultural Anthropology* 18 (2), 156–193.
Irvine, J. and Gal, S. (2000) Language ideology and linguistic differentiation. In P.V. Kroskrity (ed.) *Regimes of Language: Ideologies, Polities, and Identities* (pp. 35–83). Santa Fe, NM: School of American Research Press.

Kubota, R. (2016) The multi/plural turn, postcolonial theory, and neoliberal multiculturalism: Complicities and implications for applied linguistics. *Applied Linguistics* 37, 474–494.
Kubota, R. and Lin, A. (2006) Race and TESOL: Introduction to concepts and theories. *TESOL Quarterly* 40 (3), 471–493.
Ladson-Billings, G. and Tate, W. (1995) Toward a critical race theory of education. *Teachers College Record* 97, 47–68.
Makoni, S. and Pennycook, A. (2007) Disinventing and reconstituting languages. In S. Makoni and A. Penycook (eds) *Disinventing and Reconstituting Languages* (pp. 1–41). Clevedon: Multilingual Matters.
Makoni, S., Kaiper-Marquez, A. and Mokwena, L. (2022) *The Routledge Handbook of Language in the Global South*. London: Routledge.
May, S. (2014) Justifying educational language rights. *Review of Research in Education* 38 (1), 215–241.
Mbembe, A. (2014) *Crítica da Razão Negra*. Lisboa: Antígona.
Menezes de Souza, L.T.M. (2018) Glocal languages, coloniality and globalization from below. In M. Guilherme and L.M.T. Menezes de Souza (eds) *Glocal Languages and Critical Intercultural Awareness* (pp. 17–41). New York: Routledge.
Menezes de Souza, L.M.T. (2019) Decolonial pedagogies, multilingualism and literacies. Multilingualism and Literacies. *Multilingual Margins: A Journal of Multilingualism from the Periphery* 6, 1–15.
Moura, C. (2014) *Rebeliões na senzala: Quilombos, insurreições, guerrilhas* (5th edn). São Paulo: Anita Garibaldi.
Nascimento, G. (2016) A história não acabou: A representação da identidade de classe social, não livro didático de língua inglesa. Dissertation (Master in Applied Linguistics), Departamento de Línguas Estrangeiras e Tradução, Universidade de Brasília.
Nascimento, G. (2019) *Racismo linguístico: Os subterrâneos da linguagem e do racismo*. Belo Horizonte: Letramento.
Nascimento, G. and Windle, J. (2020) The nexus of race and class in ELT: From interaction orders to orders of being. *Applied Linguistics* 42 (3), 473–491.
Norton, B. (1997) Language, identity, and the ownership of English. *TESOL Quarterly* 31 (3), 409–429.
Pavlenko, A. (2003) "I never knew I was a bilingual": Reimagining teacher identities in TESOL. *Journal of Language, Identity & Education* 2 (4), 251–268.
Pennycook, A. (2002) *English and the Discourses of Colonialism*. London: Routledge.
Pennycook, A. and Makoni, S. (2019) *Innovations and Challenges in Applied Linguistics from the Global South*. New York: Routledge.
Phillipson, R. (1992) *Linguistic Imperialism*. Oxford: Oxford University Press.
Rosa, J. and Flores, N. (2017) Unsettling race and language: Toward a raciolinguistic perspective. *Language in Society* 46 (5), 621–647.
Said, E. (1990) *Orientalismo: O Oriente como invenção do Ocidente*. São Paulo: Companhia das Letras.
Santos, B. de S. (2007) Beyond Abyssal Thinking: From global lines to ecologies of knowledge. *In Review* XXX-I-2007, 45–89.
Santos, M. (2000) *Por Uma Outra Globalização: Do Pensamento único à Consciência Universal*. Rio de Janeiro: Record.
Saylag, R. (2014) Culture shock an obstacle for EFL learners. *Procedia - Social and Behavioral Sciences* 114, 533–537.
Silva, D.N. and Lopes, A.C. (2019) Hablar portuñol é como respirar: Translanguaging and the descent into the ordinary. In J. Lee and S. Dovchin (eds) *Translinguistics: Negotiating Innovation & Ordinariness*. (1st edn, pp. 104–114). London: Routledge.
Silverstein, M. (1979) Language structure and linguistic ideology. In P.R. Clyne, W.F. Hanks and C.L. Hofbauer (eds) *The Elements: A Para-Session on Linguistic Units and Levels* (pp. 193–247). Chicago: Chicago Linguistic Society.

Singh, J. (2018) *Unthinking Mastery: Dehumanism and Decolonial Entanglements.* Durham, NC: Duke University Press.

Skutnabb-Kangas, T. (2000) *Linguistic Genocide in Education—or Worldwide Diversity and Human Rights?* Mahwah, NJ: Lawrence Erlbaum.

Smitherman, G. (1998) Ebonics, king, and oakland: Some folk don't believe fat meat is greasy. *Journal of English Linguistics* 26, 97–107.

Souza, A.L.S. (2011) *Letramentos de Reexistência: Poesia, Grafite, Música, Dança, Hip Hop* (1st edn). São Paulo: Parábola Editorial.

Turra, C. and Venturi, G. (1995) *Racismo cordial: A Mais Completa Análise Sobre Preconceito de Cor no Brasil.* São Paulo: Ática.

Veronelli, G. (2016) A coalitional approach to theorizing decolonial communication. *Hypatia* 31 (2), 404–420.

Williams, Q. and Stroud, C. (2015) Linguistic citizenship: Language and politics in postnational modernities. *Language & Citizenship* 14 (3), 406–430.

Windle, J.A. (2018) Neoliberalism, imperialism and conservatism: Tangled logics of educational inequality in the Global South. *Discourse: Studies in the Cultural Politics of Education* 40 (2) 191–202.

Windle, J.A. and Muniz, K. (2018) Constructions of race in Brazil: Resistance and resignification in teacher education. *International Studies in Sociology of Education* 27, 307–323

4 Confessions of a Sociolinguist: A Linguistic Autoethnography

Chatwara Suwannamai Duran

In this chapter, I discuss, from both personal and professional stances, how a language ideology that privileges Standard American English and its 'correct forms' subordinates other forms of Englishes. To approach this subject matter, I utilize linguistic autoethnography, or the way in which I examine my evolving understanding while being and becoming a member in speech communities. To reflect on my own experience as an international student, an immigrant in the US and a speaker of English as a second language, I first examine how my own upbringing in Thailand, inherited values and education prior to coming the US shaped the way in which I viewed and questioned non-standard forms of English, especially at the very beginning of my residence in the US. In addition, from working with my research participants who are also immigrants in the US, I have found that insulting someone's accent and mocking/ridiculing certain speech styles may commonly appear to have an entertaining goal, and yet be underlined by inequality and hierarchy among language varieties and speakers. Nevertheless, being constantly exposed to linguistic and cultural diversity in the US can gradually change one's views and those of one's research subjects toward understanding and appreciating different varieties of English. With my experience of such possible and positive change, I use linguistic autoethnography in my college classroom in the hope of directly and indirectly teaching about linguistic diversity and to lessen linguistic ignorance and discrimination in a short period of time. I discuss the outcomes at the end of the chapter.

Introduction

Almost two decades ago I came to the US as an international student. I remember that, during the beginning of my study and stay in the US, I was irritated if a sentence ended with a preposition such as in, 'Where should we meet *at*?' when a classmate asked to arrange a study group. I was also surprised when my American cousin said, 'No food, no nothing (in the fridge)'. I questioned in my head, 'Aren't double negatives bad and nonsense?' In a conversation with a woman, I was bothered by her incorrect plural form as she said, 'two mouses'.[1] My irritated feeling, as I recalled, came from valuing prescriptive grammar rules of Standard American English that had been at the core of my English education. I held on to the rules to earn a high score in English proficiency tests and for academic purposes. Though I never confronted, questioned and corrected the speakers directly, I admitted that I was not far from being linguistically narrow minded at the time. Recalling how I felt and thought, I realize that (1) I was not exposed to enough linguistic and cultural diversity of English and its speakers, (2) I paid too much attention to grammatical form and less to key content and communicative purposes and (3) I valued Standard English most in both formal and informal communications. I feel bad now that my previous self was not far from being linguistically discriminatory against 'non-standard' forms of English, or those that look and sound different from the codified version accepted as standard forms in either L1 or L2 contexts.[2] In this chapter, I discuss how my attitudes toward non-standard languages have been shaped and how they shifted because of real-life experience, education and professional training. In doing so, I hope that my reflection and analysis of my experiences contribute to a methodological approach to linguistic self-exploration based on autoethnography. My hope is to establish a pedagogy that encourages others to celebrate language diversity, or at least to be more understanding and accepting of multiple varieties of English.

Discussing the subject matter by examining, exploring and even criticizing my own experience to better understand the construct of my language attitude and ideology, I utilize a methodological approach called *autoethnography* (Canagarajah, 2012; Ellis, 2004; Spry, 2001). This approach makes a connection between the researcher's life history and the wider 'cultural, social, and political' issues (Ellis, 2004: xix), which I pursue. Presenting the language attitudes of those I encountered, I also investigate how my belief has changed over time. By adding up the term to be *linguistic autoethnography*, I focus on specific experiences related to language repertoires, attitudes toward different language varieties in all levels (phonology, morphology, syntax and pragmatics) and perceptions toward speakers. Many scholars discuss the flaws and limitations of autoethnography because investigating one's own story is quite subjective and merely experiential (Atkinson, 2006). However, I believe that a researcher's own experience is a critical part of data analysis and interpretation, especially in qualitative research (see also Ellis *et al.*, 2011). According to Anderson (2006), autoethnography is not inferior to other methods. In fact, it can be used to enrich realist and analytical approaches to ethnography. In addition, O'Reilly (2012) adds that autoethnography encourages 'a self-reflexive and non-judgmental understanding of a phenomenon' (2012: 132). For me, in this chapter, to acknowledge and examine 'subjectivities crafted through critical reflection and experience' (Rivers, 2019: 378) toward languages and speakers is to put my bias and language attitudes in check.

Attitudes toward a certain form of language have been researched widely in sociolinguistic studies. In world Englishes, research has paid attention to language perceptions and attitudes across different accents and varieties of Englishes in many regions across the globe, for example, Africa (Wiebesiek *et al.*, 2011), Asia (Bernaisch & Koch, 2016; Tokumoto & Shibata, 2011) and Europe (Nejjari *et al.*, 2012). In many studies, the findings show that the more favorable forms of English are those with the prestigious and historical constructs that value Standard British and American Englishes. In addition, if not British or American English, positive and negative attitudes toward local Englishes usually result from socioeconomic hierarchy or social status and education levels. That is, the higher social class and educational level of speakers, the more favorable their English is considered. Another point I would like to emphasize here is that, in these studies, researchers gain access to participants and their data by using interview questions or survey forms as their research tools. In this chapter, I promote self-exploration or taking a close look at our own beliefs and feelings about languages, dialects and accents. I posit that acknowledging that we have language attitudes, and that the attitudes could bring about assumption, discrimination and stereotype (Giles & Watson, 2013) are a humble and helpful way toward being more understanding of linguistic and cultural diversity. I examine my own language attitude and its gradual changes in my three main interconnected roles: (1) as an international student turned immigrant in the US, (2) as a researcher in sociolinguistics/applied linguistics and (3) as an educator/university professor.

Theoretical Underpinning

Autoethnography is believed to be strengthened by theory and data (Anderson, 2006). Writing a linguistic autoethnography, I discuss how my take on ideology that privileges Standard American English, and its codified forms subordinate other forms of Englishes and their speakers. I see the possibility of utilizing the frameworks of language attitude socialization and language/linguistic ignorance because both frameworks help investigating one's ongoing language ideology – believing, changing and shifting over time as one is socializing with others by using a language or languages in different contexts and stages of life. I discuss the two frameworks in more detail below.

For language attitude socialization – or the process of learning and using inherited biases about language – Day (1982) found that language-based attitudes and stereotypes are shaped and settled early in life through socialization and sociocultural transmission, especially in our familiar surroundings. Children as young as three years old can spot dialect differences and yet have neutral preferences and understand that each language or dialect can be used in a certain situation (Day, 1982). Unfortunately, after extensive exposure to a standard or dominant dialect or language through formal education and a wider context of socialization, their preference for the standard dialect in their community/region increases. Apart from formal education, attitudes toward different dialects are transmitted in various ways such as through language criticism (Marlow & Giles, 2010), biased media portrayals (Dragojevic et al., 2016) and subtle linguistic biases, among others. Learning English as a foreign language, which means having limited or no exposure to native English speakers until my teenage years, I wonder how my attitudes toward different dialects and accents of English were constructed despite being a non-native English speaker.

As for language or linguistic ignorance, there is a wide range of understandings, and I had difficulty for a short while trying to decide if I used the word 'ignorance' properly. The challenge is to differentiate between naïve ignorance and intentional ignorance. The challenge to differentiate the two is also based on my experience living in the information age, when news and data are available and accessible to us more than ever before. The information age provides us with tools to gain knowledge very easily across space and time. However, it is not easy to know everything. Naïve ignorance could happen when we are not sufficiently exposed to sensitive issues, history, diversity, different ways of thinking and social settings due to our age, experience and education. Alcoff (2007) explains that 'All knowers are situated in time and space with specific experiences, social locations, modes of perceptual practices and habits, styles of reasoning, and sets of interests that are fluid and open to interpretation but that have some objective elements in regard to the conditions of the knower's material reality' (2007: 42).

With naïve ignorance, we may not be introduced to a way of thinking different from our inherited, familiar environments. For example, born and raised in Thailand, I learned that a light complexion was traditionally considered better looking than a dark complexion. People with a darker skin tone in Thailand may be bullied verbally from a very young age by family members and at school. My younger self did not question this phenomenon and thought that this was an ordinary occurrence rather than something to be questioned. Many Thai individuals with darker skin tones would buy skincare products promising to whiten their skin. Later, as a young adult, I wondered why this phenomenon occurred, but still did not clearly know how to address the issue that someone else was being shamed due to their skin color. After living in the US, I learned from being exposed to everyday life in a different place that judging people by their skin color is not only shallow but also extremely harmful and racist. Having gained an understanding of the history, sociocultural constructs and racial injustice in the US through education, conversations with friends and classmates, news and events around the country and many accessible resources, I developed an informed point of view. While starting off from the perspective of naïve ignorance, I gradually changed my view and understanding toward an appreciation of the beauty of diversity in all of its forms. I believe that when naïve ignorance is at the heart of the matter, we all can learn to be more open to different ways of thinking and embrace diversity by exposing ourselves to the world around us.

On the other hand, intentional ignorance may still occur despite accessible information. As Gilson (2011) suggested, 'Epistemologies of ignorance have made the convincing case that ignorance is no mere lack of knowledge but rather is actively produced and maintained' (2011: 308-309). When we filter what we consume depending on what we are interested in and what is related to us only, we may be operating in a framework of intentional ignorance. As an educator, whether or not it is mere lack of knowledge, I have a choice to be informed and to inform others.

In this chapter *linguistic* ignorance, refers to how a speaker of a language believes that one language or dialect is superior to others based on the sociocultural, economic and historical constructs, especially of speakers, rather than the linguistic features. In another common case, speakers displaying linguistic ignorance may be upset when people in their surrounding speak a language that they do not understand, or they feel bothered by hearing a language different from their own. An example is the viral video clip (KHON, 2017) showing a woman being angry at two non-English speaking customers (Korean as reported) sitting next to her at a Starbucks in California. The situation got worse when the woman said loudly, 'Don't you dare say that again' when she heard some non-English words from those customers. She went on, 'Especially that oriental, I hate it'. Obviously, this is a form of intentional ignorance. The woman was aware that the speakers are Asian, and they speak an Asian language. Here, when paired with negativity and discrimination against a particular group who uses a certain linguistic style, a given dialect or a language, *linguistic ignorance* leads to linguistic racism. As languages are culture-based, intellectual heritage, and 'complex implications for identity' (United Nations, 2021), I argue that this form of linguistic ignorance is dehumanizing.

In what follows, I discuss my trajectories as an insensitive speaker, as a trained researcher and, lastly, as an instructor. When I utilize a linguistic autoethnographical method, my aim is not related to differentiating naïve and intentional linguistic ignorance. I also understand that we may not be able to entirely get rid of linguistic ignorance and linguistic racism given that naïve ignorance exists when we have not been exposed enough to belief systems outside of our surroundings. In addition, intentional ignorance can strongly persist when one avoids being informed by empirical evidence that is against one's own personal belief. Rather, my goal is to use my self-exploration and experience to fill or at least reduce the linguistic ignorance gap and to find ways to educate others.

An Insensitive Novice

In this section, I recall and reflect on how I have constructed attitudes toward different dialects and accents of English from both personal and professional experiences. While basing my discussion on my own experience, I am informed by analytical autoethnography (Byczkowska-Owczarek, 2014), which is a practice believed to offer an analytical view that allows researchers to observe and note the 'situations, thoughts, and actions' that happen to them (2014: 13). This way, I can use logical reasoning to exemplify what happened in a given situation rather than using emotion and bias.

Some inherited values that I learned early in life have constructed negative attitudes toward some features of people and languages. For example, colorism or favoring a certain color, especially of human skin as mentioned earlier, affects the way I beheld beauty. In addition, my native language, Thai, has many dialects and accents. My hometown is located approximately 30 kilometers, or a 30-minute drive, away from Bangkok, the capital city of Thailand, and I grew up speaking Central Thai, which is considered a standard dialect of Thai. The understanding that I spoke Standard Thai gave me pride and also resulted in some bad linguistic behavior when I met non-standard Thai speakers. My cousins and I sometimes made fun of our babysitters' rural Thai accent. In addition, one of our babysitters was from Lao, Thailand's neighboring country. She was always a subject of our language mockery because of her Laotian-accented Thai. In retrospect, I must admit that it was an act of classism, which in turn placed the Laotian babysitter as an immigrant and a marginalized person living on Thailand's soil. As a young and insensitive girl at the time, I had fun teasing and mocking my Laotian babysitter's accent because she was different. Given her situation of power imbalance, she did not argue back. All of our babysitters throughout our years while we were growing up basically worked as our housekeepers or maids. They came from the countryside and had lower socioeconomic status than us, who were the employers. In both cases, some degree of ignorance on our part applied. Now, I believe that such ignorance resulted in bullying acts.

My pride of speaking Standard Thai was challenged when I was 13 years old and attended secondary school in Bangkok. During that time, my non-Bangkok expressions and accent were detected by my Bangkok classmates. Some of them often asked me to repeat what I said. This is particularly true of instances when they heard my question tags with a strange intonation they had not heard before. Some asked where I was from originally as I did not sound like a Bangkok native. I was embarrassed that I did not speak Standard Thai like a 'city girl' as I believed. In my experience, dialects and accents of Thai were placed in a social hierarchical order. Urban styles were more valued than their rural counterparts; native language use was more valued than non-native; and the language used by those with higher socioeconomic status was more accepted than the language of those with lower socioeconomic status.

Prior to coming the US, I learned English as a foreign language in Thailand and was rarely introduced to non-standard forms of English. Recalling my own experience, I realize that education is a major part of constructing positive and negative attitudes toward different varieties of English. Because I majored in English at a university in Thailand (1996–2000), I was taught standard pronunciation, standard British or American English and grammatical correctness (from a prescriptive point of view), all of which were highly valued.[3] English literature classes I took introduced me to well-known writers who were from the traditional literary canon. Students who were English majors at the time needed to take a course called Element of Spoken English, which followed Standard American English. If they were interested, another advanced course, Sound System of English, was available. I took both classes. Recalling the objectives of the classes, I understood that being able to explain the phonology of American English (consonant and vowel sounds, stress and sentence intonation) was not enough. Students earned a better grade when they could pronounce and speak as closely as possible Standard American English during oral examinations throughout the semester. Examples include but are not limited to the differentiation of /I/ and /ɛ/ as in pin and pen, and the interdental fricatives /ð/ and /θ/ that do not exist in the Thai sound system and Thai speakers tend to replace it with /d/.

As for standard grammar, apart from my formal education, I was extremely influenced by a test of English as a foreign language (TOEFL) preparation course I took at a well-known institute in Bangkok and many past TOEFL exam copies I practiced on. Many prescriptive grammar rules were emphasized. For example, an English sentence cannot end with a preposition, there are twelve tenses in English and strict rules such as adverbs to use are attached to each tense, tag questions have a strict formula with the use of verb and a negative word 'not' and the like.

Together with those, I brought to the US a large number of prescriptivist grammar and pronunciation rules, which were enough for me to start detecting non-standard forms of American English at the very beginning of my residency. Although I had fun learning some local styles different from my English language learning in a formal classroom, such as 'Howdy' as a greeting and 'Y'all' as a second plural pronoun commonly used in Texas, I was not comfortable using them myself. In addition, hearing non-standard, non-prescriptive forms such as double negatives (e.g. I *don't* have *nothing*), using an objective pronoun as a subjective pronoun (e.g. *Me and my mom* are going on vacation in Hong Kong), an 'incorrect' order of pronouns (e.g. *I and my dad* instead of *My dad and I*) and the use of the adjective 'different' accompanied by the preposition 'than' instead of 'from' always raised a red flag in my head. This is because they were not correct according to the prescriptive rules I had learned.

Although I brought with me a prescriptive grammar detector in my head, years of living, navigating and socializing in the US introduced me to more forms of American English with unique features different from the so-called Standard American English. I learned slang and expressions used by American peers who represented diverse cultures, ethnicities, identities and interests. I have learned many words that do not align with their prescriptive part of speech, for example, nouns as a verb as in 'Google it!' and 'Beer me!' I have also heard and been impressed by hundreds of words to express, 'under the influence of alcohol', or what we simply call, 'drunk', which is the only word I learned in Thailand. Here, in the US, battered, hammered, legless, pickled, plastered, tanked, wasted and many more are used to describe 'being drunk'. In addition, living in San Antonio, TX, Tempe, AZ and San Diego, CA introduced me to the products of Spanish-English contact, Spanglish and Chicano English. Spanglish words such as *lonche* (lunch), *googlear* (to google), *parquear* (to park) and *troca* (truck) have added to the richness and uniqueness of language in the US. I also learned many Asian-styled and accented Englishes from working at a Chinese buffet restaurant in San Antonio for three years with co-workers from China, Hong Kong, Indonesia, Japan, Malaysia, Taiwan and Thailand. I realized how much I enjoy and appreciate learning new features of English both in books and in real life. The exposure to these uses and users of English(es) gradually changed my view. There is no one correct way to communicate. Each contextualized form serves a different purpose based on audience and domain. For example, 'two waters', meaning two glasses of water, is commonly used as a restaurant lingo. However, the phrase is ungrammatical according to a prescriptive grammar rule that categorizes 'water' as a mass or uncountable noun that cannot be pluralized by adding an 's' plural marker. Pragmatically, a compliment such as 'I like your purse!' is often used as a greeting in a friendly manner to a friend and even a stranger instead of 'Good morning, how are you today?' which is more prescriptive and formal.

One of the most memorable revelatory moments happened a few years after my arrival in the US. I had a boyfriend who was a Texas native and American-English speaker. With some insecure feelings I had about my non-native English, with features of Asian-Englishes, I often asked him to teach me the 'right way' of speaking whenever he heard something wrong from me. I usually requested, 'Please correct my English'. His answer always was, 'I don't have to correct you. I understand you already'. His response was always impressively stuck in my head. It was not a compliment that meant that I spoke perfect English without any errors. In fact, I realized that the relevant element was his familiarity with my accent and styles, including his sincere attention to the content and message being conveyed beyond grammatical errors. If he did not understand what I said, he would ask me to repeat, and I would spell the questionable word or use different words to explain. In becoming more aware of such communicative strategies, I asked new questions: 'How long does it take for a person to be familiarized with an unfamiliar accent and style of English that deviate from American English norms?' and 'What makes a lay person become more accepting and appreciative of non-standard forms of English?' I can venture an answer to those questions at a personal level by positing that an intention to be friends and constant exposure to different features of language make people more patient and accepting. At a more professional level, it is not easy to answer them. In the following sections, I will answer the questions based on my professional training and experience as a researcher and college instructor.

In this section, I reflect on my years growing up, language attitude socialization prior to coming to the US and some personal learning experiences in the US. My journey as an international student and a new immigrant has added more ways to learn about language diversity. The linguistic ignorance I had has gradually faded away by the constant exposure to real speakers who introduce me to linguistic differences in- and outside of the formal classroom settings.

Researcher's Role and Interconnecting Experiences

Throughout my academic career, I have been trained as a researcher using multiple qualitative methods that primarily include interview and participant observation. With this research approach, a researcher's own experience is a major part of the research journey, from creating research questions to analyzing and interpret data. Connecting this process to autoethnography, I focus on the intersubjectivity and interconnectivity between my research participants and me in this section. Trained as an applied linguist and sociolinguist, I seek to understand language ideologies, or the beliefs about languages, among multilingual individuals and families. I interview my participants, who are immigrants, or foreign-born Americans, to explore their language learning trajectories across national boundaries. Their views on language learning, especially the English language, and the path to becoming literate were shared with me with their lived experiences and within their contexts. I often come across opinions on languages, dialects and accents from my participants. I found that conversing with my participants often meant reaching shared experiences. One of the most agreed-upon findings from the participants is that the standard form of English learned in school is the most correct and reliable form. Such teaching causes misperception or devaluation of different or other forms, especially at the initial exposure to differences.

From countless conversations and exchanges with my research participants, I have found that insulting someone's accent and ridiculing a certain speech style among minoritized speakers and within and across ethnic groups may commonly appear to have an entertaining goal, yet it is underlined by inequality and racial/ethnic hierarchy among speakers. In my previous study (Duran, 2017) with the newly arrived Karenni children and their families who were English language learners in Arizona, children often served as 'mediators of good English transmitted from school to their households' (2017: 129). This is because these new immigrants believed that formal English instruction at school in their host community provided the most reliable and correct form of English. On many occasions during my fieldwork, I observed that the children corrected their parents' non-standard pronunciation and usage of English. The parents also encouraged their children to correct the parents' English pronunciation such as stressed syllables in multisyllabic words (e.g. Colorado, California, enthusiasm), the retroflex /r/ as in *car* and *girl* that are not familiar to Karenni speakers and tongue twisting words (e.g. chicken and kitchen). I also witnessed the children ridiculing their parents' English. One Karenni teenager revealed that her mother's accented English, 'is very very bad' (Duran, 2017: 128). The mother told me that occasionally her daughter asked the mother to stop speaking English because her pronunciation and accent were embarrassing.

Learning Standard American English at school shaped a hierarchical structure of varieties of English in these immigrant homes, and inevitable in a larger American society, where Standard American English was placed at the top and other deviations and differences are less valued and/or looked down upon. The practice of correcting and ridiculing in new immigrant families resonates with my personal experience when my younger self mocked my babysitters whom I considered less capable of speaking Standard Thai. In fact, the new immigrants and my babysitters were learning and trying their best to communicate outside their home country or hometown.

Another two cases are based on my current research with female immigrants from Thailand living and working in Houston, Texas. The participants shared with me the way they learned English prior to coming to the US, which introduced them to a formal, standard form. In addition to the standard form, they have also learned Texas's most iconic and most mentioned local style, which is the second plural pronoun *Y'all*. My Thai participants did not fail to discuss this word. A 37-year-old female participant, Ladda (pseudonym),[4] who was married to an American man and had lived in Texas since 2010 revealed how she felt about it,

> Y'all, y'all, what do y'all want, man? (laughing). Like, huh? I know, 'What's up?' but my class haven't had this word [y'all] you know (laughing). Like, for, they use like a slang, you know. Too much for me. It's kind of hard for me, you know.

Ladda shared with me that she initially did not understand what *Y'all* meant. Although she has a bachelor's degree in Tourism and Hospitality, used English and worked as a tour guide for international travelers in Thailand prior to coming to the US, she pinpointed that *Y'all* was slang because she never learned about this word in her English class. Having heard it many times in her current host community, Ladda asked her husband for clarification. She said, 'I used to ask him, 'Why do you say 'Y'all, y'all, y'all' (laughing)?" Her husband explained to her, 'It's like a southern style'.

Later, when I met her again, Ladda said that she got used to *Y'all*. Although she does not use it, she understands that 'It's a Texan style', as she put it. In addition, she had been exposed more to different accented Englishes as she worked at a Chinese restaurant. She became more understanding of differences of English. She explained,

> Nobody speaks Thai with me. I have Spanish-speaking friends. I have Chinese friends. But, we need to talk together, all the friends, Spanish, Chinese. Our English is not like advanced, you know. When we speak English, sometimes we speak wrong, but when we pronounce some words with accents, we just have to pronounce. Even the accent is not the right one, we understand what they mean, you know, when we talk together, you know. Like the Chinese, they say some words, but their accent is Chinese, but I know what they mean.

From the excerpt, communicating with co-workers, who have different English accents at the restaurant, Ladda focused more on content meaning than accent. She went on,

> So, I don't have any other Thai to talk to. That means I have to learn more English to talk with them. I have to use English. Sometimes we use the Google Translate talking (laughing).

From the excerpt, Ladda's goal to communicate brought about other strategy such as using Google Translate when Ladda and her interlocutor did not understand one another. This emphasizes that she sought after a message to meet the goal of communication rather than considering different accents as a problem.

Another female participant from Thailand, Tipa, has been in Texas since 1982 when she was sixteen and attended a high school in Dallas. She discussed how Texas English was different from the way she learned English in Thailand,

> I learned English in a British way. I only went to British Council for my classes in Bangkok, Thailand, and, when I came to the US, it's very hard. I couldn't understand anything. And the Texas accent is not easy to, to get used to, right? When I get here, the whole summer that I, my first summer, I watched a lot of TV. Like, I watched CNN, and I watched Sesame Street, like all day. And then, that got my listening skill up to speech. In high school, I got As in all my classes, you know, but I couldn't speak to people. I was kind of like MUTED for three years in high school (laughing).

As Tipa explained, upon arrival, Tipa considered US English, especially Texan English was 'very hard' to understand right away because it was not the way she learned in Thailand. It took her a long time to pass through the silent period. And, one of the reasons why Tipa had been 'muted' was that she was afraid of being ridiculed, as she added,

> I spoke with the people that I know that would not RIDICULE me, like, the Filipino girls, or Vietnamese girls, or, like, not WHITE people (laughing).

Tipa explained she was more comfortable using English with friends with an Asian background and that she did not have white friends until she went to college. I asked her why. She responded,

> It was my own thinking that I can't make mistakes when I speak to white friends. So, if I don't speak well, I wouldn't, I tend not to speak at all, you know. And, then, I was exposed more in college and started speaking more in college and then, you know, after that, it's just normal.

Tipa acknowledged that her younger self thought that English had to be spoken well without 'mistakes' grammatically and phonetically, especially with white friends, the mainstream Americans. As she spoken an Asian-accented English, she was afraid that it was not 'well' enough and might get ridiculed.

Observing and interviewing my participants from the three cases above, I have found that the participants' contexts may be different, but all their language attitudes have resulted from the hierarchical structure of different dialects, where the so-called Standard Language learned from a formal classroom is expected. In the Karenni families, children's English learned from school was highly valued and placed the children in a more powerful position than their parents in the household, especially at the very beginning of their resettlement. This is because the families were expected to acquire English as quickly as possible for education and employment. I followed the families for two years, and I cannot conclude that the Karenni families' language ideology that privileges Standard American English will change and that they will become more open to non-standard forms. On the other hand, Ladda and Tipa have been in the US longer than the Karenni families. Ladda and Tipa's experiences of language attitude socialization have expanded to more domains and audiences. Exposures to diversity help Ladda and Tipa become more appreciative to differences. Ladda had learned to focus on comprehension rather than accents and errors. Tipa became familiar with American English in addition to British English. In addition, Tipa was initially afraid to make mistakes but, after years of residence in the US, she became more open to communicating in the way she does.

I asked two questions in the previous section, 'How long does it take for a person to be familiarized with an unfamiliar accent and style of English that deviate from the American English norms?' and 'What makes a lay person become more accepting and appreciative of non-standard forms of English?' Based on Ladda, Tipa, and myself, I can say that to become more accepting of unfamiliar accents, different styles of English and non-standard forms, we need exposure to those differences on a regular basis for many years. Please note that, with this finding, I cannot generalize that speakers in all other contexts will have similar experiences and consequences.

Another point is that, taking on a researcher's role exploring my participants' linguistic points of view, I have found that constant exposure to linguistic differences gradually expanded the scope of my participants' acceptance of English varieties. But, as a researcher, apart from gaining data, I can only help the participants reflect and understand their own thoughts, beliefs and experiences. To respect their individual thoughts and beliefs, I should not impose on them in any way to think the same way I do. This gap leaves me to consider how to educate a wider community to accept and appreciate linguistic diversity. One similar theme emerges in both my and the participants' experiences is that education is one of the major parts of constructing the language ideology that privileges a certain form of language. Therefore, I go on to tackle the issue by playing an instructor's role, which may be more appropriate to introducing linguistic diversity and different perspectives based on research and scientific studies.

Instructor's Role: Educating Others and Using Linguistic Autoethnography in the Classroom

In this section, I discuss my role as an instructor with a goal to educate those I can with hopes to reduce linguistic ignorance and discrimination to some extent, one class at a time. As found in my own and research participants' experiences, that constant exposures to linguistic differences can lead to more understanding and accepting language diversity, I use linguistic autoethnography in the classroom. Students share their autoethnographies with the class through presentation. Reflective journal writing is assigned at the end of the project. I reflect on the outcomes and benefits of linguistic autoethnography through the classroom experience.

As a university instructor in Houston, 'a city without a majority where more than 140 different languages are spoken' (Kirk, 2019), I have students from a wide range of cultural, socioeconomic, ethnic, linguistic and racial backgrounds. Often, my classes directly and loudly represent the city – without a majority – distributed by a nearly equal amount of Anglo-American, African-American, Asian-American, Hispanic and mixed-raced students. I have taken this opportunity to employ linguistic autoethnography to learn more about my students and my community. Although students may have already been exposed to diversity outside the classroom, the classroom itself is a useful place for guided discussions. In the process, students are trained to do a mini research project and are also encouraged to investigate linguistic diversity in detail and in a friendly, safe and supportive environment.

In a broader view of every semester, my students surprise me with their languages and/or dialects spoken at home when I informally ask them through classroom discussions and activities, including formal assignments. In addition to Standard American English that they use in an academic setting, many students presented themselves as speakers of African American Vernacular English, Louisianian Creole, Patois, Southern American English, Spanish and Vietnamese, among others. Other languages spoken at home represent the world here: Arabic, Bisaya, Dutch, French, Mbundu, Náuatl, Panjabi, Portuguese and the list goes on. Within some languages, students also claim that they speak a particular variation, for example, Belgian French, Egyptian Arabic, Northern Vietnamese and so on. In addition, many are learning an additional language such as Korean, Mandarin Chinese, Japanese, German or Latin.

Although students vary in terms of their educational background in linguistics and research experience, I incorporate linguistic autoethnography and community engagement, especially with sociolinguistics-related classes, to train my students as sociolinguists and ethnographers. To make them feel comfortable with a research project, I assign them to investigate first the closest and most familiar community to them.

That is, to explore themselves and their very own family. In doing so, I usually assign a project at the very beginning of the semester. I ask students to investigate their families' linguistic heritage, their own language(s) and dialect(s), their language attitudes and additional language learning experiences. My guiding questions include[5]:

(1) What dialects and/or languages do your grandparents and parents speak? Provide examples of words, expressions and unique features they use.
(2) What level of education did each of the family members you mention attain? What was/is their occupation? Have the languages they use shaped or been shaped by their education, occupation, social class and community they live in? Did they continue to speak all the languages they knew throughout their lives, etc.?
(3) Can you speak the dialects or languages that your grandparents and parents speak? Why or why not?
(4) What dialects and/or languages did you learn as a child? And, what dialects and/or languages do you speak now? Provide examples of words, expressions and unique features you use(d).
(5) What have been your experiences in learning another language or dialect? How long did it take you to learn another language? How well do/did you speak it? What was the context (what was the situation like when/where you learned it)? Are/were you literate in the new language? Have you lost the ability to speak any language you once knew? What are the reasons for the loss?

The assignment has three parts. First, after interviewing some family members and researching their own linguistic autoethnography, students write a five-page paper guided by the above questions. Second, each student has five to seven minutes for an oral presentation in class where they can share visuals such as PowerPoints, photos and maps. During that time, the classroom is treated as another community where all students listen to others, exchange stories and take notes. Finally, all students write a reflective and analytical journal after listening to the whole class. They are required to write what they have learned from their classmates' linguistic autoethnographies, and to elicit findings from the information they have gained. In what follows, I provide some insights and excerpts from my Varieties of English class in Spring 2020, with 30 undergraduate students.

Based on students linguistic autoethnographic papers and oral presentations, many students discovered some information that they did not know before through their research process. For example, Sally, who defined herself as a southern girl, found that her mother, who is originally from Alabama, used to say 'y'allses' as a plural second person pronoun prior to living in Texas. Yolanda did not know that her maternal grandfather could speak Japanese, but the grandfather stopped using it because it was treated as a threat during the World War II era. With this piece of information, Yolanda became motivated to learn Japanese because she wanted to fill the missing piece in her family.

My students' journals at the end of the assignment show that the students became more appreciative of their own languages, dialects and those of others. In this chapter, three themes, which meet my goal to educate students about linguistic diversity, emerged based on the students' reflection on their own experience doing this project and summarizing their classmates' linguistic autoethnographies.

First, students see differences among their stories, such as their ancestors' countries of origins and native languages and dialects, and how their occupations shaped their language use. But, more importantly, the students have found meaningful similarities that lead them to see that they shared one same human race. Myra, a female African Filipino American, expressed in her reflective journal, 'Through this activity we were able to travel the world, learn of new languages, experience different cultures, and witness how we are all connected'.

In another example, Santee, a male student majoring in Anthropology and who has a South Asian background, expressed in his journal that 'It's great to learn about our classmates' *different* lived experiences and see how we, generationally or culturally, may be *the same*'. Sally, who defined herself as a southern girl, also wrote,

> I couldn't help but notice interesting commonalities and differences between the experiences of each presenter. I then began to speculate about the implications behind these similarities and differences and compiled the experiences into a large collection that could be studied as a single entity.

These similarities students found include a requirement to learn Standard English for education no matter what their heritage languages are – whether or not their ancestors came to the US from somewhere else – a need to engage in code-switching practices, the reality of a language shift within two or three generations and the experience of multiple languages and dialects throughout their lives. Even those who claimed they and their family only spoke English agreed that there were various styles, dialects, regional and generational differences of English. In addition, knowing that they have similarities, students realize that they are not alone. Jonathan's story is a representation of this learning journey. In his linguistic autoethnography, Jonathan wrote that he is Hispanic but could not speak Spanish because English was prioritized for the sake of educational success. After listening to his classmates, he wrote in his journal,

> I grew up in a Spanish-speaking family but being able to speak the language was never a priority or necessity for me. It was interesting to

learn that I was not the only one in the same position. Eva presented her project and showed that both of her parents' side of the family had some sort of connection to the Hispanic community. Despite her family background, she has not had the chance to learn Spanish ... Both of Katie's parents' [sic] families tie to Italy and Sicily and how they spoke Italian and Sicilian; however, she was not able to speak those languages.

With the shared experience, Jonathan put it in his journal, 'After venturing into my own heritage, it was *comforting* to know that some of my fellow classmates also classify themselves within similar backgrounds'.

I discussed in the introduction that exploring one's own linguistic background is a humble way to understand language diversity and consequences. Using this same method in the classroom, I see how students learn more about themselves, as Ty put it, that the project is 'a vehicle of self-discovery'. Listening to others, students also learn more about a larger community, yet at a very personal level. While being different makes diversity, through this project, commonalities lead them to see their shared race as humans.

Second, it is prominent that my students realized the privilege of using Standard American English especially because of the formal education they received. Jenny wrote, 'With more formal education, my classmates and I began to uphold the standard American English as the "one size fits all" language'.

In addition, gaining more information about others who presented their linguistic background with pride, many students agreed that the privilege of the Standard Language brought about how other dialects of English were perceived as inferior, as Ricky wrote,

> The educational system making a deliberate effort to suppress what is viewed as an academically or professionally inferior accent. We have listened to this happening with non-native speakers of English, as well as native speakers, who use a dialect or vernacular separate from Standard American English.

And, Sara wrote,

> Stories are told about how accented English (anything perceived as non-standard) is considered a hindrance to success. This portrays language ideology in the US concerning to acceptability of English varieties.

Students' presentations and repetitions of the same stories reemphasized that the privilege of Standard American English is a learned framework, yet an enduring one in our society. Students understand that such privilege is the reason why non-standard forms receive less value.

The third theme based on students' journals after listening to all classmates' linguistic autoethnographies presents that the students became comfortably aware of language diversity, and varieties or variations. They have learned that using non-standard forms is natural and more common. Monica concluded, 'I learned that no one speaks *just English*, and everyone has some family history that traces them to different dialects of English or different languages entirely'.

In the same vein, Kyle expressed, 'In regard to the various varieties in English, throughout the class it was more common for people to speak a different dialect of a language than the perceived standard'. And, Veronica wrote,

> People create and alter their language as can be seen in all the varieties a single language there are. This project affirmed to me that language is the greatest creation of humanity, and it is a creation that is constantly being amended in conjunction with the changes humans naturally face. As humans grow and change, so does language.

Although the privilege of Standard Language, Standard American English in particular, is strongly constructed, as discussed in the previous theme, students understand that other variations are not inferior. In fact, they are more natural and commonly used. Students become gratified by the details of the English and other languages they speak and use. Utilizing and practicing linguistic autoethnography in the classroom, I feel fulfilled that I directly and indirectly introduce linguistic diversity to the younger generation. Linguistic autoethnography is a useful way to keep students' linguistic attitudes in check through their language learning and usage experiences, including sharing stories with others. The exposure to linguistic diversity in their closest communities will help students expand their understanding in a larger community.

Summary

Throughout my self-exploration using linguistic autoethnography, I found that language attitudes and ignorance can change over time depending on the exposure to linguistic differences. I started off as a somewhat insensitive speaker and language learner when I was in Thailand and at the very beginning of my academic career in the US. However, I have found through my self-exploration that my attitude toward non-standard varieties of English have been gradually changed because of my professional training, personal experiences and exposures to diversity. As a researcher, I have found these linguistic attitude changes to be similar to those shared by my participants, who have lived in the US for several years.

For others, especially my students, to have quick exposure to linguistic differences and diversity, I use linguistic autoethnography with my students as an assignment in the classroom. The outcome of the assignment has been positive. Students present their open mind to language diversity and different varieties of English. Although intentional ignorance maybe challenging to tackle, at least I hope that naïve ignorance can be reduced by guided discussion and education.

Notes

(1) A type of mammal with a long tail, not an electric device that could be pluralized as mouses.
(2) L1 means first language of a speaker. The speaker's L1 accent, while native, is influenced by their surroundings, geographical or regional ways of producing sounds. For example, an American English speaker speaks English as L1. But, they may speak L1 with a Southern American English accent or a Californian accent. L2 means second, not first or native, language of a speaker. In other word, the speaker learns the second language later. The speaker's L2 accent may be influenced or interfered by their first language, which makes him or her sound non-native or non-standard to native speakers.
(3) I discussed the traditional English education at the time I was in college in Thailand between 1996 and 2000. The current parameters of English education in Thailand may have changed.
(4) All names of research and student participants in this chapter are pseudonyms.
(5) The questions are adapted from (1) Heritage Language project designed by Dr Kellie Rolstad when I was in a PhD program at University Name and (2) Posada (2017).

References

Alcoff, L.M. (2007) Epistemologies of ignorance: Three types. In S. Sullivan and N. Tuana (eds) *Race and Epistemologies of Ignorance* (pp. 39–50). Albany, NY: State University of New York Press.
Anderson, L. (2006) Analytic autoethnography. *Journal of Contemporary Ethnography* 35 (4), 373–395.
Atkinson, P.A. (2006) Rescuing autoethnography. *Journal of Contemporary Ethnography* 35 (4), 400–404.
Bernaisch, T. and Koch, C. (2016) Attitudes toward English in India. *World Englishes* 35 (1), 118–132.
Byczkowska-Owczarek, D. (2014) Researcher's personal experience as a method of embodiment research. *Hexis. Theory, Society & Culture* 1 (1). https://doi.org/10.15584/hexis.3.
Day, R.R. (1982) Children's attitude toward language. In E.B. Ryan and H. Giles (eds) *Attitudes Toward Language Variation: Social and Applied Contexts* (pp. 116–131). London: Edward Arnold.
Dragojevic, M., Mastro, D., Giles, H. and Sink, A. (2016) Silencing nonstandard speakers: A content analysis of accent portrayals on American primetime television. *Language in Society* 45 (1), 59–85.
Duran, C.S. (2017) *Language and Literacy in Refugee Families*. London: Palgrave Macmillan.
Ellis, C. (2004) *The Ethnographic I: A Methodological Novel About Autoethnography*. Walnut Creek, CA: AltaMira Press.
Ellis, C., Adams, T.E. and Bochner, A.P. (2011) Autoethnography: An overview. *Historical Social Research/Historische Sozialforschung* 36 (4), 273–290.
Giles, H. and Watson, B. (2013) *The Social Meanings of Language, Dialect, and Accent: International Perspectives on Speech Styles*. New York: Peter Lang.
Gilson, E. (2011) Vulnerability, ignorance, and oppression. *Hypatia* 26 (2), 308–332.

KHON (2017) Woman appears to get angry at Starbucks customer for speaking Korean. See https://www.khon2.com/news/woman-appears-to-get-angry-at-california-starbucks-customers-for-speaking-korean/ (accessed May 2021).

Kirk, B. (2019) Houston named the most diverse city in recent survey. See https://patch.com/texas/houston/houston-named-most-diverse-city-u-s-recent-survey (accessed January 2021).

Marlow, M.L. and Giles, H. (2010) 'We won't get ahead speaking like that!' Expressing and managing language criticism in Hawai'i. *Journal of Multilingual and Multicultural Development* 31 (3), 237–251.

Nejjari, W., Gerritsen, M., Van Der Haagen, M. and Korzilius, H. (2012) Responses to Dutch-accented English. *World Englishes* 31 (2), 248–267.

O'Reilly, K. (2012) *Ethnographic Method* (2nd edn). New York: Routledge.

Posada, A. (2017) Linguistic autobiographies in the English class. Seehttps://aliciapousada.weebly.com/uploads/1/0/0/2/10020146/pousada_prtesol_linguistic_autobiographies_english_class.pdf (accessed May 2021).

Rivers, D. (2019) Walking on grass: Reconciling experience and expectation within Japan. *Journal of Language, Identity, and Education* 18 (6), 377–388.

Spry, T. (2001) Performing autoethnography: An embodied methodological praxis. *Qualitative Inquiry* 7 (6), 706–732.

Tokumoto, M. and Shibata, M. (2011) Asian varieties of English: Attitudes toward pronunciation. *World Englishes* 30 (3), 392–408.

United Nations (2021) International mother language day. See https://www.un.org/en/observances/mother-language-day (accessed May 2021).

Wiebesiek, L., Rudwick, S. and Zeller, J. (2011) South African Indian English: A qualitative studies of attitudes. *World Englishes* 30 (2), 251–268.

5 Narratives of Invisibility: Racism and Anti-Racism in Academic Spaces in Brazil

Clarissa Menezes Jordão, Juliana Zeggio Martinez and Eduardo Henrique Diniz de Figueiredo

In this chapter, we construct a dialogue among three scholars from the Global South, reflecting upon situations we have experienced (as students and/or scholars) in respect to race, racism, coloniality and decolonization in academia. One of the authors writes about publication experiences that bring to the fore the ways in which publishing criteria often seek to erase ontologies and epistemologies from the Global South. The second author tells a story of how participating in a community of a majority of black scholars made her perceive her own whiteness (which was often naturalized) in critical ways for the first time, and the urgency to scrutinize the privilege of being white in an unequal world. Finally, the third author shares the story of how he came to understand the ways in which participants in academic research are many times disembodied, which often leads to little problematization of issues related to race, gender and sexuality. Upon discussing these narratives, we pay particular attention to how issues related to anti-racism are often made invisible in academia. We then reflect upon ways in which we may overcome such invisibility in scholarly spaces and activities, mainly considering decoloniality as a turning point.

All there is, while things perpetually fall apart, is the possibility of acting from where we are. (Shotwell, 2016: 4)

In this chapter, you will find a dialogue among the three authors, Applied Linguistics academics from the Global South, reflecting upon situations we have experienced (as students, professors and/or scholars) in respect to race, racism, coloniality and decolonization in academia.

We begin by briefly presenting these situations (which we refer to as *narratives*), and then we move on to discuss how issues related to race and racism are often made invisible in academia, as scholarly settings are deeply grounded in the abyssal line (de Sousa Santos, 2018) and epistemic racism and sexism (Grosfoguel, 2015). We then reflect upon ways in which we may (or have) overcome such invisibility in our spaces and activities, mainly considering decoloniality as a turning point (Mignolo, 2000).

Before moving on to our narratives, we feel it is important to present our geopolitical and body-political location – which Grosfoguel (2007) calls *locus of enunciation*. We are three Latinx scholars located in Brazil, whose work has mostly focused on critical Applied Linguistics and language teaching and learning (the term Latinx is understood here in a broad sense, in reference to those of us who are from Latin America, irrespective of where we are now located in the world).

Within Brazil, we are often seen as white, privileged scholars, due to our skin colors and our position in a major public Southern university (as explained by Devulsky, 2021, skin color is the main factor of racial discrimination in Brazilian contexts, despite the fact that racial identity is defined by other biological, as well as many non-biological, traits[1]). Outside of Brazil, however, we are perceived in a number of different ways and have experienced racialized practices as well. This happens because what is defined as 'white', 'black' and so on in many Latin American contexts is different from the ways in which the same concepts are understood in other parts of the globe. This difference brings with it a number of ambiguities in terms of racial identity, especially to those of us who have living/working/studying/traveling experiences in different places. It also brings other ambiguities, of ontoepistemological nature, which we will explore throughout this chapter.

Thus, we experience race (and racism) in convoluted, often confusing ways, since our bodies, ways of speaking and gesturing and the manners in which we relate to people as a whole index very different identities and ways of knowing and being (both to those with whom we relate and to ourselves). This will be noticed in each of the narratives produced by us as we identify and interrogate our own constitutive coloniality, hoping to be able to interrupt it (Menezes de Souza, 2019). We also take as a starting point the fact that '[a]ny embodied situation is complex and dynamic, imbricated with many webs of connection, carrying ethical implications' (Shotwell, 2016: 124).

Therefore, whether we are in privileged or underprivileged positions at any given point in time and space, we are part of a world in which 'everyone is implicated in situations we (at least in some way) repudiate' (2016: 5). Being implicated does not mean, of course, accepting these situations. It does, on the other hand, bring two important considerations we wish to highlight: (1) that in order to effect change we need to understand our own complicity in these situations; and (2) that actions which denounce and seek to end racism, sexism, classism, ageism and all other isms are the responsibility not only of those who are affected by these forms of discrimination directly, but of all of us collectively and of the institutions that form our societies.

Writing the following narratives from such assumptions has allowed us to promote two of the three movements towards decolonization referred to by Menezes de Souza *et al.* (2019): *identifying* and *interrogating* racism in our lives, at least as far as the reported incidents are concerned. Although we believe that such movements will open again and again in different situations in our lives, the third movement, *interrupting*, has particularly become a never-ending project, as we are aware of the structural racism[2] (Bonilla-Silva, 1996) that constitutes us and around which our society has been constructed.

In our writing of the narratives, we also address Singh's (2021) suggestion that applied linguists should 'encourage the people who we research' [ourselves included, we add] 'to theorize their own knowledge, i.e. to assume epistemological positionalities, that are meaningful to themselves and to the communities from which they come' (2021: 1168; see also Pennycook & Makoni, 2020). The facts that we have started this text by presenting our own locus of enunciation and that we theorize about race, racism and anti-racism based on our own experiences illustrate some of the main ways in which we have taken up Singh's (2021) proposal in this chapter and in our work more broadly.

Our first narrative, then, focuses on the writer's awareness of her own whiteness during an international summer school abroad; it is titled 'International student'. The second, 'Supervisor', tells of the author's astonishment having been selected to supervise a graduate student on her research around race. The third narrative, 'Academic author', draws on academic reviews received by the writer. All of them report incidents lived by us, and the lessons we learned from them follow suit in the text.

Narratives

Juliana's narrative – International student

In 2016, I attended a summer school on decolonizing knowledge and power held abroad. I'll never forget how amazed I was to see that the majority of the participants were non-white,[3] mostly black. It was a fascinating experience to be in a classroom in which I did not associate myself with the 'norm' – in fact, it was quite the opposite from what I had experienced as a student through all my life. In the beginning, I felt unease, but the opportunity turned into a remarkable learning experience.

For the first time, I saw myself as a white person. I saw myself in such a way that I had never seen before. Being white in that classroom disrupted the taken-for-granted whiteness I had grown up with and learned to see around me in academic settings. That moment reminded me of another talk I had seen months before, in which it was explained how black people are forced to learn they are black in a racist world. The speaker shared lots of stories, highlighting how, since very young, he was seen as a body not belonging to certain places. His stories taught me about the hierarchies and the abyssal line separating and classifying different bodies.

I realized how a body impacts and affects relationships, cultural and social encounters and how our bodies shape the (negative and positive) experiences we have in life. During that summer school, I understood how unable I was to share similar stories of racism living in a white body. I do recall one professor in particular who was teaching about the decolonial project by drawing on Franz Fanon's zone of non-being and how that was an unthinkable concept from my own locus of enunciation. That experience proved what I had learned before: a concept or a theoretical framework or any scientific data cannot exist in a disembodied way; all knowledge production is always situated.

Eduardo's narrative – Supervisor

It was rather surprising for me to receive a message (in 2016) from a student who had just finished her undergraduate studies in another state in Brazil, and who was going to apply to our master's program and wanted to work with me as an advisor. My surprise stemmed from two main factors: the fact that I was very new as a professor in our graduate program; and the idea that someone who wanted to work with racial issues had chosen me to advise her. Still, I felt – from the very beginning – that if that student were to be accepted into our program, it was my responsibility to advise her.

During my time as the student's advisor, it was clear to me that I did not know near enough about racial studies and Applied Linguistics as I thought I should. Advising her often made me nervous. I became even more apprehensive – sleepless at times – when we started to decide on who should be in my advisee's thesis committee. One of the people who we knew we should invite – because of her great expertise in studies on race and language teaching – intimidated me, for two main reasons: first, because I was sure she would see me as an impostor, which I feel I still am in regards to studies on this particular subject; and second, because I did not know what attitude she would have towards me having accepted to advise someone's work in this area.

It was then that I had a second surprise. Upon contacting the fellow professor, she accepted the invitation straight away. And as I went to the bus station to pick her up for my advisee's defense – I met her personally on that very day – I had a chance to talk to her in person for the first time. I explained that I had had a very hard time advising the thesis she was about to evaluate publicly, and that I had been even more concerned about having her in my advisee's committee. That was when she taught me a lesson: she said that it was often the case that students wished to work with themes related to race, but that advisors would discourage them because they did not feel prepared to tackle such matters. She then simply said to me that non-white students needed more people to accept this task of diving into racial studies with them, because we are all learning about it every day.

I was, of course, happy with the comment, at least in the beginning. But then I became increasingly uncomfortable with the perspective I had had at first. In particular, I began to question how my own work often has not paid central attention to issues such as race, gender, and especially students' (as well as my own) loci of enunciation. I have since tried to address these issues, but I feel I have a lot to catch up.

Clarissa's narrative – Academic author

Many years ago, I dared submit a paper to a renowned international journal in language education. It was about the importance of relationality and rapport with students for teaching-learning in school. I wished its form would mirror its content, so it was written in the first person singular, my locus of enunciation was clearly stated and also my subjectivity was often brought to the foreground as a way to problematize the pseudo-absence of the body from research.

Guess what: it was rejected upfront.

I protested and asked the editors to explain why. They did: 'Unfortunately, academic discourse is also something that the English language requires in a certain way, making this a totally colonized field: Anglophone academia. Either we write as the culturally academic discourse imposes or we don't publish. Therefore, the article, although showing some glimpses of brilliant ideas, fails to follow the coherent academic discourse required for a publication in the English language'.[4]

I was astonished at what I understood as a complete oblivion of the fact that those 'glimpses of brilliant ideas' would be kept from the 'Anglophone academia' because I was not writing as the 'culturally academic discourse imposes'. I was astonished at the naivety of the editor who seemed to believe that such discourse existed on its own, disembodied, denied authorship and therefore impossible to be changed. 'Unfortunately', he said. Who is in charge here, I wondered, if not the editors themselves?

I protested, trying to justify my writing on the basis of emotion/ reason, body/mind, subjectivity/objectivity binaries. For me, at the time, it was a matter of us having different views about what was considered science, scientific knowledge and 'coherent academic discourse', for I had been widely published in Brazilian well-known academic papers by then. I thought it was a clash between two different epistemologies. I myself, in my attempts to understand what was happening, disembodied the incident and reduced it to what was considered appropriate to that context or not. I excluded ontology from the picture: my body and my locus of enunciation were not perceived as part of the discrimination I was suffering then.

The Applied Linguistics from Which We Speak

We believe it is likely clear to most readers how the narratives we have just told relate to race and anti-racism. As we have seen, Juliana shares how participating in a community of a majority of black scholars made her perceive her own whiteness (which was often naturalized) in critical ways, and the urgency to scrutinize the privilege of being white in an unequal world. Eduardo narrates how his own work with identity had been, at times, oblivious to race, gender and sexuality, and highlights the importance of engaging with such issues not only from a conceptual perspective, but also – or mainly – in the sense of co-constructing spaces with students in which these issues can be researched and discussed. Finally, Clarissa writes about academic publication experiences that bring to the fore the ways in which publishing criteria often seek to erase onto-epistemologies from the Global South.

However, there are a number of dimensions within the narratives that may be less clear. One may wonder, for instance, how those incidents can be related to the authors' loci of enunciation as Applied Linguists or, in other words, what possible associations they can have with this disciplinary field that focuses on language, communication, identity. In order to make them explicit, we need to start our discussion about anti-racism from how language is conceived in the Applied Linguistics from which we speak, and thus lay the bases from which we build our understanding of these narratives and their interconnection with language studies.

There is a wide group of researchers/educators in Brazil (e.g. Borba, 2020; Borelli *et al.*, 2020; Ferreira, 2006; Garcez, 2019; Jordão, 2016; Menezes de Souza, 2007; Moita Lopes, 2006; Monte Mór, 2007; Nascimento, 2019; Rezende, 2018), ourselves included, who have been doing Applied Linguistics informed by post-structuralism, decoloniality, critical literacies, feminist, queer and race studies, to name just a few areas, and therefore have been looking at language from the angle of its indissociability with social practice. This body of work dialogues with research by scholars located in other parts of the world, especially from the Global South. We refer to 'Global South' here in the notion brought forward by Boaventura de Sousa Santos, that is, as a geopolitical and ontoepistemological – rather than geographical – position, expressed by a decolonial attitude that presupposes taking up a plural stance and relational ways of being in the world (Mignolo & Walsh, 2018) as well as the engagement with issues of oppression and identification with struggles against the effects of capitalism, patriarchalism and colonialism (de Sousa Santos, 2018). In this sense, we often see global souths in the geographical north and global norths in the geographical south.

Influenced also by the works of Paulo Freire and the Bakhtin Circle, that group has produced a considerable body of research around the impact language praxes can exert on people and people on languages, starting from the assumption that, besides being a social practice, language is an ethical and axiological act, a responsible/responsive act (Bakhtin, 19201924). Praxis (as well as its plural, praxes) is (are) understood here as defined by Mignolo and Walsh (2018: 7):

> In our thinking alone and together, theory and praxis are necessarily interrelated. Theory and praxis are constructions that presuppose the basic praxis of living. Without our daily praxis of living, it would not be possible to make conceptual and second-order distinctions between theory and praxis. Following this line of reasoning, [we delink] from the modern concept of theory versus praxis. For us, theory is doing and doing is thinking. Are you not doing something when you theorize or analyze concepts? Isn't doing something praxis? And from praxis – understood as thought-reflection-action, and thought-reflection on this action – do we not also construct theory and theorize thought? By disobeying the long-held belief that you first theorize and then apply, or that you can engage in blind praxis without theoretical analysis and vision, we locate our thinking/doing in a different terrain. This terrain is rooted in the praxis of living and in the idea of theory-and-as-praxis and praxis-and-as-theory, and in the interdependence and continuous flow of movement of both.

This is to say that we always respond to something or someone, acting and reacting *with* the world, so language is not restricted to verbal interactions, but expanded into enunciative acts, responsively brought into existence in every enunciation, while at the same time integrating a pre-existing community: As put forth by Volosinov (1973: 81): '… language, like a ball, is tossed from generation to generation. In actual fact, language moves together with that stream and is inseparable from it. Language cannot properly be said to be handed down – it endures, but it endures as a continuous process of becoming'. Therefore, we speak from within a field of knowledge we see as deeply entangled in social issues, politics, ideology, culture, power – a field that takes on interdisciplinarity and intentionally crosses academic borders.

For us, the main goal of doing Applied Linguistics is not *simply* to present solutions to language problems, solutions to be applied somewhere else by someone else, but instead we seek to problematize the 'wor(l)d', especially in its purportedly universality, linearity, homogeneity, hierarchy, separability, one-dimensionality, single temporality – all features inherited from modernity. In this sense, we embrace the decolonial project brought forward by the Latin-American modernity/coloniality research group. Coloniality, for this group, is different from colonialism. While colonialism may be said to be over (historically, at least), coloniality refers to the ongoing violence that constructs such as race, gender, sexuality, social class, dominant/subalternized knowledges and so on, exert upon non-dominant individuals and social groups. Such constructs come from the experience of colonialism, and from the understanding that while colonialism may have ended historically (with the administrative and political independence of many nation-states), coloniality, that is, the violence and hierarchies produced by it, has not (Castro Gómez & Grosfoguel, 2007).

Alongside decoloniality, we bring to the floor of Applied Linguistics our understandings of Portuguese sociologist Boaventura de Sousa Santos, as he stresses the importance of making visible knowledges that have been silenced by European modernity and thus amplifying the ecology of knowledges in our simultaneous existences (de Sousa Santos, 2018). But we also strive to make visible our own coloniality (i.e. the ways in which we may be complicit with the violence produced by colonial experience), so that we can identify, interrogate and hopefully come to interrupt it (Menezes de Souza *et al.*, 2019). Writing this chapter is, for us as Applied Linguists, citizens, middle-classed, cisgender, participants of an educated and privileged social class in Brazil, father, CAT tutor, caretaker of parent and others, an uncomfortable exercise on deepening our understanding of the violence resulting from structural racism, something that we could only do with each other's help in collaboration. It is an 'act of insurgency'[5] (Mignolo & Walsh, 2018: 38) in which we 'reconceptualize modes of interpretation and of reading, seeing, and being in and with the world'.

Going back to our take on Applied Linguistics, we see it as a social science concerned with people more than with descriptions of language items or structures, and also as a political space where action (both collective and individual) can be taken towards building a better world – a world where the word can be agonistically fought over, disputed, negotiated, claimed and reclaimed. This Applied Linguistics encompasses Freire's 'palavra-mundo', or *wor(l)d* (Freire & Macedo, 1987), a concept that sees language and society as inseparable, and language and subjectivity as embodied-experiences. It places studies in linguistics as necessarily concerned with the implications of language to the planet. Here's where decoloniality and epistemologies of the South are more evidently in association with such Applied Linguistics (Makoni *et al.*, 2022; Pennycook & Makoni, 2020), in so far as they are deeply concerned with all forms of existence in their interconnectedness and interdependence (Viveiros de Castro, 2004).

An Interpretive Account of the Narratives

If we assume language as a social practice, as something we *do* rather than something we *have* (Lu & Horner, 2013), as explained above, we can see our narratives as constitutive of our subjectivities, as actions informed by and informing how we see ourselves in the world. This is a concept of language contrary to the now infamous *telementation* in Saussure's talking heads (Canagarajah, 2013; Harris, 1999), that placed language as an external object, a medium responsible for conveying our thoughts to somebody else. Instead, language here is seen as the very faculty allowing our thoughts to be formed, our understandings to be constructed, our selves (and egos, and alter egos, and personae) to *be*: it is central to our existence because it is 'such stuff we are made on',[6] as Prospero might put it. Embodied language makes ourselves possible. From this perspective, it is not restricted to the verbal, but includes other materialities such as images, smells, colors, emotions; it is not limited by reasoning or mental operations, but involves our bodies, our senses, our situatedness, our contexts, our geopolitical locations, our histories.

In what follows, we bring our collective, interpretive account of the narratives we have just presented. We have divided this part of the chapter in two sections: *embodiment and invisibility* and *abyssal lines and whiteness*. This was done under the assumption that the issues we are dealing with intersect, rather than separate; however, we believe that creating the subsections may help the reader (as it has helped us) focus on specific aspects of anti-racism.

Embodiment and invisibility

When we take language to be thus constitutive of who we are and how we become, we need to start from the understanding that all knowledge, as well as all language, is embodied, and that our main locus of identity is the body (Louro, 2000). As explained by Louro (2000), based on bell hooks's work, language and education are generally thought to be in the realm of the mind only, as if we were disembodied spirits, or disembodied intellects. This type of thinking is particularly evident in Eduardo's narrative, especially when he explains that he realized his own work with identity and with language as a social practice had been oblivious to race, gender, sexuality and the notion of one's locus of enunciation. In other words, he is acknowledging that he paid no attention to the bodies of those who engaged with or participated in his research, including his own, therefore making those bodies invisible.

Even though one could ask if ever a body can be made invisible or how a body is placed in the zone of invisibility, Juliana's narrative also discloses the tension between visibility and invisibility of bodies in Brazil and in other contexts as well. Based on commonsensical and local narratives, the south of Brazil, where the three of us are now located, is quite often pictured as a region of the country with an enormous concentration of white people, perhaps because of the presence of communities of European descendants supporting the myth that this part of the country is mostly populated by white people. Similarly to the schooling and academic experience lived by Juliana, many people who are white in the south of the country have not had non-white schoolmates, work colleagues, or teachers (Garcia, 2021). In fact, most of them have never thought of what it means to be born white in a racist country, or what white privilege means, and have never felt misplaced or offended due to ethnic and racial reasons.

What becomes striking in this commonsensical setting is the fact that official local data indicate the presence of non-white people as almost half of the population in the south of the country, and national data show that more than 50% of the population of Brazil identifies itself as non-white.[7] We might interpret this tension between official data and local perception as segregation or the myth of a racially mixed country, when in fact there is a spatial dimension to race relations. In our academic setting, for instance, the presence of black people is almost nonexistent, endorsing epistemic racism (and sexism, as will be shown later). It was just with the anti-racist struggle by the Brazilian Black Movement and their effort to intervene in race relations in the country that recent educational policies, promoted by the previous progressive government (from 2008 to 2013), enabled a rise of black and indigenous students' presence in our university.[8] Nevertheless, in our direct experience, such quantitative rise does not seem to be accompanied by this population reaching visibility and/or relevant positions in prestigious universities around the country, and this is even more evident in the case of black women (Nogueira, 2017).

There are significant historical aspects that elucidate the invisibility of such bodies, race relations and racism within Brazil. Brazilian sociologist Jessé Souza (2017) explains how the South and the Southeast of the country, in the 19th century, went through a massive change in terms of work conception and development, turning the local economy into a new configuration. At that time, a large population of immigrants arrived in the country to work in coffee plantations. With this new workforce available during the transition from enslavement to free labor, the previous enslaved and subaltern groups (mostly black and indigenous) were left on their own to survive. Consequently, the former enslaved people were forced to integrate in a new social order without being offered conditions to compete with the new immigrant human labor. Without equal and just possibilities, these populations became then invisible to the market, to the State, to the country, establishing the myth of Brazil as a racial democracy. Jessé Souza (2017) also emphasizes that, in academic aspects, this historical erasure of inequalities, entrenched in the history of the country, ended up 'facilitating' the life of many scholars who did not have to deal with what was made invisible, a fact which clarifies, at least in part, the complexity that lies in the experiences shared in our narratives.

For the Latin-American modernity/coloniality research group, however, racialization is a social practice and process that started long before the 19th century, a scrutiny that deepens the unjust conditions described by Jésse Souza (2017). Drawing on Peruvian sociologist Anibal Quijano's concept of coloniality of power, one can learn how *race* was a category/concept created to play a particular role in the colonial project of modernity: that of ranking, ruling and naturalizing our existence. Quijano (2000) claims that the idea of race was fundamental for modernity to be projected as a model of global power. First, it established a biological difference among people(s) that placed some in a condition of inferiority based on binary relations of identities such as modern/primitive, white/non-white, European/non-European, cultured/uncultured, civilized/uncivilized. Second, it justified the constitution of control in regards to labor, resources and products. This way, the encounter of Latin-American Amerindians with the Spanish *conquistadores* and, later on, with the population brought from the African continent to Abya Yala marked the beginning of a racialized co-existence in history that lasts until today. Labor, gender, classed divisions, for instance, have been established by coloniality through *race*. In Quijano's words (2000), 'race and racial identity were established as instruments of basic social classification ... and the idea of race was a way of granting legitimacy to the relations of domination imposed by the conquest' (2000: 534). For the past few centuries, he continues, 'race became the fundamental criterion for the distribution of the world population into ranks, places, and roles in the new society's structure of power' (2000: 535).

Clarissa's narrative, 'The academic author', in turn, allows us to perceive another dimension of invisibility, which involves epistemic and language issues more specifically. In this narrative, we can see manifest a double-folded assumption that (1) there is such a thing as *one* academic discourse, which is based on Eurocentric onto-epistemologies; and that (2) its higher manifestation is being as close as possible to whatever reviewers have in mind as the top arrangements of discourse in academia. All other forms of knowing, performing, organizing and communicating in scientific discourse are drastically, and sadly, labeled as non-legitimate, including those constitutive of bodies coming from the Global South. The issue for refusing the article, therefore, seems not to have been a concern with communicability, with readability, with reaching the audience. Rather, epistemic prejudice and self-centered arrogance seem to have influenced the reviewer's decision. In this case, we can see how the issue of embodiment is not restricted to a physical aspect, but can expand, as it usually does, to being a geopolitical one. The author's body as an academic from the Global South was silenced, projected to the other side of the abyssal line (which we will discuss later), not to be seen. From our perspective, this experience highlights the understanding of racism (which includes epistemic racism and sexism) 'as discourse, knowledge, and social practices that, by means of inferiorization, denigration, marginalization, and exclusion, construct and perpetuate unequal relations of power between groups of people defined by perceived racial difference' (Kubota, 2020: 712–713).

In our understanding, these realities are reflected in our academic work and professional bodies. We feel, therefore, that an Applied Linguistics that seeks to be anti-racist needs to engage with the body, with the issue of (in)visibility, and with the notion of situated knowledges more deeply. In terms of research, studies in areas as diverse as second language acquisition, teaching English to speakers of other languages (TESOL), English as an international language/English as a lingua franca (for distinctions between these two, see Rose *et al.*, 2020), and language minority education, to name just a few, can only benefit from closer engagements with the bodies involved in research, rather than simplifying them into binary categories such as male/female, native/nonnative, young/old, speaker of this/that language, white/non-white and so on. In fact, even some of the research focusing specifically on language and identity could benefit from closer attention to the body and to how issues concerning the embodiment of knowledge and knowing usually play a considerable part in the interpretation of results. Moreover, the well-known and established frameworks that have been informing such research fields/areas also need to be scrutinized and challenged in terms of their onto-epistemological assumptions (i.e. what counts as research, how it should be conducted, whose theories matter and so on).

Not only that: as researchers and authors, we need to be continuously aware of and explicit about our own geographical, historical, geopolitical and bodily selves (Menezes de Souza, 2019), and how these selves impact the ways in which we generate our data, discuss our findings, engage with and present our research participants, and how we position ourselves within each particular investigation we conduct. Questions that come to our minds in this respect, based on the narratives and on other aspects of our own trajectories, as well as on our discussion thus far, are: Why may some of us often fear the possibilities of addressing issues of race, ethnicity, gender, sexuality and other identity matters in our work? Why do some of us think it is not our role to engage with these issues? What is our responsibility in dealing with such issues? Would we interpret our data differently if our participants were from another race, gender, if their voices indexed a certain sexual orientation, if they dressed a certain way (not only talked a certain way, as we often focus on in Sociolinguistics and Applied Linguistics work)? In which ways does our racial, gender, sexual, class identities impact our relation with participants in the studies we conduct? How do these identities impact our own readings and interpretations? How are these identities often projected in academic settings? How has (academic) language been used to project such issues and identities? Asking oneself these and similar questions is, for us, one of the ways in which we can do anti-racist work in Applied Linguistics and in other fields.

In fact, the importance of the body in anti-racist work applies not only to our roles as researchers, but also to the positions we hold as professors, colleagues, coordinators, heads of departments, and so on (Kubota, 2020). This implies, in our view, working with students and colleagues to understand how the ways in which they/we read the wor(l)d are permeated by their/our trajectories and identities, which are indissociable from their/our embodied existences. It also implies trying to comprehend how our actions, as well as the ways in which we perceive others – and are perceived by them – are strictly related to our racialized, gender, aged/ageing, classed, sexualized selves and the ways in which certain 'markers' of identity (e.g. being a woman, a white person, a Latinx, a cisgender person) are indexed in different social groups. Studies such as those by Bhattacharya *et al.* (2020), Files *et al.* (2017), Lin *et al.* (2004) and Nascimento (2019), for instance, have shown how such identity 'markers' have pervaded the professional lives of those who are positioned as 'inferior' in hierarchies created by modernity/coloniality. These 'markers' of identity are simultaneously fixed, in so far as they are imprinted in the body, and culturally indexed, having their meanings attributed to in various assemblages that construct what has been referred to as *intersectionality* (Collins, 1998; Ferreira & Barbosa, 2019).

This perspective comes from the awareness that human beings are part of the world and cannot be separated from other existences in the world, from other beings that inhabit this planet, not even when we attempt to analyze them, as has been the case with scientific knowledge. The dismembering of bodies into parts, the dissection of units of analysis into isolated, independent elements, as if our organisms were neatly adjusted machines, has constituted an important move of modern thinking and of the modern way to make science: *separability*. Decolonial perspectives, and our current experience living a pandemic (as we will comment later), have stressed the importance of the realization that all forms of existence are related, that they matter and inform one another (Shotwell, 2016). This awareness is particularly important when we think of racism in its various manifestations, be they related to our lives as academics or to our everyday existences. It comes with the realization that when one person (or any living being, or element of culture as a whole) suffers, we all are entangled in that suffering; that is, we are all interconnected. Anti-racist work needs to highlight this interconnectedness in such a way that it problematizes how discrimination on each and every basis limits possibilities of existing in diversity, or even of existing at all.

Abyssal lines and whiteness

As we have seen, the tension between visibility and invisibility is not just an issue related to bodies, but also to languages, knowledges, cultures, histories, geopolitics. Different theoretical concepts and metaphors have been used to question separability, a founding dimension of modernity, as we have mentioned before. The division between what is visible (and counts as valid) and what is invisible (often delegitimized, devalued) has promoted visibility as vital to our relation with the world. Some knowledges, as well as some people/bodies/communities, were rendered invisible in their differences to whatever was deemed valuable, mostly in relation to Eurocentric ways of engaging with, understanding and explaining the world.

Boaventura de Sousa Santos refers to the centrality of visibility in his concept of *abyssal lines* or *abyssal thinking*. For him, non-Eurocentric ways of relating with the world have been projected to the other side of an abyss with the creation of an invisible line separating, once again, what is to be seen and what is not, what is to be considered useful, important, civilized, and what is deemed useless, unimportant, primitive or even nonexistent. In his words (de Sousa Santos, 2018: 6):

> The epistemologies of the North are premised upon an abyssal line separating metropolitan societies and forms of sociability from colonial societies and forms of sociability, in the terms of which whatever is valid, normal, or ethical on the metropolitan side of the line does not apply on the colonial side of the line. As this abyssal line is as basic as it is invisible, it allows for false universalisms that are based on the social experience of metropolitan societies and aimed at reproducing and justifying the normative dualism metropolis/colony. Being on the other, colonial, side of the abyssal line amounts to being prevented by dominant knowledge from representing the world as one's own and in one's own terms.

Because abyssal lines are themselves invisible, bringing them to light is also an important aspect of anti-racist work, in our view. In Clarissa's narrative, for instance, we interpret the mention to 'Anglophone academia' – posed as it is as a 'colonized field' which imposes norms and values that are fixed and not open for reinterpretation – as the explicit drawing of one such line; a line that divides what is possible, doable, knowable, publishable, presentable, and what is not – no matter how brilliant the ideas in question. In fact, this very episode refers us to what is known as epistemic racism, i.e. a type of racism that considers inferior 'the knowledge produced by other [non-dominant] epistemologies, cosmologies and worldviews – from the geopolitics of knowledge and body-politics of knowledge of different world-regions with diverse time/space dimensions' (Grosfoguel, 2015: 24). Our argument here is that for any of these knowledges to become visible, the abyssal lines themselves, which are drawn in many different situations between what counts and what does not count as knowledge, need to also be brought to the fore and contested.

Bringing our narratives to this chapter and analyzing them is for us one way to make the abyssal line visible, and of engaging in a self-critical process whereby we look at the ways in which we ourselves may have been complicit with the creation and perpetuation of invisibility in race relations, epistemic racism and sexism. In reading Clarissa's narrative, for instance, one might observe that the experience of suffering epistemic racism impacts our academic praxis. In our lives as professors and researchers we also reinforce acts of judgment in assessment, review and feedback practices, which may perpetuate such type of epistemic injustice. Identifying such moments is one step in making the abyssal line visible. Another step is to resignify the ways we relate to one another in our academic settings (Kubota, 2020). This experience has contributed to the author's repositioning in terms of student assessment: from then on, Clarissa has actively included students in the decision-making process about evaluation tools and benchmarks for her courses, discussing with each group the pros and cons of the various possibilities available and openly negotiating the assessment criteria with them.

In Eduardo's narrative, in turn, race seemed to be placed in a *blind spot* of his own research agenda and possibilities. It was as though it was possible to do Applied Linguistics, in the ways that we define here, without paying attention to how the bodies and existences of ourselves, our students and our research participants are constitutive of our/their language experiences. The comment made by the renowned professor about how it is actually common for scholars to steer away from racial issues in their advising work highlights, at least in our view, the need for us, working from the Applied Linguistics from which we speak, to engage with and actually *invite* racial and gender perspectives in our own work as well as in the work produced by our students. This became even more evident for Eduardo a few years later, when another one of his advisees was conducting research on recent migrant students in Brazil (most of whom were non-white). In that occasion, Eduardo had not asked his advisee to look at race and the body as a central element in her analysis. This was later pointed out by a fellow professor (who is also one of the present authors), and the student was then able to develop a more dense analysis of her participants' linguistic experiences in that particular study, which made a large difference in her final results. In this particular case, the divisions that are constructed by disciplinary, epistemological and methodological categories (which are universalized in modern science) served as the abyssal line; and this line was only brought to the fore by moments of dialogue that Eduardo later had with fellow professors and students.

In the case of Juliana's narrative, the abyssal line is implicated in the predominantly white academic space in which the 'international student' had engaged throughout her life. This line has been drawn by historical and sociocultural aspects of our country, which has naturalized the exclusion of non-white bodies in spaces of privilege, such as the university. As we have discussed previously, recent affirmative actions have been pushing for changes in this spatial, epistemic and geopolitical configurations. As a consequence, we hope that current and future students experience more inclusive academic relationships in increasingly diverse academic settings. Juliana's narrative thus shows the realization of privilege related to being white in terms of skin color, a materiality that constructs as invisible the dimension of race that hierarchizes our bodies (Quijano, 2000). It foregrounds the physical body where racism can be placed.

In fact, such whiteness seems to perpass the other narratives as well. Clarissa's narrative and its focus on the epistemic body helps us realize how power relations are connected to certain positionings whose workings are invisibilized until oppression is exerted so openly it can no longer be dodged: whiteness here relates to feeling superior not only in terms of academic discourse, but also as far as knowing what is best for everyone. The narrative illustrates how whiteness may be a concrete metaphor to the exercise of power – together with the idea of the Global North, whiteness may signal the arrogance of being placed at superior positions in the hierarchy of bodies and their knowledges. Finally, Eduardo's account illustrates the ways in which the very subjects of race and racism are often curbed and avoided in a number of research contexts, emphasizing that there is also a disciplinary body at play: the separability of modernity in which the university is founded compartmentalizes knowledge in clear-cut disciplines that limit knowers and knowing to pre-established domains.

The physical body, the epistemic body and the disciplinary body that we have referred to above materialize the abyssal lines constructed by the idea of race. Issues such as the invisibility and even prohibition of certain knowledges, certain knowers and certain ways of knowing in specific spaces have serious ontological implications that format our bodies and the ways we relate to them and to those around us. Our narratives point out/pointed us to some of the intersections that can be traced when ontoepistemologies are embodied and such embodiment is made visible. We are not talking here from a global 'hubris of the zero point' (Castro-Gómez, 2005), but from our loci of enunciation: we are bringing to the fore our lived experiences in the certainty that they represent the historical impact racism has in our bodies; languages, skin colors, positionalities, gender, sexuality, social class all intersect as embodied dimensions of our ontoepistemologies.

Closing Remarks

As we close this chapter, we must remind readers once again of our locus of enunciation as Latinx scholars who are often perceived as white within Brazil and non-white in other contexts. This often means that we need to engage with anti-racism in different ways: at times, having to remind ourselves of our own privilege in many of the circles we navigate – a privilege that many others often do not have; and sometimes having to perceive how we are being positioned by others in racist, sexist, xenophobic ways. Our work with anti-racism, as we have stated, needs to grapple with these and other complexities with which we and our colleagues/students/research participants are faced every day.

We believe the narratives we have presented in this chapter illustrate these complexities. The non-presence, nonexistence or the invisibility of certain bodies in certain places/spaces/times deeply affects and shapes our own life experiences, existences and praxes with the world. One dimension of such impact is entrenched in structural racism and seen in our three narratives, as all of them reflect a racialized social system and racialized experiences.

In Brazil, experiences of inequality, racism and violence are very much intertwined with skin color, gender, sexuality, and social class. While we write this chapter (in the first few months of 2021), it is impossible to forget the biggest increase of COVID-19 cases and deaths in our country. Coronavirus has spread all over Brazil, and the Brazilian health system, both public and private, is in complete collapse at the moment. This breakdown in the country has exposed disparities we already knew but have been hidden by the myth of a mixed-race and a friendly, welcoming country. The majority of the population suffering from the effects of COVID-19 (many of whom are black and indigenous) live in vulnerable conditions, with informal jobs or facing unemployment and fighting for survival (Galindo & Junior, 2021).

The present situation of the country is the consequence of centuries of necropolitics in Brazil, and a State founded in the mix of capitalism and slavery (Safatle, 2020). As explained by Safatle and Gandesha (2020), Brazilian democracy was created by a common past of forgetting its own history of violence. The State has been active in trying to invisibilize such history and, in a parallel move, it has also been more and more absent from the life of ordinary citizens. Without the presence of the State, communities have been inventive in promoting solidarity practices to spread care and help to the most needy in order to survive. Their creativity is a way to resist the invisibility projected on their racialized bodies and their positioning on the other side of the abyssal line. Another way to make this line visible (albeit on a smaller scale) is to see our implication into the violence of modernity and, acknowledging our own privileged loci, to look at the complexity of racism as a structural force in Brazilian society.

As we hope to have shown here, Applied Linguistics, and in our case the Applied Linguistics from which we speak, has the essential task of remembering our history, retelling our constitutive narratives and seeking to understand how they may be entrenched in histories of racial inequality, structural racism and violence. The three moves of decoloniality (i.e. identifying, interrogating and interrupting the various forms that violence has taken in our colonial societies) will be the more effective in working for anti-racism when (or perhaps only if) embodiment and situatedness are prioritized in our work. As stated in the epigraph of this chapter, we all have the possibility of acting from where we are (in fact, this is all we have) based on our histories and trajectories; when we exercise such possibility, we believe we may be able to effect change in our many contexts.

Notes

(1) This is also true in other contexts worldwide, as recently discussed by Tharps. See, for instance, https://time.com/4512430/colorism-in-america/.
(2) According to Bonilla-Silva (1996: 475), a challenging aspect of *structural racism* lies in the understanding that racism is neither a self-evident experience nor a purely ideological phenomenon. In an alternative framework, he suggests 'that racism should be studied from the viewpoint of racialization'. He goes on to affirm that 'after a society becomes racialized, racialization develops a life of its own. Although it interacts with class and gender structurations in the social system, it becomes an organizing principle of social relations in itself'. For the author, race 'is a social construct, but that construct, like class and gender, has independent effects in social life. After racial stratification is established, race becomes an independent criterion for vertical hierarchy in society. Therefore different races experience positions of subordination and superordination in society and develop different interests' (1996: 475).
(3) We use the expressions 'white' and 'non-white' for our perceived notion that questions of power are more explicit in the use of those terms, when we compare them to an expression such as 'people of color'.
(4) This 'incident' was also briefly discussed, under different lenses, in an opinion piece called 'Tradition and change: Can mainstream academic discourse ever change?', published in the Comments section of the International Journal of Applied Linguistics in 2015 (Jordão, 2015).
(5) We are aware that the word insurgency has come to be understood in a very negative light recently, especially after the invasion of the Capitol building by right-wing groups in Washington, DC, in January 2021. The way the term is understood here is different from that used in such context. It is based on Mignolo and Walsh (2018), who define it as related to knowledge and (re)existence. As explained by the

authors, 'insurgency urges, puts forth, and advances from the ground up and from the margins, other imaginaries, visions, knowledges, modes of thought, other ways of being, becoming, and living in relation' (2018: 34).

(6) We are such stuff dreams are made on – Prospero, The Tempest (William Shakespeare).
(7) Data obtained from Revista Piauí (from November 2019). Availabe at https://piaui.folha.uol.com.br/lupa/2019/11/20/consciencia-negra-numeros-brasil/ (accessed April 2021).
(8) Data obtained from The Brazilian Institute of Geography and Statistics (2019). Available at https://agenciadenoticias.ibge.gov.br/agencia-sala-de-imprensa/2013-agencia-de-noticias/releases/25989-pretos-ou-pardos-estao-mais-escolarizados-mas-desigualdade-em-relacao-aos-brancos-permanece (accessed April 2021).

References

Bakhtin, M. (1920–1924) *Para uma filosofia do ato responsável*. São Carlos: Pedro & João Editores.
Bhattacharya, U., Jiang, L. and Canagarajah, S. (2020) Race, representation, and diversity in the American Association for Applied Linguistics. *Applied Linguistics* 41 (6), 999–1004.
Bonilla-Silva, E. (1996) Rethinking racism: Toward a structural interpretation. *American Sociological Review* 62 (3), 465–480.
Borba, R. (ed.) (2020) *Discursos transviados: Por uma linguística queer*. São Paulo: Cortez.
Borelli, J.D.V.P., Silvestre, V.P.V. and Pessoa, R.R. (2020) Towards a decolonial language teacher education. *Revista Brasileira de Linguística Aplicada* 20 (2), 301–324.
Canagarajah, S. (2013) *Translingual Practice: Global English and Cosmopolitan Relations*. New York: Routledge.
Castro-Gómez, S. (2005) *La hybris del punto cero: Ciencia, raza e ilustración en la Nueva Granada (1750-1816)*. Bogotá: Editorial Pontificia, Universidad Javeriana.
Castro-Gómez, S., Grosfoguel R. Prólogo (2007) Giro decolonial, teoría crítica y pensamento heterárquico. In S. Castro-Gómez and R. Grosfoguel (eds) *El giro decolonial: Reflexiones para una diversidad epistémica más allá del capitalismo global* (pp. 9–24). Bogotá: Siglo del Hombre Editores.
Collins, P.H. (1998) It's all in the family: Intersections of gender, race, and nation. *Hypatia* 13 (3), 62–82.
de Sousa Santos, B. (2018) *The End of the Cognitive Empire: The Coming of Age of Epistemologies of the South*. Durham, NC: Duke University Press.
Devulsky, A. (2021) *Colorismo*. São Paulo: Jandaíra.
Ferreira, A.J. (2006) *Formação de professores raça/etnia: Reflexões e sugestões de materiais de ensino*. Cascavel: Coluna do Saber.
Ferreira, A.J. and Barbosa, A. (2019) Entrevista com Aparecida de Jesus Ferreira. *Revista X* 14 (3), 1–15.
Files, J.A., Mayer, A.P., Ko, M.G., Friedrich, P., Jenkins, M., Bryan, M.J., Vegunta, S., Wittich, C.M., Lyle, M.A., Melikian, R., Duston, T., Chang, Y.H. and Hayes, S.N. (2017) Speaker introductions at internal medicine grand rounds: Forms of address reveal gender bias. *Journal of Women's Health* 26 (5), 413–419.
Freire, P. and Macedo, D.P. (1987) *Literacy: Reading the Word and the World*. South Hadley, MA: Bergin & Garvey Publishers.
Galindo, E.P. and Junior, J.U.P. (2021) A cor da moradia: Apontamentos sobre raça, habitação e pandemia. *Boletim de Análise Político-Institucional* 26, 73–83.
Garcez, P.M. (2019) A (in)visibilidade da pesquisa em Linguística Aplicada brasileira: O que é publish or perish para os linguistas aplicados no Brasil?. In P.T.C. Szundy,

R. Tilio and G.C.V. Melo (eds) *Inovações e desafios epistemológicos em linguística aplicada na América Latina* (pp. 41–62). Campinas, SP: Pontes Editores.

Garcia, C. (2021) O sul do Brasil também é negro: conheça territórios produtores de cultura no passado e presente. *Educação e Território*. See https://educacaoeterritorio.org.br/reportagens/o-sul-do-brasil-tambem-e-negro-conheca-territorios-produtores-de-cultura-no-passado-e-presente/ (accessed 25 November 2022).

Grosfoguel, R. (2007) The epistemic decolonial turn: Beyond political-economy paradigms. *Cultural Studies* 21, 211–223.

Grosfoguel, R. (2015) Epistemic racism/sexism, westernized universities and the four genocides/epistemicides of the long sixteenth century. In M. Araújo and S.R. Maezo (eds) *Eurocentrism, Racism and Knowledge: Debates on History and Power in Europe and the Americas* (pp. 23–46). New York: Palgrave Macmillan.

Harris, R. (1999) Integrational linguistics and the structuralist legacy. *Language & Communication* 19, 45–68.

Jordão, C.M. (2015) Tradition and difference: can mainstream academic discourse in applied linguistics ever change? *International Journal of Applied Linguistics* 25 (3), 422–425.

Jordão, C.M. (ed.) (2016) *A linguística aplicada no Brasil: Rumos e passagens*. Campinas: Pontes Editores.

Kubota, R. (2020) Confronting epistemological racism, decolonizing scholarly knowledge: Race and gender in applied linguistics. *Applied Linguistics* 41 (5), 712–732.

Lin, A., Grant, R., Kubota, R., Motha, S., Sachs, G.T., Vandrick, S. and Wong, S. (2004) Women faculty of color in TESOL: Theorizing our lived experiences. *TESOL Quarterly* 38 (3), 487–504.

Louro, G.L. (2000) Corpo, escola e identidade. *Educação e Realidade* 25 (2), 59–76.

Lu, M., and Horner, B. (2013) Translingual literacy, language difference, and matters of agency. *College English* 75 (6), 58607.

Makoni, S., Kaiper-Marquez, A. and Mokwena, L. (2022) *The Routledge Handbook of Language in the Global South*. London: Routledge.

Menezes de Souza, L.M.T. (2007) Entering a culture quietly: Writing and cultural survival in indigenous education in Brazil. In S. Makoni and A. Pennycook (eds) *Disinventing and Reconstituting Languages* (pp. 135–169). Clevedon: Multilingual Matters.

Menezes de Souza, L.M.T. (2019) Glocal languages, coloniality and globalization from below. In M. Guilherme and L.M.T. Menezes de Souza (eds) *Glocal Languages and Critical Intercultural Awareness: The South Answers Back* (pp. 17–41). New York: Routledge.

Menezes de Souza, L.M., Martinez, J.Z. and Diniz de Figueiredo, E. (2019) 'Eu só posso me responsabilizar pelas minhas leituras, não pelas teorias que eu cito': Entrevista com Lynn Mario Trindade Menezes de Souza (USP). *Revista X* 14 (5), 5–21.

Mignolo, W. (2000) *Local Histories/Global Designs: Coloniality, Subaltern Knowledges, and Border Thinking*. Princeton, NJ: Princeton University Press.

Mignolo, W. and Walsh, C. (2018) *On Decoloniality: Concepts, Analytics, Praxis*. Durham, NC: Duke University Press.

Moita Lopes, L.P. (2006) *Por uma linguística aplicada indisciplinar*. São Paulo: Parábola Editorial.

Monte-Mor, W. (2007) Investigating critical literacy at the university in Brazil. *Critical Literacy* 1, 41–51.

Nascimento, G. (2019) *Racismo linguístico: Os subterrâneos da linguagem e do racismo*. Belo Horizonte: Letramento.

Nogueira, A.M.H. (2017) O lugar das professoras negras na Universidade Federal de Santa Catarina. *Proceedings of Seminário Internacional Fazendo Gênero 11 & 13th Women's Worlds Congress*, 1–12.

Pennycook, A. and Makoni, S. (2020) *Innovations and Challenges in Applied Linguistics from the Global South*. New York: Routledge.

Quijano, A. (2000) Coloniality of power, Eurocentrism, and Latin America. *Nepantla: Views from South* 1 (3), 533–580.

Rezende, T. (2018) A semiótica dos corpos na literatura goiana: O corpo negro de Leodegária de Jesus. *Revista Plurais* 8 (1), 131–159.

Rose, H., Syrbe, M., Montakantiwong, A. and Funada, N. (2020) *Global TESOL for the 21st Century: Teaching English in a Changing World*. Bristol: Multilingual Matters.

Safatle, V. (2020) Welcome to the suicidal state. Contactos. See https://contactos.tome.press/welcome-to-the-suicidal-state/ (accessed 22 November 2022).

Safatle, V. and Gandesha, S. (2020) The Brazilian matrix: Between fascism and neoliberalism. *Krisis: Journal for Contemporary Philosophy* 40 (1), 215–233.

Shotwell, A. (2016) *Against Purity: Living Ethically in Compromised Times*. Minneapolis, MN: University of Minnesota Press.

Singh, J.N. (2021) Commentary: Epistemological positionalities. *Applied Linguistics* 42 (6), 1168–1175.

Souza, J. (2017) *A Elite do Atraso: Da Escravidão à Lava Jato*. Rio de Janeiro: Leya.

Viveiros de Castro, E. (2004) Perspectival anthropology and the method of controlled equivocation. *Tipiti* 1 (2), 1–22.

Volosinov, V.N. (1973) *Marxism and the Philosophy of Language*. Cambridge, MA: Harvard University Press.

6 Positionality, Creativity and Linguistic Prejudice: The Challenges of Honoring Multiple Identities and Being an Anti-Racist

Patricia Friedrich

When it comes to positionality, Maher and Tetreault (2001: 164) state that that 'people are defined not in terms of fixed identities, but by their location within shifting networks of relationships, which can be analyzed and changed'. At the intersection of race, ethnicity and language, the fluidity of these identities can become even more apparent, given that language is such a meaningful aspect of identity. Therefore, a person might hold a lot of linguistic power in one environment and hardly any in another. Understanding these dynamics is paramount to devising surroundings that are inclusive and openly anti-racist, where individuals feel a sense of belonging. In this chapter, I will discuss and use examples to illustrate how this plays out in different environments and across different languages and varieties. The definition of anti-racist I adopt is that of Kendi (2019: 13): 'One who is supporting an antiracist policy through their actions or expressing an anti-racist idea'. Linguistic prejudice is featured in this chapter in so far as many decisions about which languages 'count', which ones are 'correct' and which ones are to be taught cannot be separated by prescriptive rules that in themselves are driven by racial and ethnic biases. Ultimately, becoming an anti-racism linguist necessitates an understanding of how we embody these different identities, how we see the 'Other', and how we create environments where difference is represented in terms of creativity and accomplishment rather than deficit and deviation from 'the norm'. Examples will come primarily from world Englishes, English Language Teaching and literature. Since positionality also refers to the location of the researcher in relation to their research, I will use personal narrative as another tool to access these important considerations.

Identity

Two apparently small interactions that occurred in the last couple of years have stayed with me because of the importance they have for the work I do. The first one concerns a friend from my adolescence who recently reached out to me on social media. It was a delight to reconnect after so many years, to learn that she had become a medical doctor, and to exchange information about what we had been doing. At some point, she asked to read my work, and one of the items I recommended to her was Files *et al.* (2018), given that it bridges together our interests by focusing on women and forms of address in medicine. I also suggested some of my writings in world Englishes. She seemed to really enjoy these articles, and later we swapped text messages about them.

It was very interesting to me that, at a certain point, after we had talked about content and the research itself, she wrote to me about the use of first person 'I' in my writing, explaining that she wished I did not do it so much because without it the papers would sound more scientific. In turn, I commented that these were disciplinary differences, that I understood that many of the articles and books she read to inform her medical practice likely did not use that first-person recourse, but that the 'I' was increasingly common in the social sciences and in the humanities, especially as people engaged in autoethnography and other forms of self-reporting and self-research. It was a rich and meaningful exchange, and I felt like both of us came out of it having learned something new.

A few months later, as I prepared a manuscript for submission, I received some feedback from external reviewers on a proposal for work on equity, anti-racism and inclusion. While both scholars doing the review had enjoyed the premise of my proposal very much and recommended that I go ahead with completion and publication of the text, one of them commented that there was something to be said about my status as an Anglo-American woman writing that work.

Since the review was anonymous, I do not know if I ever met the scholar in question, but I imagine I have not. For if they had ever met me, they would likely know that I was born and raised in Brazil (to a Brazilian mother, whose family has been in Brazil for many generations) and identify as a Latinx scholar. English is my second language, and to this day I get commentaries about how I only have 'the slightest of accents' after being interrupted mid-sentence because people *have to know* where the accent is from. I imagine that the reviewer made the assumption about my being Anglo-American solely on the basis of my name, which obviates my father's German ancestry but does not address the other aspects of my positionality or identity (for more on names, see McHenry's Chapter 7 in this volume). Even more so, they were not aware of the fact that, as a person who inhabits an in-between space, I often have my identity chosen for me, and that people, often and without asking, do exactly what they had done: decide on the basis of my name or another individual, real or presumed feature, what my identity is. For illustrative purposes, here are some of the conclusions that people have, over the years, arrived at about my identity and expressed to me directly:

'*You, as a white woman ...*'.

'*We, as people of color...*' (pointing to both me and themselves, as the subjects of 'we').

'*Clearly, you are Hispanic*' (unsolicited).

'*You don't count because you were not born in the US*' (speaking of my Latinx status).

'*Brazilians don't count because you don't speak Spanish*' (regarding celebrations of people of Latin-American background).

'*Are you German?*' (because of my last name).

'*Are you French?*' (I was wearing a silk scarf).

'*Is your husband German?*' (assumed because of my last name, which is actually from my father).

'*Are you Italian?*' (hearing my husband and I speak Portuguese while on an elevator).

'*You don't look Brazilian*' (given that Brazil is a very diverse country in terms of race and ethnicity, I am not sure of what this means).

'*Where does your blond hair come from?*' (to which I could not resist but respond quite truthfully, 'the drugstore down the street' as my original hair color, before age took it away, was brown).

As a side note, the idea of 'not counting' deserves its own discussion although it is regrettably outside of the scope of this chapter. Not counting or counting can have significant consequences in the real world, so I hope meaningful work is conducted on those ideas. The whole point of including 'belonging' as part of diversity and inclusion work is closely connected to the harm of 'not counting'. As we – researchers, teachers, advocates, leaders – forward ideas of diversity and inclusion and more closely align them to the notion of belonging, the more we will have to investigate the effect of 'not counting' on the latter.

In the end, both those seemingly innocuous occurrences, my friend's commentary on the 'I' and the reviewer's assumption that I was Anglo-American, triggered in me the memory of the interactions I illustrate above, and they stayed with me because they speak so strongly of the importance of one's positionality and the ways in which language is used (or at times, not used) to convey one's place in the world and, consequently, the perspective from which they speak, write and issue a point view.

Every time, a person did not pay attention to what I was saying – despite my being intelligible to them – because they believed they had to decipher my background, every time my name took precedence over my self-assigned identity, every time my speaking Portuguese in public in the US caused someone else to turn around and study me, the fact that I, like so many others, inhabit a linguistic and cultural in-between became more obvious and helped define how I interact with the world. It also indicated to me that many 'decisions' by other people about my racial and ethnic background were being made on the basis of language. That is, often people tried to guess my identity solely on the very small window of access they had to my linguistic networks. If I used Portuguese, I must be an immigrant: yet, many people can use such a language because they enjoy language learning, because they are a scholar of its literature, because they lived abroad for a period of time, among so many other reasons. If I came from South America, then I must be a native speaker of Spanish (Spanish is an additional language to me but not native) even though places such as Brazil, Suriname and French Guiana (the latter an overseas department of France), have languages other than Spanish as official and local in their territories.

For members of certain minoritized groups, these dynamics are clearly much more impactful than they are to me, and at no point do I forget that the phenomenon I experience is minute if compared to the overt racism, prejudice, disparity and inequality that so many other individuals face. As a woman of European ancestry, I indeed have access to the kind of privilege that is not extended to all and is openly denied to many, even when my status as user of English as a second language is brought to light. In fact, I often wonder in how many ways I am still unaware of nuances of this privilege that are imperceptible to me for having always been there. For instance, I wonder how many times I have made erroneous assumptions about the identity of others as well, given externalities. What is more, not for a second do I forget (or not struggle with) my positionality and the possible things that I do not know that I do not know while I am writing for and editing this book.

Yet the point remains that my linguistic power (and power in general) is affected by my environment and my positionality in relation to that environment. If I am in Brazil, speaking to a large audience of (predominantly) Brazilians in the context of Teachers of English to Speakers of Other Languages (TESOL), for example, the way my power is perceived in relation to others (i.e. Brazilian-born but American, successful scholar, writer, subject-matter expert), is very different from what I get when I speak Portuguese to a family member in a supermarket in the US (i.e. immigrant, second-language user of English). In many academic contexts, I am praised for the fact that I speak four languages. Being a polyglot in those contexts is a marker of achievement and is thought to give me a communicative advantage, whether I am helping host guests from abroad or publishing in other languages. Outside of academia, especially in public places, my achievement can even put me at risk.[1] Therefore, to assume that my linguistic power is uniform across all of my possible interactions and realms of language use would be not only naïve but also misguided.

Likewise, linguistic status can never be understood in a vacuum. It is a feature of one's environment and, as such, liable to change continually, sometimes even within minutes. I can be at a supermarket one moment, having my public use of Portuguese challenged, and then go home to a synchronous internet video meeting with other academics and have it considered laudable and sophisticated.

This fluid, context-specific positionality matters a lot. Thus, the approach to positionality by Maher and Tetreault (2001: 164) is very apt because it states that that 'people are defined not in terms of fixed identities, but by their location within shifting networks of relationships, which can be analyzed and changed'. The fact that I, one person, can be differently perceived as an expert and authority in one context and can have my language use questioned in another clearly illustrates the fluid nature of the concept. Likewise, the realization that one person will conclude I am 'clearly white' when another will deem that I am 'certainly not' puts in perspective the reality that we might all be coming to linguistic interactions expecting to share basic assumptions with our interlocutors that are indeed, in the end, not shared at all. In these first paragraphs, what I tried to do relates to the first of the two elements in Maher and Tetreault's quote – the analysis – in this case, focused on myself. I will spend the rest of this chapter: (1) giving examples of how language further features in this examination; (2) considering what part linguists can play in analyzing language in the context of positionality and promoting positive change in the world; and (3) arriving at some suggestions to help us all practice the anti-racism linguistics that so many of us believe in (i.e. the 'change' part). My reflections are influenced by many different lines of thought, but I want to highlight the words of Singh (2021: 1168) that suggest the following:

> instead of simply giving previously colonised people bits of European modern knowledge (such as access to inner-circle Englishes), applied linguists must encourage the people who we research to theorize their own

knowledge, i.e. to assume epistemological positionalities, that are meaningful to themselves and to the communities from which they come.

The idea to theorize one's own knowledge sits at the heart of autoethnographies, elements of which are present and highlighted throughout this book. It is a central aspect of research in sociolinguistics and related fields now, from anthropology to sociology. The idea to not simply communicate bits of European, and, I would add, Anglo-American knowledge to other communities in the inner circle of English as well as in the outer and expending circle (Kachru, 1983, and after) but rather encourage the theorizing of their own knowledge through lenses that make sense to them is a much more elegant approach to inclusion than earlier attempts, such as those grounded on ideas of Linguistic Imperialism (Phillipson, 1992) because the latter necessitates a certain exclusion of Western knowledge (in this case, of colonial languages) from the repertoire of different groups.

We should not confuse, however, the notion of an epistemological positionality with a rejection of the concept of expertise. In fact, it is just the opposite. In acknowledging the value of a group's own perspective, we are recentering their expertise, represented by their scholars, teachers, elders, writers, etc., and we are establishing an anti-racist epistemology in the process, too. This is very different from the societal trend, arguable borne out of (or at least made more salient by) social media, of delegitimizing expert knowledge in a misguided attempt to claim that everyone's knowledge is 'just an opinion' and therefore as good as anyone else's. Instead, I would argue that expertise matters, positionality matters, and that the combination of lived experience and expertise makes for a powerful knowledge base. For allies, it is important that individuals recognize that their experience of the world is not everyone's experience of the world, linguistic and otherwise. That means being able to listen to the concerns, suggestions, and arguments of those directly impacted by a linguistic phenomenon and taking those perspectives as valid, even in face of disagreements.

Ultimately, becoming an anti-racism linguist necessitates an understanding of how we embody different identities, how we see the Other, and how we create environments where difference is represented in terms of creativity and accomplishment rather than deficit and departure from 'the norm'. It also requires that we reconsider expertise in light of the needs of a community and the specialized knowledge it already possesses.

Creativity

Not very long ago, I submitted a novel for consideration to a large publisher. The feedback came back, with a lot of praise for the story, the writing itself, the resolution of the central conflict, but unfortunately, despite all of the acknowledgement of the merits of the story, the publishing house decided not to offer a contract. Their reasoning was that the story had as the target audience Anglo-American and Anglo-European individuals (I never said that was the intended audience) who might not identify with my characters nor with the representation of places such as Brazil in an 'everyday' kind of way. The implication was that Brazil and characters living there had to be made more stereotypically 'the other' for the book to sell, or else, it seemed to be the point the editor was making, there was no reason for the story to take place there. Since common themes of the Amazon forest, soccer, carnival, the beach were either not present or secondary to the main conflict, there was suspicion of inauthenticity or lack of common ground with American readers' perceptions of that country.

I was confused and frustrated by this event. I had tried to depict Brazil from the perspective of a person who grew up there, and for whom living there *was* everyday life. Once I started looking at the feedback from a sociolinguistic point of view, I realized how our different positionalities were impacting our perceptions of creativity. Our memberships in different linguistic networks and our proximity to or distance from the environment being portrayed also played a part. Yet, the result, given the power imbalance of the situation, was still that my novel would not reach the wider audience that such a large publishing house could deliver to an author. And this practice, when repeated many times, leads members of certain linguistic networks to have their discourse, language and lived experience magnified again and again, while others do not.

That is, if readers are told often enough, by way of what is widely available, what discourses count and what linguistic practices should be observed, they might start believing that such discourses and practices are all there is. An homogenization of linguistic and sociolinguistic features follows, and creativity shrinks. One simple exercise that will demonstrate that is looking at titles of novels at a given period in time and noticing how similar they are, to the point that it is often difficult to tell them apart (until another naming trend happens and the same patter, with different words, is repeated).

Linguistic creativity is thus many times curbed down in the same ways that dialectal variation is: with repeated acts of disapproval, or more subtly, by the editorializing of content or the denial of a larger platform to those who do not conform to the expected sociolinguistic patterns. In practical terms, this results, among other things, in the very low percentage of authors of color and other minoritized groups in publishing. At the end of 2020, *The New York Times* published an opinion piece[2] by Richard Jean So and Gus Wezerek based on their field research that had led to the following conclusion:

> Author diversity at major publishing houses has increased in recent years, but white writers still dominate. Non-Hispanic white people account for 60 percent of the U.S. population; in 2018, they wrote 89 percent of the books in our sample.

That same piece – which I read after formulating my own argument on the reinforcement of trends by the publication of books that are alike – makes a similar point by stating that, if a publisher decides on whether to publish (or more importantly, not publish) a book on the basis of the stereotypes and beliefs their public already has, they only end up reinforcing those stereotypes. The more difficult it then becomes for those authors who break the mold to get published. A perpetual circle of underrepresentation ensues.

In a similarly elucidating essay[3] author KX Song creates a taxonomy of reasons why publishing has remained so non-diverse. In one of the categories (A Narrow Definition of Literature), she argues that,

> Conventional western narratives favor a focus on conflict and individualism, with common tropes such as man versus man or man versus nature …. But to characterize "literature" as only fitting within these styles is to exclude a plethora of non-western literary traditions…. [I]f instead we recognize our subconscious biases and shift our understanding of what a novel is, we can grow to appreciate stories with a focus on community rather than individuals, constancy rather than change.

The tools available for subversive action are not always optimal. Without the backing of large institutional forces and conglomerates, even in an age of digital communication, it is difficult to make a dent in the system: algorithms reinforce those who are already strong, and financial investment (which cannot be matched by individuals), which cause broadcasting, advertising and distribution to be possible, make it all the more unattainable for those going at it alone. However, there is beauty and power in repeated grassroot action by individuals and their linguistic networks, by independent publishers, podcasters, associations and co-authors.

My novel is now in print and available by a mid-sized publisher. It has received three awards. While the process of making it known to the public and arguing for its worthiness is work-intensive, it is also extremely rewarding. As readers, we can do our part by (1) buying books by indie (self-published) authors or those authors published by independent publishing houses (typically small or mid-sized publishing presses), which are more open to taking a chance on a new writer and on writers of different linguistic/ethnic/racial/cultural backgrounds; (2) amplifying the voices of those authors by recommending their books, reviewing them in popular sites, blogs, etc.; (3) writing to publishers and commending them when they do publish diverse voices; or (4) identifying publishers who focus on a particular minoritized group and then supporting them (there are, for example indie presses that focus on publishing LGBTQ+ authors and stories or stories by other minoritized authors).

While finishing this chapter, I also came across the good news[4] that the number of independent bookstores in the US has grown significantly and many cater to interests in stories by authors of particular identities (e.g. Asian-American writers). Clearly, there is an audience for these stories, and this increased access should be celebrated and built upon.

How about Creativity and Academia?

If we take the same arguments to a scholarly sphere, we will find parallels with a publishing system that does not always foster inclusion of different voices, varieties of language, and thought philosophies. For example, it is a well-known fact that scholars whose first language is not English face much greater barriers for entry in a publication system where allegedly 98% of the indexed work (Ramírez-Castañeda, 2020) – or in the very least 90% in certain areas, according to other authors (e.g. Lillis & Curry, 2010; Strauss, 2017) – is in English. Not only that, but many international scholars, when not comfortable expressing themselves at such a complex level of communication in English, have to incur in steep translation and editorial expenses before they can even be considered for publication. Furthermore, 'mistakes' deemed as resulting from second-language status are often scrutinized and criticized to a degree that is unmatched by mistakes by users of English as a first language, even when the occurrence of the former impacts communication and intelligibility less than the occurrence of the latter. It is as if first-language users employed their intuition of what constitutes a 'non-native' mistake and then applied different rules to handling them.

For example, I know a scholar – a user of English as a second language – whose use of one 'wrong' word in a paper (meaning a use perceived to be non-native) led to chastising by the editor along the lines of 'you need to improve your English', even though the perceived single mistake could have been addressed in no more than two seconds. While this is just anecdotal information, it seems emblematic of what many researchers report. This double standard has professional and personal ramifications for the scholars in question (in the very least, it is demoralizing to have one's linguistic knowledge challenged that way, but it is often much more than that) and more broadly for the state of knowledge and who gets to disseminate what to broad audiences. Furthermore, interactions like this tend to evidence how monolingual thought is prevalent in certain areas of knowledge, power, and influence, even though bi- and multilingualism are the rule in terms of number of users around the world.

To be an anti-racism linguist in this case means advocating for those scholars, doing our part when we are in the editorial position and disseminating the technical expertise in linguistic that would allow other to see how unsound that kind of behavior really is.

Embodiment

The notion that who speaks or writes matters brings with it an awareness that people are not detached from their bodies, their cultures, and indeed their positionality when they communicate. I like the way positionality translates into Portuguese as *lugar de fala* or 'the place from where one speaks'. That place is where one's body is located at a certain moment in time, with all of the identities it takes, and all that means in the environments it inhabits. It is part of the reason for the positioning that many researchers in the humanities, for example, have started to take when they write, disclosing their gender, disability status, racial and ethnic identity, etc. at the beginning of their texts, both oral and written. Rather than an exercise in selfish individuality, it is an acknowledgement that what they are about to say and write is shaped by the place their body occupies in the world. And because bodies interact with the environment in equally dynamic ways, that kind of 'checking in' needs to become a recurring exercise. Just as in the example I provided earlier, if my body is at a supermarket in the US, and the words that come out of such body happen to be in Portuguese, the reaction to them is equally shaped by that environment and the other bodies there represented. I change my location, and the response changes too.

In the case of languages like English, positionality has everything to do with attitudes toward it and its varieties. Part of the reason why world Englishes scholars often reject the term dialects is well explained in Nascimento (Chapter 3 in this volume). When used in opposition to language, dialect tends to have a strong connotation of a hierarchical classification among linguistic expressions, and in a world where Western thought has often been equated with 'the standard,' languages associated with people of color around the world end up more often being called 'dialects' than languages with European (white) associations. When Phillipson (1992) wrote of linguistic imperialism, and openly called the places where English was used non-natively (or represented by post-colonial varieties) 'periphery', he was very literally centering native Englishes to the detriment of every other variety, in the modern (not post-modern) tradition of center versus periphery, oppressed versus oppressor.

The problem with that centering is that it reinforces the very elements we are trying to rebalance, and it causes us to have to think of language varieties in terms of distance from the standard. And not rarely do individuals conclude that the more distant something is from the standard, the least acceptable it is as well.

There are of course no linguistic bases for this distinction, which is a social construction created on prejudice and misperceptions. Every living language is functional, (internally) rule governed, and changes to adapt to the needs of the communities it serves. Those are the very elements that define its being a living language. On the other hand, language purism is a harmful fiction. When it comes to the English language in particular, any of us would be hard pressed to find arguments for its 'purity' given that, since its formation, it has been a hybrid of the languages of the Jutes, Saxons, Angles and Frisians (and the displaced Welsh), later heavily influenced by Latin, Old Norse and Old French, only to mention the best-known European ancestors, before we even take into account the many contributions from other continents. Any consideration of the superiority of one language over another is mere fantasy, fueled by sociopolitical, ideological and potentially discriminatory forces.

Hage (2016: 124–125) lists six functions of anti-racism, which I paraphrase here: (1) reducing the occurrence of racist practices, (2) nurturing forms of non-racist culture, (3) supporting/sheltering those who suffer racism, (4) giving power to racialized subjects, (5) effecting change on racist relations, (6) forging an a-racist culture. Hage uses these categories to 'recall' both in the sense of 'remember' but also in the sense of 'take back' (as when a product is defective) the discourse of anti-racism as it stands in opposition to the discourses of racism. In this process, Hage contributes a very important insight in the following terms:

> While racists have happily moved from one form of racism to another, caring little about logical contradictions, inconsistencies, and discrepancies in their argumentations, too many anti-racist academics spend an inordinate amount of time trying to judge racists on precisely such grounds. In a classical case of what Pierre Bourdieu (1990) calls 'projecting into the object one's relation to the object' (27), they criticise racists as if the racists are fellow academics with whom they are having disagreements in a tutorial room about how to interpret reality. The performativity of racist statements and more obviously racist practices, which is what is most important to the racists themselves, is given far less attention than needed. Instead, the racists' greatest sins are made to be interpretative/intellectual ones. (2016: 126)

This is of course one of the difficulties of 'being in the right' (meaning correct, not the political end of the spectrum). Those who act by principle, hoping to make positive contributions, try to stick to the rules, to not lie, to show integrity, not only in *what* they pursue but also *how* they pursue it. One of the difficulties in making progress in anti-racism linguistics, as well is any other anti-racism effort, lies then in exactly this. We can, and should, therefore, be principled without letting our preoccupation with frameworks and academicism take over the bigger goal of making significant advancements in the world.

In Bourdieu (1990: 34), this situation is explained in the following terms:

> Intellectualism is inscribed in the fact of introducing into the object the intellectual relation to the object, of substituting the observer's relation to the practice for the practical relation to practice.

If I can be permitted one more moment of venting, I have now, at this stage in my career, withdrawn from consideration for inclusion in anthologies three chapters of my work, and in all three cases the reason was exactly the same and exactly covered by what Bourdieu writes. At some point of the editorial process, I realized that what I was writing, or the change that I was proposing, had stopped being the central consideration. Instead, the form the text took and a desired perfect alignment between mine and other contributions in the volume had taken over. The meticulous attention to whether in any one passage I had been completely congruent with what I had written before and what others had written about stifled creativity and invention. In the meantime, the planet had continued to turn, and the forces contrary to the inclusive practices, language and cultural shifts I was proposing had continued to operate in as haphazardly a manner as they had always done. I hope in this volume, both in terms of my contributions as well as those as the other scholars featured here, I, as an editor have been able to privilege content over academicism, and impact over conformity. Language and anti-racism are too important for us to behave otherwise.

Notes

(1) For readers not familiar with language politics in Arizona, there is a long history in the state of both unsuccessful attempts and successful passing of 'English-only' laws, for example in schools, which has created an environment where immigrants are at times afraid to use other languages in public spaces.
(2) So, R.J. and Wezerek, G. (2020) Just How White is the Book Industry? *The New York Times*. See https://www.nytimes.com/interactive/2020/12/11/opinion/culture/diversity-publishing-industry.html (accessed 5 November 2022).
(3) Song, KX (2022) Why Is The Publishing Industry Still So White? *Includr*. See https://includr.org/perspective/why-is-the-publishing-industry-still-so-white/?fbclid=IwAR03x0WtmNEYAcQiYtmKHEMMkwgU8_ZRhUjCCrSJVGl2aN2bO6oz4BjPl4g.
(4) Alexandra Alter and Elizabeth A. Harris. Some Surprising Good News: Bookstores Are Booming and Becoming More Diverse. *The New York Times*, 10 July 2022. See https://www.nytimes.com/2022/07/10/books/bookstores-diversity-pandemic.html?fbclid=IwAR1s3pgOjzpC_BVTflk9bv3aQx_fT2o-aB6bncBowXWoiGl9xVXeiE3Ly-I.

References

Bourdieu, P. (1990) *The Logic of Practice*. Cambridge: Polity Press.
Files, J., Mayer, A.P., Ko, M.G. and Friedrich, P. *et al.* (2017) Speaker introductions at internal medicine grand rounds: Forms of address reveal gender bias. *Journal of Women's Health* 26 (5), 413–419.

Kachru, B.B. (1983) Regional norms of English. In S.J. Savignon and M. Berns (eds) *Communicative Language Teaching: Where are we Going? Studies in Language Learning 4* (pp. 54–76). Urbana, IL: Language Learning Laboratory, University of Illinois at Urbana-Champaign.

Hage, G. (2016) Recalling anti-racism. *Ethnic and Racial Studies* 39 (1), 123–133.

Kendi, I.X. (2019) *How to be an Anti-Racist*. New York: One World.

Lillis, T. and Curry, M. (2010) *Academic Writing in a Global Contexts: The Politics and Practices of Publishing in English*. London: Routledge.

Maher, F.A. and Tetreault, M.K.T. (2001) *The Feminist Classroom: Dynamics of Gender, Race, and Privilege* (expanded edn). New York: Rowman & Littlefield Publishers, Inc.

Phillipson, R. (1992) *Linguistic Imperialism*. Oxford: Oxford University Press.

Ramírez-Castañeda, V. (2020) Disadvantages in preparing and publishing scientific papers caused by the dominance of the English language in science: The case of Colombian researchers in biological sciences. *PLOS ONE* 15 (9), e0238372.

Singh, J.N. (2021) Commentary: Epistemological positionalities. *Applied Linguistics*: 42 (6), 1168–1175.

Strauss, P. (2017) "It's not the way we use English" – Can we resist the native speaker stranglehold on academic publications? *Publications* 5 (4), 1–7.

7 'No One Can Say it Anyway': Personal Names in the Classroom

Tracey McHenry

> In this chapter, I address the intersection of teaching praxis and the 'political', when teachers grapple with the personal names of their students. I touch upon topics such as the construction of racial identity, the politics of surnames, the challenges presented by names that do not conform to Western expectations, gender and ethnicity issues connected to names and the legal aspects of names and name changes. In my discussion of the issues, I hope to clarify the importance of personal names, especially for students in K-16 classrooms. Lastly, I discuss one program developed by the Santa Clara County (California, US) Office of Education called 'My Name, My Identity'.

Introduction

In my childhood in Alaska, we all revered the tallest mountain in North America as 'the Great One', called 'Denali' in the language of the Koyukon Athabascans who have lived in Alaska for thousands of years, long before white Americans. However, I was always confused by the fact that we'd call the mountain both 'Denali' and 'Mount McKinley'. As a child, I puzzled over this discontinuity, never understanding the political drama going on underneath. Little did I know that this name inconsistency was politics and power and White privilege trumping Native practices. A gold prospector in 1896 unofficially named the mountain after the recently elected President William McKinley of Ohio, who never even visited Alaska.

For 75 years, the mountain and its surrounding national park were known by competing names, but in 1980, an 'awkward compromise' lead to the national park being called Denali National Park and Reserve whereas the mountain itself would be known as Mount McKinley

('Mount McKinley Will Again Be Called Denali', 2015). In 2015, then-President Obama visited Alaska and declared that the mountain would be officially called Denali, which angered residents of Ohio, a state far removed from Alaska but very politically important in the Electoral College aspect of American presidential elections. Even now, there is a simmering feud ongoing over the 'appropriate' name of this majestic mountain. While mountains are not people, and politicians and elections are not involved in most personal naming decisions, this anecdote shows the importance of names. Names can indicate cultural inclusion, in the case of the name Denali, or they can suggest respect for tradition and power, in the case of the name McKinley. In similar ways, personal names often straddle this gap between inclusion, exclusion and power dynamics.

It is clear that names are an important part of our identity. Names are more than just a simple way to refer to other humans. We attach strong feelings and powerful meanings to our names. Parents agonize over the perfect name for their new baby, and in some cultures, parents consult naming specialists before the baby arrives. After the baby's birth, the name instantly becomes part of the child: in their immediate family and local culture, the name is part of who they are and where they are from.

However, when children enter the public school system in the US, these names become a signifier – of a different language or different country or of just difference itself. Even children from the dominant culture represented in the school may struggle with teachers' attempts to say their name. For example, when we gave my oldest daughter the well-known Irish name 'Maeve', we anticipated little reaction. However, she has spent most of her life correcting others who misread her name as the color 'mauve'. She always had the 'weird' name that few can seem to remember to write or pronounce accurately, and while it does one job we intended it to – that of connecting her to both sides of her family tree – it has not helped her 'fit in', especially in school. This experience, combined with my years of teaching students from non-English dominant countries, has shaped my interest in how teachers deal with the 'name problem' in ESL classrooms.

As names are often the first or second thing that we notice about a person we've newly met, they're inescapable. It's impossible to be a teacher and not be faced with the reality of your students' names. For some part of the 20th century, teachers may have felt obliged or mandated to use an 'American' name for their newly arrived students. It was common practice for students from language backgrounds unfamiliar to the teacher or the school culture at large to choose an 'American' (often Biblical) name. Fueled by the long-held belief in the 'melting pot' theory of assimilation, many older teachers expect students to become part of the myth of a shared singular American culture. And for many, the first step to joining this culture is acquiring a name that allows students to blend in. As Keller and Franzak (2016) and Mitchell (2016) tell us, the teacher-student name dance is the first demonstration of the tension between assimilation and acceptance. It is my belief that the role that names play in education – particularly in ESL education – is not given enough attention, and it is my intent in this chapter to tease out the threads of this discussion.

Literature Review

The importance of personal names has been studied across the academic spectrum. From the law (Kushner, 2009) to sociology (Allen, 2019) to sociolinguistics of branding (Wong, 2013) to economics (Aura & Hess, 2010; Betrand & Mullainathan, 2004; Biavaschi *et al.*, 2013; Fryer & Levitt, 2003) to names in specific multicultural contexts, such as Brazil (Thonus, 1992), many researchers have addressed the roles names play in our daily lives. For the purposes of this research, I will focus exclusively on research connected to names and psychology, names and diversity and naming in the classroom.

Names and Psychology

For an early review of literature on the importance of names, Dion (1983) provides a thorough review of the psychological aspects of names. Of special note is his summary of research linking liking of one's own name and liking oneself. According to him, as a name is part of our identity, it is linked with our self-perception (1983: 251). While dated and not focused on non-Western names, his insights are useful as we consider the impact names have on our students. He notes that names tend to ground us to our identities and that children often connect their vision of themselves in the future to the reality of having the same name throughout their life thus far (Dion, 1983: 249). Names are more than personalities that we can change on a whim: names connect us (or distance us) from family, history and culture.

Naming decisions can be a reflection of parental attitudes or wishes about assimilation into the dominant culture. Sue and Telles (2007) and Alba and Nee (2003) discuss patterns of naming in their sociological analyses of naming and assimilation. As Sue and Telles (2007: 1387) state, naming is an easy variable to study because everyone has a first name, they're all recorded in government documents, and they 'can be quantified on a continuum from ethnic to nonethnic'. They note, as others have as well, that female children tend to be given more 'assimilated' or non-ethnic names while ethnic names are reserved for male children. In this way, we can see that gender plays a role in naming decisions, further complicating the decisions newly arrived parents must face when they chose a name for their children.

Also important is the role naming has played historically in American immigration. Many Americans families have last names that were changed upon arrival in the US. Most well-known are the many Eastern European immigrants who altered their last names to hide their Jewish ancestry (see Fermaglich, 2015, for an overview), but in the last 100 years, people arriving from countries deemed 'less desirable' have sometimes anglicized their last names to 'fit in'. I had a student whose great grandfather, arriving in New York City at Ellis Island, took the last name of the person in line ahead of him. So, while the family knows he was Jewish and from Russia, there is no written record of his real name. Kaplan and Bernays' (1997) book outlines this history of name change and assimilation.

It is relevant to my work here to emphasize that this awareness is essential. Teachers with European-American origins may themselves have a history of name changes in their families – either by the name bearer or by a government worker – which can provide a common ground with their students. Most important, however, is to note that name changing to 'fit in' is not a new practice in America. However, in the past, names may have been changed without consent or under duress. We need to acknowledge this history as we navigate names, meaning and assimilation with our students.

Names and Diversity

Names as a reflection of ethnic diversity is a topic of growing interest. Some earlier research may be less culturally aware than we may expect from scholarship, such as Levine and Willis (1994) article on 'unusual names', which focuses on the negative reaction to names given to African American children. Much early research on this topic focuses on African American names and negative public reaction to these names, but more recent research (discussed below) teases out the nuances of this topic. The impact of an American president with an African American name of Barack Obama has been studied as well. Anderson-Clark and Green (2017) document the rise of first names associated with African Americans after the election of the US first African American president in 2008.

There is much research addressing the challenges facing students or employees with distinctively African American names. Betrand and Mullainathan (2004) find that resumes with African American names are 50% less likely to be called (2004: 998). They also are careful to note that their research (involving manipulating 'quality' of the resumes and addresses to reflect social class) suggests that it is not neighborhood location or resume strength that affects the callback rate – it is race, as signaled in the choice of first name. An early paper on name changes is Kang's (1971) article studying Chinese students at a midwestern university. In his work, Kang notes that 36% of the almost 300 students anglicized their names, a decision which he refers to as a 'striking phenomenon' (1971: 159).

This century has seen research on what Allen (2019) calls 'stigma management' by Muslim men who change their names to deflect scrutiny. The author documents a very common pattern of men with the name Mohammed going by the name 'Mo'. The author's use of the term 'stigma' is not to be ignored: many recent researchers mention non-familiar names serving as 'verifications' of a non-American, non-white identity. Similarly, Zhao and Biernat (2017) use the term 'cross categorization' to refer to the complex situations of individuals who have names with elements from both the birth culture and Western culture. The action movie star Jet Li was born in China with the name Li Lianjie. Only when his name was determined to be 'unpronounceable' in the Philippines was he given the new name 'Jet', which alluded to how fast his career was growing. In this way, an English word became his new first name and his family name Li became his Western 'last' name.

Sometimes, name can signify political or religious battles in a home country. Girma's (2020) article on naming practices in Ethiopian immigrant communities in the US addresses the disconnect when Ethiopian immigrants are lumped in with African Americans in the US, both sharing skin color and other attributes, but not sharing the same history of oppression and slavery. However, Ethiopians and others must negotiate the competing ethnic divisions in their country of origin even as they create lives in the US. Girma discusses how names are 'used to draw symbolic boundaries vis-à-vis African Americans' (2020: 28) while simultaneously being either 'familiar' Biblical/Hebrew names or being easy-to-pronounce but nonetheless African names. Her work demonstrates the complex social positions that recent arrivals to the US often inhabit and specifically shows how names are often the first indicators of difference or familiarity for immigrant children.

Naming in the Classroom

While there is a vast amount of research in education, not much of it focuses solely on names. In his widely cited paper for The National Bureau of Economic Research in the United States, Figlio (2005: 4) uses test scores, giftedness/nongiftedness classifications and other data for every student in a Florida school district from 1994–1995 through 2000–2001. This huge data set includes 55,046 children in 24,298 families with two or more children. His aim was to see if teachers 'take cues' from student names and then 'systematically lower expectations for students with names that are associated more with low socio-economic status, names that are disproportionately given to Black children' (Figlio, 2005: 3). Note that he is an economist writing for the National Bureau of

Economic Research and not a linguist or an educator, so his terminology can seem dated and off-putting.

According to Figlio (2005), teachers 'may expect less from children with names that "sound" like they were given by uneducated parents. These names, empirically, are given most frequently by Blacks [sic], but they are also given by White and Hispanic parents as well' (2005: 4). His conclusions suggest a correlation between 'Black sounding' names – which he differentiates from non-Black sounding – and lower achievement in terms of standardized tests and referrals for gifted programs. He concludes that racially identifiable names 'may trigger differences in perceptions' (Figlio, 2005: 4) and are actually associated with low socioeconomic backgrounds rather than 'just' racial differences. Fryer and Levitt (2003) conclude that 'carrying a black name is primarily a consequence rather than a cause of poverty and segregation' (2003: 801). Concluding that names associated with African American ancestry is a result of poverty and segregation still misses the point that names are a 'signal' of Otherness to some White Americans, which then may contribute to continued discrimination at school or in the workplace. This conclusion, like that of Figlio (2005), attempts to separate names from educational and social issues that these name holders may experience but obscures the reality that names are representations of the complex realities that many students from diverse backgrounds live with every day. We need to work towards a future where 'unusual' names are not automatically linked to socio-economic struggles and discrimination.

Other scholarly work addressing personal names focuses on student-faculty interactions connected to names. One large study addressed the dynamics between students and faculty communication. Milkman *et al.* (2012) analyze the constellation of race and distant versus future events in emails to 6548 professors, using personal names as one variable. One test group included emails from students whose names signaled their race – discussed in their research as either Caucasian, African American, Hispanic, Indian or Chinese – and gender. When the requests were to meet in one week, males with Caucasian names were granted access to faculty members 26% more often than were women and minorities; also, compared with women and minorities, males with Caucasian names received more and faster responses.

However, these patterns were essentially eliminated when prospective students requested a meeting that same day. According to Zhao and Berniat (2017: 62), 'these results support the hypothesis that Anglo names lead to more positive outcomes than use of original names: Professors were more likely to respond to an email request from a Chinese student using an Anglo name than one using a Chinese name'. In other words, professors seem to respond more quickly to students with names that seem familiar.

This research contributes to a better understanding of student-teacher relationships while it also urges us to pay attention to how we respond to students from various backgrounds. Knowing that teachers at all levels tend to respond to students with 'familiar' names and that teachers subtly expect less from students with African American names should make us wonder how this bias may manifest itself in other ways in teacher-student interactions. Teachers who want to embrace an anti-racist pedagogy must address names as part of their classroom practice.

What, then, are educators to do when faced with the challenge of remembering all our students' names, and how to pronounce them, as well as matching them to specific faces? How can an English monolingual teacher pronounce and spell names from varying languages? These are questions for a bigger project than this chapter, but before I attempt to answer them, I want to highlight a program in California (US) that encourages students and teachers to claim ownership of their real names.

Discussion of 'My Name, My Identity' program in California public schools

The Santa Clara County Office of Education has many initiatives, including 'Strong Start', focusing on early childhood and 'The Power of Democracy', addressing civic engagement, among others. Of interest to this research is the 'My Name, My Identity' initiative. The campaign – a partnership between the National Association for Bilingual Education, the Santa Clara, California, County Office of Education and the California Association for Bilingual Education – focuses on the role personal names play in student success. In this next section, I will discuss this campaign and its materials and offer commentary.

Objectives of this campaign

According to the campaign website, the campaign has two objectives:

(1) Bring awareness to the importance of respecting one's name and identity in schools as measured by the number of community members making a pledge to pronounce students' names correctly.
(2) Build a respectful and caring culture in school communities that values diversity as measured by my name stories posted on social media.

The website is multi-faceted, with a focus on encouraging people to sign up to officially take their pledge. But along with this focus, there are also materials on education and advocacy.

Campaign pledge

The campaign website has an engaging front page that has images of students holding up signs with their diverse first names. There is a link to a video about students talking about the importance of their names and navigational boxes linking to pages with content, such as Investigate the World, Recognize Perspective, Communicate Ideas and Take Action. Numerous buttons on this page lead to 'Take the Pledge', which loads another page with a statement about the importance of names and then immediately tells respondents to ask students how to say their names and then says 'agree to respect their names' before the large green 'TAKE THE PLEDGE NOW' button (see Figure 7.1).

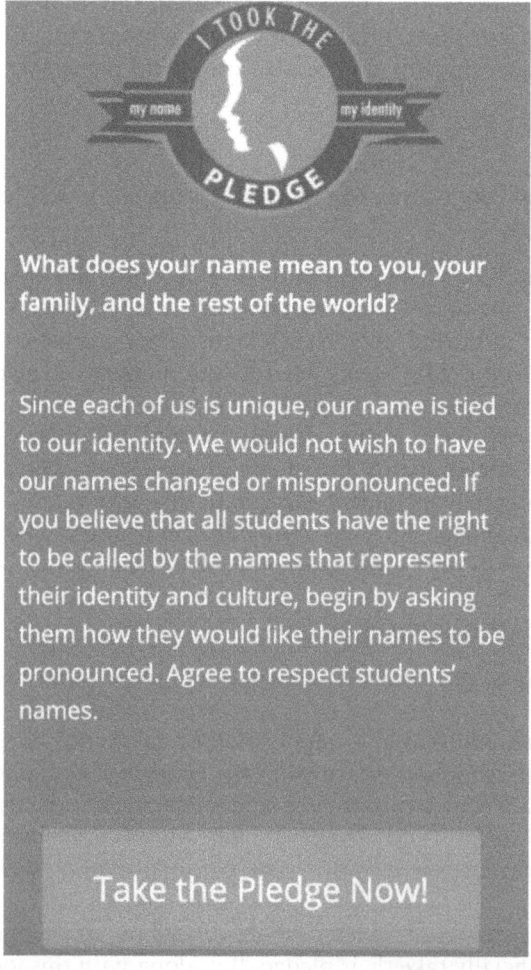

Figure 7.1 Screenshot of the 'My Name, My Identity' website

Figure 7.2 'My Name, My Identity' certificate (shared with permission)

The pledge itself asks for name and city, state, and school district (which auto fills to the appropriate public school district in the US). Figure 7.2 shows the pledge certificate users can generate when they sign up on the website. Note that the pledge's wording seems to be directed at teachers as the first line confirms that we pledge to show respect for others' names and identities in schools by pronouncing students' names correctly.

Education

The website has many well organized and comprehensive materials for teachers, including an online course that 'is for those educators looking to strengthen their personal and professional skills in building an inclusive classroom environment for students from culturally and linguistically different backgrounds' and many reading lists. Most useful and informative is the 30-minute panel presentation by the creators of this campaign made for the (virtual) 2021 National Association for Bilingual Education conference on YouTube. In addition, there is a downloadable PowerPoint and many PDFs full of information and ideas.

Advocacy

There is a sample resolution template from the Santa Clara County Office of Education to encourage others to consider a resolution for their local school organizations. Also impressive is that the one-page PDF is shared in English as well as ten additional languages. Most useful are the curriculum guides on the website. There is a four-unit curriculum (see Appendix B). In addition, there are downloadable google slides that can be customized, links to all sorts of media for many grades, and even template name badges that can be downloaded and printed for in-person use.

While this is a comprehensive and useful campaign, there are some potential pitfalls. Some teachers may lack the linguistic awareness – or drive – to learn how to pronounce their students' preferred names. However, as the campaign's materials make clear, it's not merely learning how to articulate unfamiliar sounds. Teachers are asked to consider the roles their names have played in their identity and then also to consider the ways that students have been silenced in schools unintentionally. Santa Ana's (2004) book discusses this in detail. Learning what the student names mean, even in translation, can be a brief glimpse of a culture new to the teacher as well as a quick peek into the students' home life. Hearing a story about being named after the grandmother they live with or being named after an uncle killed in a war can connect students and teachers before they start to get to know each other.

I suggest making learning your students' names and their meanings and pronunciations should be a first activity. This can be a way to head off any effort by students or teachers to use an American name without giving thought to what they're doing. Thompson (2006) notes that birth names that happen to conform more closely to American English sound patterns or that can be reduced to an American name may be less likely to be changed by the student whereas 'difficult' names are frequently changed (2006: 203), so it is worth being aware that students with 'difficult' names may be more likely to change them. Of course, some students may want to change their names and that is fine, but teachers should introduce the topic so that students understand that changing their names is not required to 'fit in' or 'become American'.

Why Teachers Need to Make the Effort

As I have shown, naming has always been an important topic, and when viewed with an awareness of assimilation in America, personal names rise in importance. Some teachers don't rise to the challenge, as seen in the as in the case of the New Jersey (US) teacher who had her teaching license suspended for a year after she made posted a screenshot of a student's name on Facebook and laughed about how the name also had a bad word in it ('Ex-N.J. teacher suspended for mocking student's name online', 2014). While some teachers may mock their students' names, it's perhaps more common for well-meaning teachers to 'Americanize' student names, all with the hope of making it easier for them – and for the teacher.

Teaching is already a demanding occupation and asking teachers to work to learn how to say their students' chosen name is yet another thing to add to their work. Yet, we know now that students benefit from their school communities – teachers, staff and other students – using their correct names. If such a small thing as learning the correct way to say someone's preferred name can help create a supportive learning environment, is it really too much to ask from teachers? I would say no. In fact, it's a small, easy, but important way to build a relationship with your students and in your classroom.

Ways to Engage with this Topic in the Classroom

There are several ways teachers can help students claim their names in the classroom. One first step is to introduce the topic through age-appropriate books. Keller and Franzak (2016) analyze the words and images of four children's books explicitly about K-12 students and names. These books are a fast way for K-6 teachers to engage with students at a basic level. Reading these books aloud to the class can provide an opening in which to discuss the topic at an introductory level.

For a deeper activity, teachers may ask students to investigate naming practices in their families or communities of origin. This is activity that all students can participate in by simply talking to family members or community members. Note that this may be problematic for some students, regardless of their cultural background, so, as always, an alternative assignment should be provided. The activity can begin by students asking other classmates about their names before the students ask family or community members questions. Some of these questions could be taken from this list.

(1) Is there a list of acceptable names from which parents must choose?
(2) Are specific family or community members consulted about names?
(3) Are there different rules to follow when naming boys versus girls?
(4) Are there prohibitions against naming a baby after a living family member?
(5) Can the same name be used by several family members in the same generation? If so, how do you differentiate between children with the same name?
(6) Are nicknames given and by whom?
(7) Do children change their name at puberty or adulthood?

At the curricular level, there are many resources available to teachers to help them integrate this into their lesson planning. Gavigan (2010) provides resources and ideas for K-6 teachers to address the topic of names. Wicht (2015) offers a lesson plan for addressing the importance of names (both historical/geographical and personal) appropriate for students in K-12. Appendix A is a list of resources provided by the 'My Name, My Identity' campaign.

The 'My Name, My Identity' campaign builds this into their curriculum. They provide robust materials for a weeklong lesson called 'Getting to Know Our Names'. Appendix B is a brief outline of this week. One important lesson can address how to say students' names. This could be done by having students slowly and carefully say their names before they explain how the letters 'sound'. Older children could do this by saying 'ae as in play' whereas younger children or those learning English phonology may need more help. One small way to help people remember how to say the names is to make specific syllables of the name rhyme with common English words. My friend with the last name Gapen reminds people to say 'the rapping Gapens' to keep us from pronouncing their last name as Gape-in.

For middle-high school students, teachers could ask students to brainstorm some celebrity names or even some celebrity baby names. A discussion of babies named Apple (Gwyneth Paltrow), X Æ A-12 (Elon Musk and Grimes) or Kal-El (Nicolas Cage) can then be turned into a discussion of how those names do or do not present challenges in communication. This could be a low-threat way to address gender identity and naming, and in this way, students could practice ways to introduce the topic if it's relevant to them. Additionally, 'odd' celebrity names can provide a springboard to discussing what makes names 'odd' and how some names have in-group meaning that can be misunderstood by others. In this way, students and teachers both can begin to see that names – not just 'foreign' names – carry symbolism and meaning that may be inaccessible to the larger population.

Another activity can involve students sharing what challenges they have experienced with their own names and then the class can discuss how to make 'difficult' names more accessible to English speakers who may be unfamiliar with these names. Teachers should make it clear that students are not obligated to share their personal information if they don't want to and that they can share name challenges from friends or family members. It's important that students do not feel compelled to discuss the challenges their names can offer as some students may have trauma connected to names from integrating into US society or even from ethnic or racial strife in their countries of origin. Students can ponder the idea of shortening names or using nick names or using only part of their name in lieu of a longer, multipart name.

Final Thoughts

As we have seen in the research discussed, naming is complex topic, particularly when the children in school are compelled to anglicize or otherwise make their name 'easier' for teachers. Culturally sensitive pedagogy means being aware of past practices that may no longer be suitable (such as having students choose 'an American name') and selecting new ways of addressing the challenges of names in the classroom. Acknowledging that students have the right to have their real names in the classroom is a crucial aspect of anti-racist pedagogy. Learning our students' names on the first day of class – whether they are familiar names like 'Emma' or new-to-us names like 'Omnia' – remains an important part of teacher-student connection. It's up to teachers to make sure that the names we learn are the names the students want to be called.

References

Alba, R. and Nee, V. (2003) *Remaking the Mainstream*. Cambridge, MA: Harvard University Press.

Allen, J. (2019) 'He goes by Mo': Drawing boundaries around Muslim identities. *Interdisciplinary Journal of Research on Religion* 15 (1), 1–22.

Anderson-Clark, T.N. and Green, R.J. (2017) Basking in reflected glory: The election of President Obama and naming behaviour. *Ethnic & Racial Studies* 40 (1), 63–76.

Aura, S. and Hess, G.D. (2010) What's in a name? *Economic Inquiry* 48 (1), 214–227.

Bertrand, M. and Mullainathan, S. (2004) Are Emily and Greg more employable than Lakisha and Jamal? A field experiment on labor market discrimination. *American Economic Review* 94 (4), 991–1013.

Biavaschi, C., Giulietti, C. and Siddique, Z. (2013) The economic payoff of name Americanization. (IZA Discussion Paper No. 7725). See http://ftp.iza.org/dp7725.pdf.

CBS (2014) Ex-N.J. teacher suspended for mocking student's name online. *CBS News*, 19 October. See https://www.cbsnews.com/news/ex-n-j-teacher-suspended-for-mocking-students-name-online/.

Dion, K.L. (1983) Names, identity, and self. *Names: A Journal of Onomastics* 31 (4), 245–257.

Fermaglich, K. (2015) "What's Uncle Sam's last name?" Jews and name changing in New York City during the World War II era. *Journal of American History* 102 (3), 719–745.

Figlio, D.N. (2005) Names, expectations and the Black-White test score gap. Working Paper 11195, National Bureau of Economic Research. See http://www.nber.org/papers/w11195.

Fryer Jr, R. and Levitt, S. (2003) The causes and consequences of distinctively Black names. *The Quarterly Journal of Economics* 119 (3), 767–805.

Gavigan, K. (2010) What's in a name? Honoring students' cultural identities. *Library Media Connection* 29 (3), 26–27.

Girma, H. (2020) Black names, immigrant names: Navigating race and ethnicity through personal names. *Journal of Black Studies* 51 (1), 16–36.

Hirschfeld Davis, J. (2015) Mount McKinley will again be called Denali. *The New York Times, 30 August*. See https://www.nytimes.com/2015/08/31/us/mount-mckinley-will-be-renamed-denali.html.

Kang, T.S. (1971) Name change and acculturation: Chinese students on an American campus. *Pacific Sociological Review* 14, 403–412.

Kaplan, J. and Bernays, A. (1997) *The Language of Names*. New York: Simon & Schuster.

Keller, T. and Franzak, J.K. (2016) When names and schools collide: Critically analyzing depictions of culturally and linguistically diverse children negotiating their names in picture books. *Children's Literature in Education: An International Quarterly* 47 (2), 177–190.

Kushner, J.S. (2009) The right to control one's name. *UCLA Law Review* 57 (1), 313–364.

Levine, M.B. and Willis, F.N. (1994) Public reactions to unusual names. *Journal of Social Psychology* 134 (5), 561–568.

Milkman, K. L., Akinola, M. and Chugh, D. (2012) Temporal distance and discrimination: An audit study in academia. *Psychological Science* 23 (7), 710–717.

Mitchell, C. (2016) Bungling student names: A slight that stings. *Education Week* 35 (30), 1–11.

Santa Ana, O. (2004) *Tongue-Tied: The Lives of Multilingual Children in Public Education*. Lanham, MD: Rowman & Littlefield Publishers, Inc.

Santa Clara County Office of Education (2021, April 28–29). *My Name, My Identity: Building Student Social, Emotional/Cultural Well-Being*. Santa Clara, CA: Santa Clara County Office of Education presentation to National Bilingual Education Association. See https://www.youtube.com/watch?v=5wjRfqIzGrA.

Sue, C.A. and Telles, E.E. (2007) Assimilation and gender in naming. *American Journal of Sociology* 112 (5), 1383–1415.

Thompson, R. (2006) Bilingual, bicultural, and binominal identities: Personal name investment and the imagination in the lives of Korean Americans. *Journal of Language, Identity & Education* 5 (3), 179–208.

Thonus, T. (1992) Anderson, Maicon, and Thyago: 'English' names in Brazil. *American Speech* 67 (2), 175–189.

Wicht, S. (2015, September 9) Names do matter. *Learning for Justice*, 9 September. See https://www.learningforjustice.org/magazine/names-do-matter.

Wong, A.D. (2013) Brand names and unconventional spelling: A two-pronged analysis of the orthographic construction of brand identity. *Written Language and Literacy* 16 (2), 115–145.

Zhao, X. and Biernat, M. (2017) 'Welcome to the U.S.' but 'change your name'? Adopting Anglo names and discrimination. *Journal of Experimental Social Psychology* 70, 59–68.

Appendix A: Resources

Resources for All Lessons
Hyperlinks are embedded in the electronic copy of the brochure.
Visit mynamemyidentity.org

Community Building Activities/Tools:
Stories of Your Names Icebreakers
(Grades PreK-12)
Identity Charts
(Grades PreK -12)

Picture Books:
Chrysanthemum
by Kevin Henkes (Grades PreK-2)
Chrysanthemum
Read Aloud in YouTube
My Name is Sangoel
by Karen Williams and Khadra Mohammed
(Grades 1 and up)
My Name is Yoon
by Helen Recorvits (Grades 1-3)
The Name Jar
by Yangsook Choi (PreK-Grade 2)
The Name Jar
Read Aloud in YouTube (PreK-Grade 2)
Three Names of Me
by Mary Cummings (Grades 3-5)

Poem:
My Name Is Jorge on Both Sides of the River
by Jane Medina (Grades K-6)
My Name Is Jorge on Both Sides of the River
by Jane Medina (Grades K-6)
Read in both Spanish and English

Chapter Book:
My Name is Maria Isabel/Me Llamo Maria Isabel,
by Alma Flor Ada (Grades 2-5)

Short Novels:
Names/Nombres
by Hulia Alvares (Grades 6-8)
The House on Mango Street
by Sandra Cisneros (Grades 9-12)

Units:
What's in a Name? A Back-to-School Literacy Unit
(Grades 1-2, 3-5)
Developing Empathy
by Teaching Tolerance (Grades 6-8)
Investigating Names to Explore Personal History and Cultural Traditions
(Grades 6-8)
Exchanging Stories--Names
(Grades 6-12)
From Word Stories to Name Stories
Lesson Plan ideas (Grades 6-12)
Becoming American: Exploring Names and Identities
Facing History Unit (Grades 9-12)

Videos:
Do Names Matter?
Lion Lee explained the importance and surprising impact of names (Grades 9-12)
My Name My Identity Flipgrid Activity
Martin Ricardo Cisneros, Academic Technology Specialist at the Santa Clara County Office of Education demonstrated how teachers can have students tell them about their names on Flipgrid, a video discussion platform (Teachers)
My Name, My Identity of Our Teachers
A group of teachers shared the meaning of their names
(Grades 6-12)
Student Voice: Respecting the Name, Respecting the Identity
Bhargavi Garimella, Director of Management at Redefy shared students' perspective on the importance of pronouncing students' names correctly (Grades K-Adult)
Respecting Students' Identities: Names Matter
Students at Washoe County School District shared their names (Grades 2-12)
Say My Name
A group of Chinese college students shared the meaning of their names and why their names are important to them (Grades 6-Adult)
That Moment You Learn The Meaning of Your Name
Siaka Massaquoi shared how he felt about his name when he was growing up and after he learned about the meaning of his name (Grades 9-Adult)

Santa Clara County Office of Education
1290 Ridder Park Drive • San Jose, CA 95131-2304
SCCOE.org

Appendix B: Sample Week Curriculum from 'My Name, My Identity'

Sample Lessons

Lesson 1

Objectives:
Learn about each other's name and the name that each person prefers to be called

Inquiry Question:
How is your name unique?

Activity: Inside/Outside Circles or Lines of Communication
Here are suggested prompts that can be used with an interactive activity:
- What is your name?
- How do you pronounce your name?
- How is it spelled?
- Do you have a nickname? Who are the people who call you by your nickname?
- What are different names people have called you?
- What is the name you prefer to be called at school?

Honoring Student Voices: As a group, discuss how names are unique to people.
Extending Learning: What would you like to know more about the importance of names to people?

Lesson 2

Objective:
Bring awareness of the importance of names and their rich family and cultural history

Inquiry Question:
Why are names important to people?

Activity: Partner Introduction
Have people interview each other in pairs. Each person will have three minutes to interview another person. Each person will have one minute to introduce his/her partner.
Suggested interview questions:
- Is there a story behind your name? What is it? For example, was your name given to honor someone?
- Who gave you your name?
- Where does your name originally come from?
- What does your name mean? For example, the name Yee in Chinese means friendship.
- What is something positive about you or your name that no one can forget?

Honoring Student Voices: As a group, discuss the reasons why names are important to people.
Extending Learning: Why is it important to pronounce others' names correctly?

Lesson 3

Objective:
Develop empathy on respecting others' names

Inquiry Question:
How would you feel if someone repeatedly mispronounced your name?

Activity: Fishbowl
Show a video "Getting Students' Names Right: Why It Matters" by Education Week
Use Fishbowl strategy to process the suggested questions:
- Have you had someone repeatedly mispronounce your name or try to change your name? How did it make you feel?
- As a show of respect, what could you do to try to pronounce others' names correctly?

Honoring Student Voices: Share one word that describes your understanding of people's feelings based on the fishbowl discussion.
For example, "I feel **safe** when I know that I can ask people, 'Did I say your name correctly?'"
Extending Learning: What are ways that you can show respect and empathy?

Lesson 4

Objective:
Express your name and identity

Inquiry Question:
How does your name badge represent who you are?

Activity: Create Your Personalized Name Badge
- Think of key words or visual representations that describe you. Create your name badge that will help people to learn your name and attributes that are important to you.
- The name badge can be in the form of a name tent, poster, infographic or a digital image.
- Have each person share his/her name badge.

Honoring Student Voices: Invite people to share their name badges with the group.
Extending Learning: What do you think students can do collectively to ensure that everyone in our community is included?

Lesson 5

Objectives:
Empower each person as a change agent in building a culture of respect and honoring everyone's name by pronouncing it correctly

Inquiry Question:
What can we do to ensure that everyone in our community is included?

Activity: Create a Pledge
- Brainstorm ideas to answer this question: What can we do to ensure that everyone in our community is included?
- Record ideas.
- Discuss the ideas and perimeters for determining actions.
- Have each person create a pledge of what he/she will do to build a community of respect.
- Each person can also take the pledge for the My Name, My Identity Campaign at http://bit.ly/mnmidpledge.

Honoring Student Voices: Invite people to share their pledges with the group.
Extending Learning: What can you do to promote a culture of respect beyond your classroom/school/district/city/state?

8 Anti-Racist Linguistic Practices in the History Curriculum

Luciana C. de Oliveira and Joy Beatty

This chapter provides an overview of what it means to be an anti-racist educator in a history context. Drawing on the notions of culturally sustaining pedagogies, anti-racist practices and Southern epistemologies, we use examples of curriculum developed through an anti-racist lens to show a dual focus on language and content. We use the concept of counter-narratives as an important component of teaching history. The goal is to highlight the need to interrogate history. Counter-narratives are born by interrogating what is 'normal'. There are particular actors and actresses in history who have never been interrogated for a number of reasons. Helping students interrogate history (text/media/social media) is a transferable skill-set to other content areas and aspects of life.

Culturally Sustaining Pedagogies

Our frame is embedded in culturally sustaining pedagogies. Culturally sustaining pedagogies (Paris & Alim, 2017), an expansion of the previously widely used concept of culturally responsive teaching (Ladson-Billings, 2014), go beyond being responsive to students' needs or cultures or making sure classroom materials and instruction are relevant to them. Paris (2012: 95) claims that culturally responsive or relevant programs do not necessarily help 'sustain and support bi-and multilingualism and bi- and multiculturalism' and therefore, being responsive or relevant is not enough. Culturally sustaining pedagogies help sustain 'the cultural and linguistic competence of their communities while simultaneously offering access to dominant cultural competence' (2012: 95). Paris advocates a pedagogy that maintains (hence the word *sustaining* in its title) the practices of students while also expanding their repertoires to include 'dominant language[s], literacies and other cultural practices' (2012: 95) so students are also able to critique such practices. Paris and Alim (2017) suggest that, 'culturally sustaining pedagogy exists wherever education sustains the lifeways of communities who have been and continue to be damaged and erased through schooling' (2017: 1).

The examples that we use in this chapter identify culturally sustaining approaches that incorporate the linguistic and cultural repertoires of students and their communities in the joint co-construction of knowledge. They also show that students and teachers should be encouraged and supported in addressing what we call counter-narratives. All examples showcase explicit, equitable language practices that encourage, validate, and extend students' cultural and linguistic affordances, backgrounds, and experiences and show how these practices integrate language into instruction in history.

Anti-Racist Practices and Curriculum

Anti-racism involves practices of identifying and opposing racism by challenging and changing values, structures, and attitudes that perpetuate systemic racism and implementing policies which actively oppose oppression in its many forms. Anti-racist practices include consideration of various forms of oppression, including discrimination based on language, gender, sexual orientation, ability and class, for example. We operationalize anti-racist practices and curriculum in social studies as actively rejecting 'the institutional and structural aspects of race and racism and explains how racism is manifested in various spaces, making the social construct of race visible' (King & Chandler, 2016: 4). An anti-racist pedagogy recognizes the role of educational institutions, practices, and people in producing and reproducing racial inequality. It offers the classroom as a place to explore the effects of racism.

Southern Epistemologies and Linguistic Citizenship

We also draw on Southern epistemologies and the role of Southern voices in conceptualizing anti-racism. We draw on the notion that the South refers to the conditions of suffering and inequality that capitalism and colonialism have brought to the forefront and to the resistance to such conditions (de Sousa Santos, 2012). Therefore, Southern epistemologies also include excluded and silenced peoples of the North, including undocumented immigrants, ethnic minoritezed individuals, religious minorities and other marginalized populations (Pennycook & Makoni, 2020; de Sousa Santos, 2012). It is concerned with the construction and validation of knowledges based on resistance by these excluded voices that have endured oppression and injustices (de Sousa

Santos, 2018). In drawing on Southern epistemologies, we also use the notion of Linguistic Citizenship as an approach to agency and voice (Stroud *et al.*, 2020; Williams & Stroud, 2015) used to highlight the power of marginalized voices to open them up as meaning-making through which alternative voices are articulated.

Building Counter-Narratives in the History Classroom

Joy: Author Boaventura de Sousa Santos's call 'to change the conversation' encourages many to question core ideological structures of history and how teachers teach history. A way to 'change the conversation' would be to develop stronger questions that challenge weak answers rooted in Eurocentric cognitive paradigms (de Sousa Santos, 2016: 40). My primary goal as a history teacher is to create counter-narratives that help to decolonize history. When decolonizing history, I constantly interrogate popular narratives that have been traditionally rooted in centering Eurocentric experiences. These Eurocentric perspectives lay the foundation for us to understand history through colonized lenses. When I began to interrogate history, I realized that the 'Western gaze' or the 'Eurocentric gaze' trivialized or omitted other groups' histories. In fact, de Sousa Santos (2016: 41) refers to these omissions as a clear detriment to our understanding of the reach and impact of 'decisive cultural and political experiences and initiatives in the countries of the Global South'. My belief is that counter-narratives are born through an interrogative process that will allow learners to understand history from colonial and non-colonial lenses. This is an act of an anti-racist educator as strong questions create a distance from Eurocentric traditions and begin to challenge weak answers rooted in colonial ideologies (de Sousa Santos, 2016). The act of decolonizing by interrogating history can happen daily within a K-12 history classroom.

In the next section, we present several examples of how Joy has integrated counter-narratives into her curriculum.

Sample Curriculum Materials

Using sample curriculum materials for teaching history, we identify examples of oppressive language and concepts by connecting them with how history is taught so they can inform lesson planning and teaching. We emphasize how educators can notice, address and challenge oppressive linguistic systems that have been normalized so that educators can implement anti-racist practices.

Example 1: Calendar

A simple study of a calendar can help students begin the process of interrogating history and therefore, discuss counternarratives and the

Definitions: Narratives and Counternarratives

Narrative

- Tells a story
- Sequence of events
- Tells history of
  - Events of past/present/future

Counternarrative

- A narrative(story) that goes against another story.
- A new/revised narrative that challenges the main or dominant narrative(story)
- A *counternarrative* may question the accuracy of popular narratives

Figure 8.1 Calendar Example

need for continued academic discussions that center and promote cultural pluralism. For example, the month of October shows Indigenous Peoples' Day and Columbus Day on the same day (Figure 8.1). Within a K-12 learning context, this is an excellent opportunity to engage students to interrogate history by helping to hone their critical thinking skills. I have chosen to center dominant and marginalized narratives of US history as a springboard to engage students in academic discussions about monoculture, cultural pluralism and the need to create counternarratives.

As previously stated, de Sousa Santos places emphasis on having strong question-sets that help to facilitate conversations. He highlights the need to develop strong questions as these questions address the 'societal and epistemological paradigm that has shaped the current horizon' in which we understand colonial and decolonial histories (de Sousa Santos, 2016: 20). Strong question sets critique Eurocentric structures and challenge current paradigms of historical thinking that shape our understanding of history. In this instance, these question-sets are unique to Indigenous Peoples' Day, Columbus Day, and help to develop counter narratives within a high school setting:

(1) Whose narrative was included on the calendar first?
   a. Why was this narrative told?
   b. To what extent is this person/group considered a winner in history?
(2) Whose narrative is now included on the calendar?
   a. Why is this narrative included now?
   b. To what extent is this person/group considered a winner in history?
(3) Of the two narratives,
   a. Which was the dominant narrative? Explain.
   b. Which is considered the counter-narrative? Explain.
(4) To what extent are counternarratives relevant? Explain.

These questions help students interrogate history by challenging dominant narratives while centering marginalized narratives, by highlighting the voices of marginalized populations as part of a Linguistic Citizenship approach in social studies. These question-sets also facilitate meaningful conversations about inclusivity and the perceived winners and losers of history. I recognize that including Indigenous Peoples' Day as a federal holiday is a step in a better direction. However, as an anti-racist educator, I still question the 'lingering inheritance of coloniality' that could be present when teaching about Indigenous Peoples' Day. We understand that much of my student's understanding of history is rooted in Eurocentric perspectives and so consequently; they will provide well-intentioned Eurocentric responses (Pennycook & Makoni, 2020: 75). For this reason, it becomes necessary to challenge their colonial ideologies so that the origins of counter-narrative can begin. This is an act of unlearning and is necessary cognitive dissonance for young learners.

Example 2: Textbook of American stories

As most educators continue to move away from using traditional textbooks, I still find it useful to include popular history textbooks into academic discussions with learners. Schools have reinforced the colonial project by centering whiteness as the dominant narrative (Alim *et al.*, 2020). While textbooks can serve as a main teaching and learning tool, some textbooks use 'white gaze measures' to sustain colonial ideologies and structures. As a result, exploring the titles and content of American textbooks should be a practice of an anti-racist educator.

While a textbook can be a tool of useful information, I have come to experience that most mainstream US history textbooks do not sustain and/or center independent positive narratives of minorities but rather mention minority experiences as struggles in comparison to the dominant narrative. In an effort to unlearn and to engage students of different cultural practices in creating counternarratives, I created two exit ticket assignments that explored a timeline of book titles from American history. The objective of the first exit ticket focused on overt wording and subtext. I used a standard history textbook as a primary resource of study. Learners responded to the following questions:

(1) Based on the title and cover image, what story and whose story is being told? Explain.
(2) When considering the subtitle, 'Beginnings to WWI', how important is the word, beginning? Explain.
(3) According to this text, the beginning of American history starts with what narrative?
(4) To what extent is the subtitle inclusive?
(5) To what extent is the subtitle oppressive?

Exit ticket questions two and three focus on the word beginning and its colonial implications. The word beginning is used as an apparatus for time that is rooted in colonial origins and understanding. As historians continue to use colonial linguistics like beginning, first and only, Makoni suggests that these colonial linguistics continue to promote a Eurocenric analytical grid of understanding that has historically trumped the origins of black, indigenous and people of color (BIPOC) groups and experiences. There is a traditional Eurocentric grid for understanding the past which sustains present-day colonial ideological structures part of the language experiences in colonial and postcolonial contexts (Makoni, 2011). By interrogating the title of this textbook, students can analyze the historical intent and wording in an effort to develop decolonized historical thinking skills.

Example 3: Book titles

This last exit ticket assignment continues to identify overt wording of book titles and students also analyze the imagery of the textbooks. When becoming an anti-racist educator, learning experiences should evolve to sustaining continuous discourse about the relationships and experiences between and among marginalized groups in history (Paris, 2012). So that this happens, I presented to students a diverse group of titles that decenters whiteness and America's monocultural experience to centering the cultural plurality of the US. After the titles were presented, students responded to the questions.

(1) Based on the titles and images, what stories and whose stories are being told? Explain.
(2) How important is it to include marginalized narratives in history classes?
(3) To what extent are these books counter narratives? Explain.
(4) How can these pluralistic experiences become the dominant narratives of US history?
(5) Who would consider these titles/books counternarratives? Explain.
(6) To what extent are these books examples of progress in US history? Explain.
(7) To what extent are these books examples of struggles in US history? Explain.

Question four has always prompted rich discussions in my classes as students consider how historically marginalized narratives could become dominant narratives. Question four suggests that the Global North, or historically dominant groups, should be learning from the Global South, or historically marginalized groups. I understand that colonial history and linguistics 'has disabled the global North from learning in non-colonial terms', which means that students may find these types of conversations as challenging to their Eurocentric grids of understanding history (de Sousa Santos, 2016: 38). Titles that include the experiences between and among marginalized communities, like Indigenous, Black and Latinx communities, should be centered in academic discussions as this supports the journey to becoming an anti-racist educator.

Example 4: Working to identify and address oppressive language

Pennycook and Makoni's (2020: 83) research 'analyzes the Eurocentrism or northern perspective that underlies much of applied linguistics' in Western educational systems. Challenging these perspectives is critical in the work of applied linguists as we engage in anti-racist practices in classrooms. It became a professional and personal goal for each history lesson to address and challenge oppressive linguistic systems. Acts of linguistic oppression became a strong focus as I continued my practice of decolonizing and disrupting traditional history narratives.

Figure 8.2 is an image from a lesson that highlights historical and modern-day examples of linguistic oppression that have been normalized and accepted in academic canons. The primary goal is to disrupt the dominant narrative and to debunk common mistruths and misconceptions about US history. Through these lenses, this lesson addresses examples of linguistic oppression.

According to the figure, concepts of power and oppression are highlighted by studying the 19th Amendment. I used a popular electronic dictionary as an information source. Popular narratives that do not

Journey to understanding... not necessarily in this order

Definitions...

1. Suffrage - right to vote in political elections
2. Women's suffrage - right for women to vote in political elections
3. 19th Amendment (1919) - U.S. constitution granted women the right to vote
4. Voting Rights Act (1965)- outlawed discriminatory voting practices

Definitions...

1. Suffrage - right to vote in political elections
2. Women's suffrage - right for women to vote in political elections
3. 19th Amendment (1919) - U.S. constitution granted White women the right to vote
4. Voting Rights Act (1965)
   - It outlawed the discriminatory voting practices
   - An act to enforce the 15th Amendment (passed in 1869, granted African American men the right to vote.)
   - Prohibits racial discrimiation in voting

Figure 8.2 Oppressive Language Example

re-address the mistruth that all women were granted the right to vote in 1919 should certainly be interrogated as we now know that all women were not granted the right to vote at the same time. This popular narrative is perpetuated in on-line educational spaces, like dictionaries.

As students studied and responded to the questions below, power and privilege were common terms of dynamics that were expressed among learners.

Oppressive language examples – 'granted':

- Who were the main authors of the US Constitution?
- To what extent are the words grant and allow similar?
- According to the definition (3), who granted White women the right to vote in 1919?
- According to the definition (4), when were women of color granted the right to vote? How do you know this? Explain.
- Based upon today's activity, how would you explain oppression to a student who was absent from today's class?

Example 5: Interrogating linguistic racism

Teachers, especially history teachers, must understand how to recognize 'the everyday' examples of linguistic and systemic oppressiveness. I have encountered examples of linguistic racism in curriculum guides, lesson overviews, teacher toolkits, presentations etc. If everyday practices are not disrupted, teachers and students will continue to report inaccurate and distorted accounts of history.

For example, this email was sent by me to another history teacher. We worked together as expert curriculum writers for US history. The curriculum that we were creating was slated to be used by teachers in specific regions of the state of Virginia. There was a particular emphasis on reaching White teachers in the rural areas of Virginia. As writers, we often provided feedback to each other about our lessons, curricula, artifacts, etc. According to the email, I provided feedback to another writer. This particular writer posits that Africans were born slaves and were brought to the Americas as slaves (see Figure 8.3). I challenged her normal and popular narrative of history through an interrogative process. My questions decentered Whiteness as the goal of attainment and challenged her to refocus her efforts towards disrupting the dominant narrative that Africa and Africans are synonymous with slavery and slave.

In this instance, as an anti-racist educator, this experience brought into focus how marginalized communities, or the Global South, are still 'understudied, unattended to or, worse, actively suppressed' even among well-intentioned history teachers (Pennycook & Makoni, 2020: 84). There is still an idea that the Global South's existence is contingent upon

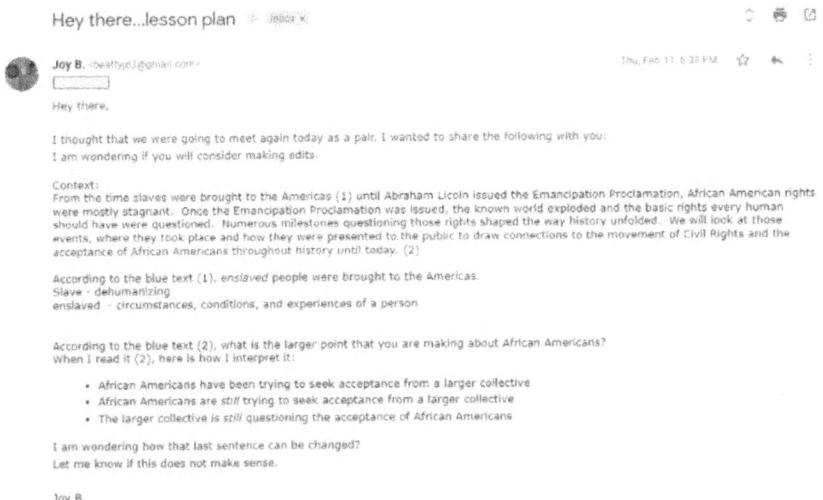

Figure 8.3 Interrogating Linguistic Racism Email Example

needing the support of the Global North and this type of ideology is foundational to sustaining the colonial mindset.

Protocol for Educators

We present a protocol for educators to identify and address oppression and acts of linguistic racism in various texts, including textbooks, websites, posters, announcements, among others. This protocol was influenced by the works of Dr Gholdy Muhammad. In her book, *Cultivating Genius: An Equity Framework for Culturally and Historically Responsive Literacy* (Muhammad, 2020), she centers equity as a framework for teaching and learning. I was inspired to develop a Culturally Responsive Teaching Protocol (CRT Protocol) that centers equity. This protocol presents cognitive and actionable steps that should happen for the teacher when lesson planning and helps cultivate the learner's experience.

I use the protocol while lesson planning and then again during reflection. As a history teacher, I understand the traditional pathways of power and how those pathways have changed. As education continues to promote advancements in STEM learning, the power and impact of computer science has been integrated into my history lessons as computer science and its systems are operated, programmed and/or used by humans who can continue to perpetuate dominant narratives.

As a result, I developed a geography lesson that integrated computer science principles as it relates to algorithms and computer programming.

Table 8.1 Suggestions for curriculum analysis and lesson planning

Questions to guide curriculum analysis and lesson planning	Potential actions
1. How does power show up in your curriculum? 2. How do you teach topics about equity and inequity? Equality and inequality? 3. How does anti-racism and anti-oppression show up in your curriculum?	• Look through curriculum materials to identify traditional systems of power and interrogate them through an anti-racist lens (e.g. who are the people in charge of government systems; who are your local leaders – race, gender etc.) • Identify what is centered in terms of topics – what has historically been the central narrative and how can you center equity and equality to disrupt this central narrative? What specific act must be done or unlearned to become more anti-racist? • Create opportunities for students to promote positive change that challenges racism and oppression (among other -isms)

After reading Dr Ruha Benjamin's *Race After Technology: Abolitionist Tools for the New Jim Code* (Benjamin, 2019), I was inspired to develop a lesson that focused on concepts like urbanization, gentrification, navigational systems (GPS) and street names. My use of the protocol while lesson planning continued to acknowledge the absence of pluralistic narratives and histories and so consequently; the need to create counternarratives became and more urgent. I have developed lessons that share examples of un-learning while on a journey of becoming an anti-racist. I am confident that by centering equity, the process of unlearning will continue to highlight America's diverse histories. Refer to Table 8.1 for suggestions.

Conclusion

Teachers must understand that decolonizing curriculum is a daily task. It will not happen in one lesson and it should not happen in one lesson. Lessons should help students learn how to navigate different cultural spaces by providing them with historical and modern-day examples of how to understand, learn and re-learn history. While systems of oppression may still exist today, intentional acts of using educational spaces to center equity can yield empowerment among learners thereby, moving the needle forward. An act of becoming an anti-racist educator is to validate marginalized experiences and perspectives by decentering the dominate narrative. This can be done by creating counternarratives.

Using a CRT Protocol like the one presented here can help history teachers implement anti-racist practices in their teaching. Our examples of curriculum developed through an anti-racist lens to show a dual focus on language and content drew on the notions of culturally sustaining pedagogies, anti-racist practices and Southern epistemologies. History teachers can consider these examples as ways they can start to build counter-narratives as an important component of teaching history as they engage in highlighting the agency and power of marginalized, alternative voices. Counter-narratives develop by interrogating what is 'normal', how marginalized voices can be placed in the forefront of history and other subject areas There are particular actors and actresses in history who have never been interrogated for a number of reasons. Helping students interrogate history (text/media/social media) is a transferable skill-set to other content areas and aspects of life.

References

Alim, H.S., Paris, D. and Wong, C.P. (2020) Culturally sustaining pedagogy: A critical framework for centering communities. In N.S. Nasir, C.D. Lee, R. Pea and M. McKinney de Royston (eds) *Handbook of the Cultural Foundations of Learning* (pp. 261–276). New York: Routledge.
Benjamin, R. (2019) *Race after Technology: Abolitionist Tools for the New Jim Code.* Cambridge: Polity Press.
de Sousa Santos, B. (2012) Public sphere and epistemologies of the south. *Africa Development* 37 (1), 43–67.
de Sousa Santos, B. (2016) *Epistemologies of the South: Justice Against Epistemicide.* New York: Routledge.
de Sousa Santos, B. (2018) *The End of the Cognitive Empire: The Coming of Age of Epistemologies of the South.* Durham, NC: Duke University Press.
King, L.J. and Chandler, P.T. (2016) From non-racism to anti-racism in social studies teacher education: Social studies and racial pedagogical content knowledge. In A.R. Crowe and A. Cuenca (eds) *Rethinking Social Studies Teacher Education in the Twenty-First Century* (pp. 3–21). Cham: Springer.
Ladson-Billings, G. (2014) Culturally relevant pedagogy 2.0: A.k.a. the remix. *Harvard Educational Review* 84 (1), 74–84.
Makoni, S. (2011) A critical analysis of the historical and contemporary status of minority languages in Zimbabwe. *Current Issues in Language Planning* 12, 437–455.
Muhammad, G. (2020) *Cultivating Genius: An Euity Framework for Culturally and Historically Responsive Literacy.* New York: Scholastic Press.
Paris, D. (2012) Culturally sustaining pedagogy: A needed change in stance, terminology, and practice. *Educational Researcher* 41 (3), 93–97.
Paris, D. and Alim, H.S (eds) (2017) *Culturally Sustaining Pedagogies: Teaching and Learning for Justice in a Changing World.* New York: Teachers College Press.
Pennycook, A. and Makoni, S. (2020) *Innovations and Challenges in Applied Linguistics from the Global South.* New York: Routledge.
Williams, Q.E. and Stroud, C. Linguistic citizenship: Language and politics in postnational modernities. *Journal of Language and Politics* 14 (3), 406–430.

9 On Human and Linguistic Dignity

Patricia Friedrich

> In this short, concluding chapter I weave together ideas of anti-racism, linguistics and human dignity to argue that the latter concept is central to better linguistic interactions and language-based institutions.

Introduction

When we stated writing this book, we were, in our own lives, searching for ways to cope and respond to both the COVID-19 pandemic and the increased acts of racism in the US in the summer of 2020. While we wrote it, we witnessed the sociopolitical cracks that resulted from extreme views of public policy on the health crisis (i.e. attempts at disqualifying public policy in the name of individualism); natural disasters across the world; and unrest at the US Capitol on 6 January 2021. We witness the increase in 'fake news;' a growing suspicion of science as a source of knowledge; disregard for sanitary measures against the pandemic; the rise of misogynistic, gender- and sexual-identity-based discrimination; racist discourses in places like Brazil, where several of us are from; the rise of deforestation; threats to indigenous peoples; and disregard for climate change. And now, as we wrap up writing, we continue to witness, perplexed, the invasion of Ukraine by Russian forces.

In a short period of time, there have been too many events of world-wide impact to count, and of course, our resolve when it comes to moving forward with ideas for inclusive, anti-racism practices is shaken in face of so many challenges. Shaken but not extinguished.

Under these extreme circumstances, it is sometimes hard to see the incredible work that many people are engaged in to counteract the effects of these phenomena and to create better, more inclusive structures, linguistically and otherwise. While the pandemic threatened all of us, many scientists dedicated all of their days and nights to finding a vaccine, to coming up with protocols to slow the spread of the virus; strategists tried to find logistic solutions to problems in the supply chain or in the production of goods affected by the pandemic. Vaccine distribution was a Herculean task. Millions of teachers learned new technological applications and pedagogical innovations to help their students learn even under the most trying conditions. And millions of others simply volunteered their time to do good to the extent of their possibilities – be it to talk to an older adult on the phone, so that they would feel less alone while quarantined, or to take supplies to a community hit particularly hard by crisis. So while not everything is bleak, all of it is serious. We have been humbled by how much we still need to learn and how much our reality can change in so little time. These events have changed us, but we get to decide in which direction we take that change.

I would like to spend this last, concluding chapter, writing about a concept that has been a guiding principle in my scholarship and moral code, and a guiding light when the situation in the world gets particularly trying: respect for human dignity. I will attempt to interweave it to ideas of linguistic peace, anti-racism and multicultural expression. It is of course a challenging time to do this, which probably makes it all the more necessary.

The concept of human dignity I adopt here is not very different from Kant's and is explained by Hill (2014: 215) as follows: 'all persons, regardless of rank or social class, have an equal intrinsic worth or dignity. Human dignity is an innate worth or status that we did not earn and cannot forfeit'.[1] A more modern, compelling view of human dignity is provided by Frederick Douglass (1894) and Buccola (2015: 234) explains that, in Douglass's case, in his essays, the concept is used not only to point out the absurdity of enslaving human beings but also to evidence how human dignity applies to the rights of women (including in the political sphere). Despite the 'universal he' in his quote, Douglass proclaims that 'In the essential dignity of man as man, I find all necessary incentives and aspirations to a useful and noble life'. I think it is particularly inspiring that he too found dignity to be a guiding element for living ethically.

Because of its unalienable nature, human dignity has been both proposed and opposed as an alternative to the concept of human rights, which tends to have more currency and certainly more legal uses in modern time than dignity does. While it is outside of the scope of this book to veer too far into the legal aspects of human-rights discussions (the importance of linguistic rights in the context of anti-racism discussions notwithstanding), I would like to spend a few moments examining human dignity in the context of language use, borrowing from political science and global human rights lines of thought where appropriate.

In fact, I find great resonance between my beliefs on human dignity and the direction Regilme Jr (2019: 287) suggests for a framework of global human rights. That author considers a focus on human dignity to be essential for bringing a sense of equity to the different societies around the world, with different political dynamics, social values and beliefs, etc. He posits that:

> To accommodate perspectives from both the Global North and the Global South, our understanding of human rights needs to be reframed, involving a shift from the discourses of *rights* to one of *dignity*. Human dignity should not be considered as ideological antithetical to civil and political rights. Rather, human dignity encapsulates all forms of human rights claims including civil and political rights, social rights, economic rights, physical integrity rights and cultural rights, among many others. (Emphasis in the original)

I would argue that covered 'among many others' are linguistic rights, the right to one's own language, as well as the right to learn any language one finds useful, important, or simply interesting, and then the right to have such language uses acknowledged, respected and uplifted. The advantage of a dignity framework, the author continues, lies in that, 'It guarantees equal normative value for both socio-economic rights, which are often dismissed by the global North, and political and civil rights that many regimes in the Global South perceive as less important' (2019: 287). That is, while dignity is not a-cultural *per se*, it carries, in its intrinsic form, the ability to exist regardless of cultural orientation and local norms. What is more, it is recognized both in civil, secular domains as well as by many religious denominations as a helpful and necessary concept.

But it is not only in big, normative and political spaces that claiming a dignity framework can help. Consider individual interactions in which a person can, before writing or speaking, ask themselves, 'in what ways will what I say/write next support or threaten the human dignity of my readers or interlocutors?' or 'how will what I communicate next aid or hamper the upholding of human dignity?' It is possible to have an immediate, both intellectual and emotion reaction to the word 'dignity'. Even if a definition should elude us, the understanding of its implication is tangible, and it is applicable in a very broad scope of situations.

Consider as well a classroom, in which a teacher was to pose one of those questions to a student, and ask that they use it as a guide to their interactions. What kinds of changes could that provoke? How about professional meetings, where there are likely going to be many disagreements, but each participant in the interaction makes a commitment to preserve human dignity and focus on the merits of each argument?

Finally, if we bring to mind situations involving diplomacy and negotiation, and apply a human dignity framework to the realization of those talks, we might end up with outcomes that are much more favorable to all involved than a winner-takes-all approach.

Disrespect for human dignity lies at the core of most, if not all, of our sociopolitical problems, from war to social inequality, from racism to misogynistic behaviors. I know it is a radical claim to make. Yet, close examination of the steps that lead to such catastrophes show that in each and every one of them there is no upholding of human dignity. If one is fully aware of the intrinsic value of another human being, they cannot get themselves to treat another in ways they would not themselves like to be treated. By the same token, if people and societies lose track of the idea that each human being is worthy just for being, separation and 'othering' can then occur.

If we take this discussion further, we can also conclude that the problem extends itself to non-human dignity. To use de Sousa Santos's concept of an abyssal line (2007), one could argue that there exists, too, a zone of non-being for non-human creatures, the maintenance of which is necessary for humans to inflict the harm they do on animals and on nature. Again, if the dignity of animals and the natural environments was to be upheld, human beings would have to see themselves as part of that world, not proprietors of it. Many people, native to the Americas, for example, have tried to live in that manner – as elements of the environment, not rulers of it – and colonial practices and abyssal thinking desecrated and destroyed their worlds and their lives.

Regilme Jr (2019: 287) also recognizes this interplay between the global/societal and the individual – while writing about 'emphasizing human dignity in the global norms order' – by stating that, 'we allow individuals to deliberatively determine and actualize how and in what ways they can fully realize their individual worth in relation to their immediate community – based on the intricacies of their cultural, economic and political conditions'.

Linguistically, that means we have to be constantly, and in context, questioning the effects of our words, and we have to treat words like the actions they are. More strictly speaking, it is only performative verbs that do things in the world, but if we consider the matter more broadly, all of our words do. Our words have the potential to transform ourselves and those around us, and that power is directly related to how we preserve or threaten human dignity.

In the context of anti-racism linguistics, human dignity must be a central concern. Racism is so wrong and so damaging exactly because it is an attempt to hurt human dignity at its very core. When one uses racist language, or adopts racist practices they are directly affronting the idea of a human being's intrinsic worth. On the other hand, with our words we get to uplift, to shine light, to amplify voices, and those possibilities – it is never too much to remind the reader – are always available to us. Even the very simple (but wise) advice by Bernard

Meltzer[2] conveys that sense of preservation of dignity: 'before you speak ask yourself if what you are going to say is true, is kind, is necessary, is helpful. If the answer is no, maybe what you are about to say should be left unsaid'.

In that same spirit, here are a few suggestions to start non-racist, non-discriminatory, and dignity-enhancing practices in the classroom and beyond:

(1) Help students practice linguistic empathy by saying to themselves the words they are about to say to another and then exploring how those words make them feel.
(2) Help students by offering alternative vocabulary and experimenting with substitutions in sentences.
(3) Practice revising texts for content based on principles of dignity. Suggest to students that they move sentences that do not create the best results to a different document where they can be reformulated or deleted.
(4) Roleplay situations of communication where conflict may arise (for example, debates) and model responses that focus on the arguments themselves, without *ad-hominem* attacks.
(5) Bring awareness to the difference between critiquing an action and criticizing a person. For example, ask the students to comment on the impact of 'You're so lazy' as opposed to 'It seems work on Tuesday was not very productive. How can I help change that?'
(6) Model behavior by treating the students in ways that help uphold and protect their dignity. There is no better example than our own actions in the real world.

With a bit of creativity, the ESL classroom, the composition classroom, the teacher preparation course, the business English seminar can all serve as educational spaces where not only linguistic elements are learned but also all of their sociolinguistic baggage is examined and improved.

Multilingualism in itself can be seen as a tool, a vehicle for anti-racism. Multilingualism brings us closer to our shared humanity, provides insight into different cultures, promotes understanding and empathy, changes our ways of seeing the world. There is nothing more humbling than realizing that one's way (of thinking, doing, being) is not the only way, and participating in the exciting venture of expanding one's horizons. Human dignity and multilingualism are also intrinsically connected. We honor another by communicating in a language dear to them. We achieve a better grasp of their cultural artifacts, their literature, their music by engaging with their language. They stop being 'the Other' if we participate in what is foundationally important in other communities.

In this book, we attempted to bring together ideas about language and anti-racism practice because we believe linguistics, TESOL, sociolinguistics and world Englishes are important loci of inclusive action. In a compelling introduction to the book *Raciolinguistics: How Language Shapes Our Ideas About Race*, Alim (2020: 25) argues the following:

> Given that race continues to covertly and overtly structure the lived experiences of millions of People of Color around the world—as well as hegemonically dominant populations (even if unbeknownst to them)—our work must continue to resist and transgress the overwhelmingly White fields of anthropology and linguistics that continue to, at worst, marginalize and, at best, sidestep issues of race and racialization.

One of the reasons why my work has been conducted in world Englishes primarily is the openness of that field of research to issues of gender, ethnicity, national origin and diversity in general from its very inception. As we expand in linguistics proper to highlight considerations of those aspects of identities and their intersection with language, we hope you will join us in considering your role in this very important endeavor, both as an individual and as a catalyst of change in the institutions where you are a member and a leader.

Notes

(1) My reference to Kant's conceptualization in this particular regard does not constitute an endorsement of his other views.
(2) The widely known quote is attributed to Bernard Meltzer, who was a radio show host for a call-in show that ran from 1967 to the 1990s.

References

Alim, S. (2020) Introducing raciolinguistics. In S. Alim, J.R. Rickford and A.F. Ball (eds) *Raciolinguistics: How Language Shapes Our Ideas About Race* (pp. 1–32). Oxford: Oxford University Press.
Alim, S., Rickford, J.R. and Ball, A.F. (eds) (2020) *Raciolinguistics: How Language Shapes Our Ideas About Race*. Oxford: Oxford University Press.
Buccola, N. (2015) "The essential dignity of man as man": Frederick Douglass on human dignity. *American Political Thought* 4, 228–258.
de Sousa Santos, B. (2007) Para além do Pensamento Abissal: Das linhas globais a uma ecologia de saberes. *Revista Crítica de Ciências Sociais*. See http://journals.openedition.org/rccs/753; https://doi.org/10.4000/rccs.753.
Douglass, F. (1894) *Blessings of Liberty and Education*. Speech, Manassas, Virginia, 3 September 1894.
Hill, T. (2014) Kantian perspectives on the rational basis of human dignity. In M. Düwell, J. Braarvig, R. Brownsword and D. Mieth (eds) *The Cambridge Handbook of Human Dignity: Interdisciplinary Perspectives* (pp. 215–221). Cambridge: Cambridge University Press.
Regilme Jr, SSF (2019) The global politics of human rights: From human rights to human dignity? *International Political Science Review* 40 (2), 279–290.

Appendix: Q&A with Contributors

How to be a Responsible (and Responsive) Language User – Suggestions by Contributors

We, as contributors to this book, have tried to convey our effort and goal to make anti-racism linguists an applied endeavor. In that spirit, we would like to close this volume with a brief set of questions and answers in which the authors address some practical but meaningful ways to navigate language use in its potential for anti-racism and anti-prejudice action. We hope that the multiplicity of formats and genres that we explore in this volume also speak to our commitment to making academic discourse less colonial and more inclusive of communication modes that are utilized around the world for knowledge sharing and exchange of information. Initials were used for expediency.

How can I avoid making quick judgements about people given their language use?

AM: Call me a pessimist, but I do not believe that we ever stop making quick judgements about people based on their language. What we can and should make sure is not to act on such hasty judgements. I would encourage all of us to start by acknowledging that we make such judgements, and get better at catching ourselves when we do. Have an honest conversation with ourselves about what judgement we made, where it came from, and whether it is accurate and fair. And if it is not, do not act on it. And be responsible for our actions, if we act on such a judgement.

TM: I find it useful to remember that language is just one aspect of a person's presence in the world, and while I as an English professor may have 'good' English language skills, it's unlikely that most English speakers I encounter will have language skills like mine, not to mention most English language learners. I could be quickly judged as a failure for my lack of prowess in skiing or football/soccer, and I need to remember that we are different in our skills.

CD: It is difficult to avoid quick judgements and/or to have no judgement at all. As I discuss in my chapter, 'Confession of a Sociolinguist:

A Linguistic Autobiography', we, at least I, have inherited values or biases about language. My strategy is: if we can't avoid it, be aware of it. Recognizing our own judgments that bring about both negative or positive attitudes toward other speakers and understanding how our attitudes and judgments have been constructed are a process of self-exploration. With this process, we understand that we can be insensitive and ignorant at times. But, the good thing is our attitudes can be changed over time as we are exposed to more and more language diversity.

PF: The problem is not necessarily making quick judgements – our brains are wired to react before we can rationally analyze why we are doing so. Therefore, it is my estimation that rather than feel guilty for such judgements, one does better for themselves and for others to then stop and consider what is behind such attitudes and then revise them accordingly if they come out lacking in empathy and/or linguistic bases.

How do I see different accents and how do I move beyond stereotypes that I associate with those accents?

AM: Although I may be more 'aware' and 'informed' than many 'lay people', I still definitely associate various stereotypes with different accents. As I said before, I don't believe that I will move beyond them completely. One thing I try to do, just as I said above, is to recognize my bias and recognize it is a stereotype, and do everything I can not to act on it. The other is to engage in experiences involving different accents and to do so with an open heart and willingness to be transformed, so that my life experience overwrites the stereotype I have.

TM: Many Americans have immediate responses to certain accents based on their experience with those accents in media (often movie or TV). We need to remind ourselves daily that the life we experience via movies and TV may reflect real peoples' lived experiences but the characters are not actually real people, and we need to keep our minds open as we encounter real people, even those with accents that sound familiar.

How are people who speak more than one language seen in different contexts? How can I make more positive assumptions about multilingualism?

TM: I like to remind my students that in the history of human inhabitation of this world, multilingualism was most likely the norm, not the exception. So Americans living in a mostly monolingual reality are 'abnormal'.

PF: One only needs to remember the many advantages of multilingualism – access to different people, different cultures, an enriched linguistic and cultural repertoire, greater capacity for abstraction and imagination, further development of empathy, rapport and understanding of human dynamics. What is not to like?

CJ, EDF, JM: The first part of this question helps us understand the intrinsic relation between language and society. Many scholars (e.g. Hymes, 1992) have discussed the fact that languages are valued in different ways in societies, depending on a number of factors. These include the socioeconomic and political prestige of those who speak each one of these languages within each context, as well as the status that they have internationally (which, by the way, is also tied to matters of prestige and power of those who speak them).

A good example is that of the case of Spanish in the US. While elites in the US often want their children to learn different languages, Spanish included, the practices of Hispanic Spanish-English bilinguals (García & Lin, 2016), many of whom are not from elite backgrounds, are generally stigmatized. What this example illustrates is that the ways in which people who speak more than one language are seen in different contexts depends on: (a) what language(s) they speak; (b) the status of these languages within their local environments; and (c) how those who speak these languages are viewed (which, in fact, is closely tied to 'b').

As for the second part of the question, we feel that the one of the best ways to make positive assumptions about multilingualism is to understand that the belief that the majority of the population in the world is monolingual is indeed a myth (Canagarajah, 2013; Li, 2000). This, in turn, helps us comprehend that being multilingual is not something about which one should be concerned (as believed by many not so long ago), but that it is actually very common worldwide.

Another important factor that can help us make positive assumptions about multilingualism is to understand that knowing more than one language may actually: bring new perspectives about life in general and about other people (including those around us); and lead us into other ways of conceptualizing things we often take for granted, even time and space (see Cook & Li, 2016).

References

Canagarajah, S. (2013) *Translingual Practices: Global Englishes and Cosmopolitan Relations.* New York: Routledge.
Cook, V. and Li, W. (eds) (2016) *The Cambridge Handbook of Linguistic Multi-competence.* Cambridge: Cambridge University Press.
García, O. and Lin, A. (2016) Extending understandings of bilingual and multilingual education. In O. García, A. Lin and S. May (eds) *Bilingual and Multilingual Education* (pp. 1–20). Cham: Springer.
Hymes, D. (1992) Inequality in language: Taking for granted. *Penn Working Papers in Educational Linguistics* 8 (1), 1–30.
Li, W. (ed.) (2000) Dimensions of bilingualism. In Li Wei (ed.) *The Bilingualism Reader* (pp. 2–21). New York: Routledge.

How do I make sense of the fact that language is changing all the time and that different groups use language differently to show solidarity, cohesion, but also to fulfill specific needs? How does this manifest in my practice?

TM: It's worthwhile for all language professionals to remind themselves that English is not and never was monolithic, and while we may have been taught that English teachers were to teach a standard, it's not clear that 'a standard' has ever existed. This can be unsettling as we can respond 'well, what do we teach then?' but the goal is to make us always aware that the 'standard' English we're using or teaching is always in flux.

PF: There are two questions that I get all the time for being a linguist. The first one is how many languages I speak (the last time this happened was only two days ago!), to which I respond truthfully, four, but then feel inclined to qualify my answer by explaining that this is not what being a linguist is about. To me it is about being riveted by and always trying to figure out how languages (those we personally use or not) work. The second is about right and wrong in language (I once received an email from a person who found my name and wanted to set a bet with a friend regarding whether 'dreamt' existed as the past of 'to dream').

I believe not acknowledging that languages are always changing is about that preoccupation with right and wrong. It concerns deciding 'for sure' whether something is a grammatical mistake or a result of language change, and the truth is that the line between the two is really faint (perhaps here lies another form of abyssal thinking?). How many linguistic innovations started as a deviation from prescriptive norm? Certainly too many to count. From the perspective of sociolinguistics, just like any cultural artifact, languages do not exist independently from the societies they serve, and using languages in particularly ways to show solidarity and belonging are important features of our interaction with the world. This can take many forms, including respecting another person's pronouns, using titles similarly and with the same frequency across genders, honoring people's traditions through language and accepting people's varieties as legitimate and functional in a multiplicity of communication contexts.

What can we do in the classroom to raise linguistic awareness and foster more inclusive practices?

PF: We start with ourselves. We scan our own environments and practices to decide whether we are honoring others and their linguistic use the same way we would like to be honored. We lead by example, modeling positive and healthy language use ourselves. As a person involved in Peace Linguistics, for example, I try my best to not use metaphors of war for trivial things or violent language for analogies and the like. It is my way of trying to engage more positive uses of language, but each person can find their own.

TM: Even in mostly monolingual societies such as many parts of America, linguistic diversity is never more than a few generations away. Many monolingual Americans come from immigrants who fled other countries, and many American families have stories of discrimination and changing family names to hide ethnic identities. We are not that different from contemporary new arrivals to the US.

CD: As discussed in my chapter (Duran), as instructors we can use an autoethnographic approach in assigning students' tasks. Students can have an opportunity to explore their own language heritage, dialects and languages used in their families, where they are originally and geographically from and how their language use has changed over time. In the process, students will be trained to do a mini research project (depending on the content of the classroom and/or length of the course. Students can share their heritage and findings to their classmates in a friendly, safe and supportive environment. In my own classes, with this assignment, I have found that students recognize both differences and similarities among themselves. Understanding one another and how language varies is the outcome.

How does language interact with the concepts of race, ethnicity, gender, disability, diversity, inclusion and belonging?

CJ, EDF, JM: As discussed in our chapter (Jordão, Martinez & Diniz de Figueiredo), our main locus of identity is the body (Louro, 2000). It is through, from and within our bodies that we speak, write, feel and relate to others. In addition, we see the body and mind as one, and not as separate structures or systems (cf. Damásio, 2021; Maturana, 2002). There are a number of implications of such conceptions. One is that we understand language not as an abstract entity that exists outside of individuals, and also not as a product of our minds alone; instead, our view of language is that it is embodied in all of us, and that it constitutes us in every sense. Therefore, our *languaging* practices (Mignolo, 2000) occur through, from and within our bodies, which means that they are intrinsically related to who we are, and thus to our race, ethnicity, gender, abilities and disabilities and so on. We cannot speak of language without individuals, and we cannot isolate individuals from their bodies. Thus we cannot isolate language from such physical characteristics.

References

Damásio, A. (2021) *The Strange Order of Things: Life, Feeling and the Making of Cultures*. London: Robinson.

Louro, G.L. (2000) Corpo, escola e identidade. *Educação e Realidade* 25 (2), 59–76.

Maturana, H. (2002) *Emoções e linguagem na educação e na política*. Belo Horizonte: Editora UFMG.

Mignolo, W. (2000) *Local Histories/Global Designs: Coloniality, Subaltern Knowledges, and Border Thinking*. Princeton, NJ: Princeton University Press.

Index

abyssal lines, defined 4–6, 98, 149
abyssal thinking 98
academic discourse 20–1
academic focus of this book 23–4
accents 57, 153
access paradox 17, 37
Alba, R. 121
Alcoff, L.M. 68
Alim, H.S. 51, 136
Alim, S. 151
Allen, J. 123
American English 72
analytical autoethnography 70
Anderson, L. 67
Anderson-Clark, T.N. 122
anti-racism
    defined 6
    functions of 116
    and multilingualism 150
anti-racist linguistics 1–3
    abyssal lines 4–6
    anti-racism 6
    belonging 6
    BIPOC 7
    decoloniality 7–8
    disability 9
    diversity 9–10
    epistemological racism 10–12
    equity 12–13
    gender 13–14
    inclusion 14–15
    institutions 15–16
    intersectionality 16–17
    language and its challenges 3–4
    linguistic justice 17
    linguistic prejudice 18, *18*
    minoritized individuals 18–19, 24n5
    the work in this book 19–24
anti-racist practices and curriculum 136
Anya, U. 52
Applied Linguistics 90–3, 96, 99–100, 102
autoethnography 66–7, 70

Bakhtin, M.M. 55, 56
Bakhtin Circle 91
Baltimore Sun, The 19, 24n5
Baumeister, R.F. 6
Beatty, Joy 23
Bebout, Lee 27–8
belonging 2–3, 6, 156
    see also DEIB (diversity, equity, inclusion and belonging)
Benjamin, R. 144
Bernays, A. 122
Berniat, M. 124
Beserra, B. de L.R. 57
Betrand, M. 122
Bhattacharya, U. *et al.* 97
Biernat, M. 123
bilingualism, asymmetrical 17
BIPOC (black, indigenous, people of color) 3, 7, 24
black activisms 56
black as a sign 55
Black Lives Matter (BLM) movement 29, 41n3
black teachers in ELT and linguistic racism in Brazil 44–6
    dis-inventing languages as zone of non-being 54–6
    language as zone of non-being 47–51
    linguistic racism 51–4
    racism in 45, 61n1
    zone of being and zone of non-being 46–7, 49
black teachers in ELT: surviving linguistic racism and language as zone of non-being 56–8
    accents 57
    methods and participants 58–9
    Paulo Freire Program 58, 61n6
    surviving zone of non-being 59–60
    conclusion 61

Index

BLM *see* Black Lives Matter (BLM) movement
Blommaert, J. 57
body as locus of research, the 20
Bonilla-Silva, E. 87, 102n2
Bourdieu, P. 37, 116, 117
Bowles, N. 3n2
Brazil 5, 11
    see also black teachers in ELT and linguistic racism in Brazil; (dis)inventing language as zone of non-being; narratives of invisibility: racism and anti-racism in academic spaces in Brazil
Brazilian Black Movement 94
Brazilian Portuguese 13
Buccola, N. 147
Byczkowska-Owczarek, D. 70
Byram, M. 52, 53

Camões, Luís de: *The Lusiads* 46
Canagarajah, S. 54
capitalism 46, 52
Castro-Gómez, S. 46, 101
challenges of honoring multiple identities and being an anti-racist 22, 106–7
    creativity 111–14
    creativity and academia 114–15
    embodiment 115–17
    identity 107–11
Chandler, P.T. 136
Chicano English 72
classism 70–1
colonialism 46, 48, 49, 52, 92
coloniality 8, 31, 50, 92, 95
colonization 28
color blindness 50
color-blind ideologies 49
confessions of a sociolinguist: a linguistic autoethnography 65–7
    an insensitive novice 70–3
    instructor's role 78–82
    linguistic ignorance 67–9, 70
    reflective journal writing 78
    researcher's role & interconnecting experiences 73–7
    theoretical underpinning 67–70
    summary 82–3
COVID-19 pandemic 1, 2, 101, 146–7
creativity 111–14
    and academia 114–15
    see also challenges of honoring multiple identities and being an anti-racist

Crenshaw, K. 16
Critical Race Theory (CRT) 46, 52
Crump, A. 52
Cummings, K.W. 24n5

Day, R.R. 68
de Sousa Santos, B. 4–5, 24n3, 90–1, 92, 98, 137, 138, 149
decoloniality, defined 7–8
DEIB (diversity, equity, inclusion and belonging) 3
Denali National Park and Reserve 119–20
dialects 54, 115
dignity 23, 146–51
Diniz de Figueiredo, Eduardo Henrique 19, 22
Dion, K.L. 121
disability 9, 156
Disability Studies (DS) 9
(dis)inventing language as zone of non-being 44–6, 54–6
    language as zone of non-being 47–51
    linguistic racism 51–4
    zone of being and zone of non-being 46–7, 49
diversity 14–15, 68–9, 156
    and inclusion 2
    of language 9–10
    and names 122–3
    see also DEIB (diversity, equity, inclusion and belonging)
Douglass, Frederick 147
Duran, Chatwara Suwannamai 22, 74
Dussell, E.D. 46

ELF (English as a lingua franca) 32
Ellis, C. 66
ELT (English language teaching) 31, 41n1, 51
embodiment 93–8, 115–17
Enlightenment 46
'entertainment' 2
environmental injustice 1–2
epistemic racism 86, 94, 96, 99, 100
epistemological racism 10–12, 136–7
equity 2, 3, 12–13
    see also DEIB (diversity, equity, inclusion and belonging)
'ethnic minority' 18–19
ethnicity 2, 6, 9, 18–19, 22, 23
    and names 121, 122, 156
    and racism 45
Europe 46

Fanon, F. 45, 46–7, 48, 49, 50, 54, 55, 56, 88
Faustino, M. 45
Ferreira, A.J. 52, 60
Figlio, D.N. 123–4
Files, J. et al. 107
Files, J.A. et al. 97
Flores, N. 47, 50, 51
Franzak, J.K. 121
Freire, Paulo 91, 92
Friedrich, P. 22
Fryer Jr, R. 124

Gandesha, S. 101
García, O. 48
Gates Jr, H.L. 55
Gavigan, K. 129
gender 13–14, 156
Gilson, E. 69
Girma, H. 123
Global English Language Teaching (GELT) 32
'Global South' 5, 90
globalization 31
González, L. 56
Google Scholar 29–30
Green, R.J. 122
Grosfoguel, R. 86, 99
Gunaratnam, Y. 18–19

Hage, G. 116
Hill, T. 147
history curriculum 23, 135
　　anti-racist practices and curriculum 136
　　building counter-narratives in history classroom 137
　　culturally sustaining pedagogies 135–6
　　protocol for educators 143–4, **144**
　　Southern epistemologies and linguistic citizenship 136–7
　　conclusion 144–5
history curriculum: sample materials 137
　　book titles 140–1
　　calendar 137–9, *138*
　　interrogating linguistic racism 142–3, *143*
　　textbook of American stories 139–40
　　working to identify & address oppressive language *141*, 141–2
hooks, bell 93
Horner, B. 93
human and linguistic dignity 23, 146–51
humanism 46, 48, 49

identity 97, 107–11
ignorance 69
inclusion 2, 14–15, 156
　　see also DEIB (diversity, equity, inclusion and belonging)
inclusive practices 155–6
injustice 1–2
Inoue, M. 50
institutional racism, defined 23
institutions, defined 15–16
insurgency 92, 102n5
intersectionality, defined 16–17, 97
Irish-Americans 27–8

Janks, H. 37
Jordão, Clarissa Menezes 19, 22, 102n4
Joshi, P. et al. 9–10
judgements 152–3
justice 2

Kachru, B.B. 34, 35
Kang, T.S. 122–3
Kant, I. 147, 151n1
Kaplan, J. 122
Keller, T. 121
King, L.J. 136
Kirk, B. 78
Kubota, R. 10–11, 16, 29, 30, 38, 57, 96

L1 66, 83n2
L2 83n2
Ladson-BIllings, G. 52
language
　　as culture 48
　　definitions of 46, 53
　　as ideology 48
　　and its challenges 3–4
　　and languaging 50
language as zone of non-being 22, 44, 45–6, 47–51
　　dis-inventing languages 44–455
language attitude socialization 67–8
language change 155
language ideology 22
language/linguistic ignorance 67–8
languaging and racialization 50
Latin America 8
Latinx 86
Lavergne, R.F. 57
Leary, M.R. 6
Leonard, W.Y. 7
Levine, M.B. 122
Levitt, S. 124
LGBTQ+ 14
Li, W. 48

Li Lianjie (Jet Li) 123
liberalism 46
Lin, A. *et al.* 29, 30, 38, 52, 97
linguistic autoethnography *see* confessions of a sociolinguist
linguistic awareness 155–6
linguistic capital 37
linguistic changes 13–14
Linguistic Citizenship 137, 139
linguistic diversity 9–10, 78
linguistic ignorance 67–9, 70
linguistic imperialism 21–2, 111
linguistic justice 17
linguistic prejudice 18, *18*
  see also challenges of honoring multiple identities and being an anti-racist
linguistic racism 69, 70
  on inventing languages as zone of non-being 51–4
  and linguistic prejudice 18, *18*
Liyanage, I. 54
local languages 5
Lodge, H. 37
Louro, G.L. 93
Lu, M. 93

Macedo, D.P. 92
Maher, F.A. 110
Makoni, S. 46, 53, 54, 140, 141
Martinez, Juliana Z. 19, 22
Martinique 48
Maslow, A.H. 6
mastery 12
Matsuda, Aya 21–2
Mbembe, A. 52, 53, 55
McHenry, Tracey 23
media 2
Meltzer, Bernard 149–50, 151n2
Menezes de Souza, L.M.T. *et al.* 52, 87
Mignolo, W. 91, 92, 102–3n5
Milkman, K.L. *et al.* 124
minoritized individuals 18–19, 24n5
Mitchell, C. 121
modernity 46, 47
Motha, S. 28–9, 31, 33–4, 36
Mount McKinley 119–20
Moura, C. 56
Muhammad, G. 143
Mullainathan, S. 122
multilingualism 150, 153–4
Muniz, K. 51
'My Name, My Identity' in California public schools 125
  advocacy 127–8
  campaign pledge *126*, 126–7, *127*
  education 127
  objectives of campaign 125
  sample week curriculum 134

names
  and diversity 122–3
  and ethnicity 121, 122, 156
  and psychology 121–2
naming and racism 45
  see also personal names in the classroom
narratives of invisibility: racism and anti-racism in academic spaces in Brazil 22, 85–6
  abyssal lines and whiteness 98–101
  Applied Linguistics from which we speak 90–3, 96, 99–100, 102
  Clarissa: academic author 87, 89–90, 95–6, 98, 99, 100
  Eduardo: supervisor 87, 90, 93, 99–100
  embodiment and invisibility 93–8
  interpretive account of the narratives 93
  Juliana: international student 87–8, 90, 94, 100
  locus of enunciation 86
  supervisor 88–9
  closing remarks 101–3
Nascimento, G. 22, 51, 56, 57, 97
National Bureau of Economic Research, US 122–3, 146
native speakers 52
Nee, V. 121
Nero, S. 35–6
NESs (native English speakers) 27, 33–5, 41n1
(N)NESTs, racialization of 37–8
New York Times 112
NNESs (non-NESs) 27, 33–5, 41n1
'No One Can Say it Anyway' *see* personal names in the classroom
Norton, B. 52, 53

Obama, Barack 120, 122
Oliveira, Luciana C. 23
O'Reilly, K. 67
outer-circle varieties 21

Palmares Republic 56, 61n3
Paris, D. 135–6
Paulo Freire Program 58, 61n6
Pavlenko, A. 52, 53

Pennycook, A. 46, 52, 141
personal names in the classroom 23, 119–21
    literature review 121
    'My Name, My Identity' in California public schools 125–8, 130, 134
    names and diversity 122–3
    names and psychology 121–2
    naming in the classroom 123–5
    resources for all lessons 133
    ways to engage with this topic 129–30
    why teachers need to make the effort 128–9
    final thoughts 130–1
Peterson, Jordan 3
Philipson, R. 52
Phillipson, R. 115
Portuguese, Brazilian 13
positionality *see* challenges of honoring multiple identities and being an anti-racist
positivism 46
power 8, 95
praxis 91
pre-modern languages 53–4

Q&A with contributors 152
    accents and stereotypes 153
    avoiding making quick judgements 152–3
    language change 155
    linguistic awareness and inclusive practices 155–6
    multilingualism 153–4
    race, ethnicity, gender, disability, diversity, inclusion and belonging 156
Quijano, Anibal 8, 95

race and racial identity 86, 95, 151, 156
    Black Lives Matter (BLM) movement 29, 41n3
    and TESOL 27–31
    see also narratives of invisibility: racism and anti-racism in academic spaces in Brazil
racialism 48–9
racialization 19, 50–2, 102n2
    and ELT 31
    and naming 45
    of NESs/NNESs 33–5
    of (N)NESTs 37–8
    of 'standard' English 35–7
    unmarked 47

raciolinguistics 52
racism 86–7, 149
    epistemic racism 86, 94, 96, 99, 100
    epistemological racism 10–12, 136–7
    institutional racism 23
    and language 48
    linguistic racism 51–4, 69, 70
    and naming 45
    and racialization 50, 51
    structural racism 29, 30, 31, 39, 87, 102n2
    in TESOL 30–1
racism in Brazil *see* (dis)inventing language as zone of non-being
reflective journal writing 78
Regilme Jr, SSF 148, 149
Rivers, D. 67
Rosa, J. 47, 50, 51
Rudolph, N. 31

Safatle, V. 101
Said, E. 46, 47
Santa Ana, O. 128
Saussure, F. de 55, 93
self-exploration 67
separability 97
sexism 87
Shotwell, A. 85, 86
Silva, J.M. *et al.* 8
Singh, J. 12, 47, 49
Singh, J.N. 21, 87, 110–11
So, R.J. 112–13
Song, K.X. 113
South America 5
Southern epistemologies 136–7
Souza, A.L.S. 52
Souza, Jessé 94–5
Spanglish 72
Spanish 154
Standard American English 66, 67, 71, 72, 74, 77, 81
'standard' English, racialization of 35–7
stereotypes 153
structural racism 29, 30, 31, 39, 87, 102n2
Sue, C.A. 121
Swedish 13

Tate, W. 52
teacher qualification and hiring 37–8
TEIL (Teaching English as an International Language) 21
TEIL as a tool for anti-racist pedagogy 26–9
    coloniality of ELT 31
    defined 31–2

race and/in TESOL 29–30
racism in TESOL 30–1
used to fight racism 32–3
concluding remarks 39–41
Telles, E.E. 121
terminology 4–5
TESOL (Teaching English to Speakers of Other Languages) 27, 41n1
race and/in 29–30, 96
racism in 30–1
TESOL International Association 30
TESOL Quarterly 29
TESOL Quarterly-TESOL Journal 30
Tetreault, M.K.T. 110
Thai language 70–1
Thompson, R. 128
time 4
TOEFL (test of English as a foreign language) 71
traditions 54
translanguaging 48
transracialization 52

United Nations 69
United States 4, 7, 11–12

Van Parijs, P. 17
Veronelli, G. 47, 49
Volosinov, V.N. 91

Walsh, C. 91, 92, 102–3n5
Welton, A.D. *et al.* 18 20
Wezerek, G. 112–13
whiteness 27–8, 36, 98–101
Wicht, S. 129–30
Willis, F.N. 122
Windle, J. 57
Windle, J.A. 51, 52, 57
work in this book, the 19–24
World Englishes (WE) 21, 32, 34, 67, 151

Yazan, B. 31

Zhao, X. 123, 124
zone of being and zone of non-being 46–7, 49

For Product Safety Concerns and Information please contact our EU Authorised Representative:

Easy Access System Europe

Mustamäe tee 50

10621 Tallinn

Estonia

gpsr.requests@easproject.com

www.ingramcontent.com/pod-product-compliance
Lightning Source LLC
Chambersburg PA
CBHW071427160426
43195CB00013B/1836